# YOU'RE THE

# PRINCIPAL!

## Now What?

JEN SCHWANKE

YOU'RE THE

PRINCIPAL!

*Now What?*

Strategies and Solutions for
New School Leaders

**ASCD**
Alexandria, VA USA

1703 N. Beauregard St. • Alexandria, VA 22311-1714 USA
Phone: 800-933-2723 or 703-578-9600 • Fax: 703-575-5400
Website: www.ascd.org • E-mail: member@ascd.org
Author guidelines: www.ascd.org/write

Deborah S. Delisle, *Executive Director;* Robert D. Clouse, *Managing Director, Digital Content & Publications;* Stefani Roth, *Publisher;* Genny Ostertag, *Director, Content Acquisitions;* Susan Hills, *Acquisitions Editor;* Julie Houtz, *Director, Book Editing & Production;* Katie Martin, *Editor;* Masie Chong, *Graphic Designer;* Mike Kalyan, *Manager, Production Services;* Cynthia Stock, *Typesetter;* Kyle Steichen, *Senior Production Specialist*

All web links in this book are correct as of the publication date below but may have become inactive or otherwise modified since that time. If you notice a deactivated or changed link, please e-mail books@ascd.org with the words "Link Update" in the subject line. In your message, please specify the web link, the book title, and the page number on which the link appears.

PAPERBACK ISBN: 978-1-4166-2221-5    ASCD product #117003                    n8/16
PDF E-BOOK ISBN: 978-1-4166-2223-9; see Books in Print for other formats.
Quantity discounts: 10–49, 10%; 50+, 15%; 1,000+, special discounts (e-mail programteam@ascd.org or call 800-933-2723, ext. 5773, or 703-575-5773). For desk copies, go to www.ascd.org/deskcopy.

**Library of Congress Cataloging-in-Publication Data**

Names: Schwanke, Jennifer.
Title: You're the principal! now what? : strategies and solutions for new
  school leaders / Jennifer Schwanke.
Description: Alexandria, Virginia : ASCD, [2016] | Includes bibliographical
  references and index.
Identifiers: LCCN 2016018791 | ISBN 9781416622215 (pbk.)
Subjects: LCSH: School principals—United States. | Educational leadership—
  United States. | School management and organization—United States.
Classification: LCC LB2831.92 .S395 2016 | DDC 371.2/012—dc23 LC record available at
https://lccn.loc.gov/2016018791

25  24  23  22  21  20  19  18  17  16          1  2  3  4  5  6  7  8  9  10  11  12

# YOU'RE THE
# PRINCIPAL!
## Now What?

# Acknowledgments

Piles of thanks to the mentors who have taught me so much along the way, including Dr. David Axner, Richard Baird, Carol King, and Rick Weininger. I am extremely grateful for the support of my current leadership, including Dr. Todd Hoadley, Jill Abraham, Kim Miller, Tracey Miller, and Jill Reinhart.

Thank you to Susan Hills and Katie Martin, the ASCD editors who helped this book come to fruition.

Thank you to my father, Dan Moorefield—the writer—and my mother, Carli Moorefield—the relentless supporter.

I am so grateful to my in-laws, Carol and Fred Schwanke, whose help and support make it all possible.

And there aren't words enough for the appreciation I have for my children, Jack and Autumn, and my amazing husband, Jay. My family!

# Preface

When I first started on my journey as a principal, supportive resources for beginning principals were quite limited. Most publications were written by, and for, principals who were already fully functioning on the job; the content spoke to those who had already conquered the early challenges of the role. These publications tended to propose elaborate, complicated initiatives that a new principal would find overwhelming, if not impossible. In other words, I didn't see much available for *beginners*. I was looking for a practical, helpful, concise resource that could be referenced quickly and on an as-needed basis.

This book is intended to be that kind of resource. It may be useful for you to read it cover to cover, but it is designed with stand-alone chapters you can peruse when you have a few free moments or reference when you need quick guidance on how to tackle one of the specific common challenges it addresses.

So who am I to write this book? I was someone who never, *ever* thought I would be a principal. But after teaching for seven years and watching the work of my principal—who was inspiring, intelligent, and incredibly effective as a leader—I was moved to cross over into school leadership. In the years since, I have worked as an assistant to two other principals, and I now serve as a principal myself. In my current position, I have the good fortune to be surrounded by a large, talented, driven, and skilled group of colleagues who challenge my thinking every day. The work is challenging, but I love it, in large part because it affords me the opportunity to make a genuine difference, each and every day, in the lives of young people.

An unexpected hiccup early on my administrative path broadened my perspective on school leadership. When I was pregnant with my first child, I grew concerned about the impact the job would have on my family. I worried about late nights, stressful days, and balancing my commitment to family with my commitment to doing good work for my school. So, after many long discussions, my husband and I decided I would step back from administration and return to teaching while we raised our family. I resigned as assistant principal, and happily took up the reins of my own classroom again.

It turned out to be a short-lived return. After just one year, I was offered an assistant position by a principal I deeply admired and respected. He convinced me to join him by reassuring me he would do the majority of the after-school events while my children were still young; his son was grown, he pointed out, so he had the time to spare. He promised I would be able to give whatever was necessary to be fully present for my family. Eager to go back to a leadership position, and eager to work for someone with his knowledge and skills, I quickly accepted his offer.

Yet, that short time back in the classroom had a powerful impact on me. I was shocked to realize that during the four years I had been an administrator, I had "crossed over" and let myself forget what it was like to be a teacher—the person who was working closest with students, who spent so much time reassuring and managing parents, who was expected to respect and support leadership decisions, no matter what. In short, I had become the proverbial principal who was too mired in leadership to remember the perspective of those whom I had been trusted to lead.

That experience taught me a profound lesson: As a principal, I must cling fiercely to the perspective of the teachers and students. Being a mother helps, for sure; I am watching my children grow through their school journey and learning a lot about teaching and leadership along the way. But the fact is, my comprehensive perspective is largely the result of taking a step back. It renewed my commitment to the mission of education and to the people who make that commitment alongside me.

I've been back working as a school leader for seven years now. I find great joy and satisfaction in leading a school to a place of happiness and success, and it's an honor to share what I have learned with you—someone who is just beginning the journey. But here is an important disclaimer: There is no perfect school principal, and there is no leadership manual comprehensive enough to cover every situation you may encounter in this job. I stepped up to the principalship from the classroom—not once but twice—and I still get caught off guard and make occasional missteps. I have my off days; I say silly things once in a while; I sometimes regret a decision I have made. Indeed, some of the suggestions in the following pages are based on a time when I made a *wrong* decision. But my "errors" have always served to make me better at my job. I can honestly say that I look forward to what each new day brings.

It can be the same for you. Every day over the next few years, you will be learning, changing, and growing as a leader. The job will teach you the value of communication, empathy, respect, and understanding. Some days you won't believe how much you love the work you are doing; other days, you'll question why you ever took the job. Ultimately, though, being a principal will leave you feeling fulfilled. Why? Because this is a job that lets you spend your days supporting and guiding your people—the students, teachers, and parents in your school community. And what could be better than that?

# Meeting Your Staff, Students, and Parents

### Scenario 1: The Staff Meeting

*You have been working as a literacy coach in a large elementary school, in which most of your work has been with 4th and 5th grade teachers. When the principal of your school retires, you decide to apply for the job. Many interviews later, you are named as principal. As you think about your new role, you come to a realization: While the teachers with whom you worked closely know you well, most others know you by name only. How should you present yourself so the school is ready—and able—to accept you as their new leader?*

### Scenario 2: The Individual Teacher Meeting

*You have just gone through a rigorous interview process for a job as the principal of a middle school. There were interviews with a human resources director; a committee composed of parents, students, and staff; a group of other principals in the district; and, finally, the superintendent. Late on Friday afternoon, you receive a call from the superintendent notifying you that the job is yours. Your first principal job! "Well, you've got your work cut out for you," the superintendent says. "This is a tricky building." Excitement quickly turns to anxiety: What does that mean? And where do you begin?*

### Scenario 3: The Aggressive Parent

*After taking over a large high school, you have begun the long process of getting to know the students and their parents. You have just finished your welcoming remarks at the school's annual Open House. You told the*

*attendees a little bit about your experience, your goals as their new prin-*
*cipal, and how eager you are to be part of their community. Immediately*
*after you conclude, a parent in the front row seems to bolt toward you. She*
*asks if you have a few moments to talk . . . now. You can tell by her body lan-*
*guage that she is an aggressive parent—one with whom you probably need*
*to build a good relationship. What are the wisest first steps?*

When you are hired as a new principal, the buzz throughout the school community will be palpable. Everyone will want to know who you are, what you value, what experience you have, and—above all—what *changes* you will bring to the school. As with most situations, your initial interaction with your staff and community will set the tone for the future. A positive start will create momentum that will carry you through the year.

The strategies and solutions in this chapter are divided into two parts: those focused on managing initial meetings with your staff and those focused on handling initial interactions with parents and students.

## Strategies and Solutions for Meeting Your Staff

It's difficult to know who will be more nervous when you first meet your staff—you or them! In my experience, a tiered, two-step approach is the best bet for introductions. The first step is to meet your entire staff as a group and tell them a bit about yourself as a person and as a leader. The second step is to have short meetings with individual staff members. In an extremely large school, this may be difficult, and you may find it more efficient and effective to meet with departments or teams. Regardless, your goal is to get to know a little bit about each of the teachers in your building.

## Step 1: Conduct a Whole-Group Meeting

Once you have been officially named principal of your school, you will need to determine the best time to meet your new staff. It's never a neat process, because there isn't a standard time line in administrator hiring practices. For example, if you are hired in the spring for the upcoming school year, it may not be appropriate to meet your whole staff until months later when they report to start the new school year; similarly, if you are hired in the summer, it may be hard to get your staff together before the start of the year. On the other hand, if you are hired to be a principal in the same building where you are teaching, or for a building within your current district, it may be possible to meet the staff within a few weeks of your official hire date. Consulting with the superintendent may help you determine the best course of action.

In my first year as a principal of an elementary school, it was particularly important that my initial interaction with the staff be a good one. The situation was unconventional: midway through the school year, the current principal had unexpectedly retired, and the superintendent needed someone to step up and fill in for the remainder of the year. He pulled me from the role I held as an assistant principal in a middle school and named me interim principal. He said he hoped I would eventually be named the official principal, but he made it clear that I would have to earn it: "We are still going to post the position, and you will interview like everyone else. The hiring committee will decide who will be the official principal for next year."

He went on to tell me about the staff. "They are in a difficult position," he explained. "Their current principal was often unkind and handled the teachers in a punitive manner. There is very little trust between him and the staff. Worse, there is a culture in which a small group was 'in' with the principal, while the others felt undervalued and mistreated." He summed it up with his trademark frankness: "The school culture is awful."

With an opening like that, I was quite anxious the day I first met the staff. I walked in with the superintendent, and we headed into the library where the staff had been called to assemble. After a brief introduction, the superintendent turned to me. "Why don't you tell them a bit about yourself?" Sixty pairs of eyes stared at me, wary and suspicious. I tried to relax.

I began by telling them about my qualifications and experience. I told them a bit about my family, my leadership experiences, and my hopes and goals for my future as a leader. I even talked about my weaknesses. "I'll be learning from you," I told them. "It's no secret that I have no elementary experience, so I'll be asking a lot of questions. But I hope you'll find that I am a good listener and a quick learner." I finished by assuring them, "I am here to lead you, not micromanage or make any big unnecessary changes. I want *my* work to support *your* work. With that approach, I think we can make this school into a pretty special place."

Although I am sure the staff was still a bit cautious, I felt a sense of calm settle over the room. The message that I didn't intend to make sweeping, reckless changes was what they needed to hear in order to step back a little and give me a chance.

From the perspective of a school staff, the first exposure to a new principal is a reasonable occasion for anxiety and worry, even when there is not an existing culture of doubt or distrust. Members of a staff want to know what their future holds—and they know your leadership will affect the future environment of their school. There are several things you can do to make the first interaction a success.

**Be yourself.** Don't change your personality or your leadership style to fit a vision of how you feel your first meeting *should* go. Think about the skills you bring to the position, and showcase them for the staff. If you're the calm, serious type, be calm and serious. If you are good-humored and casual, be so. You were hired to be the building's principal because of who you are—so make it your business to be the best possible "you."

**Outline a verbal résumé.** Give the staff a picture of your journey to this principalship. Where did you go to school, and what degrees do you hold? Where and what did you teach? What led you to administration? Outlining your credentials shows the staff why you are qualified to lead them.

**Don't be afraid to get a little personal.** Tell the staff who you are outside of your work—tell them about your family, your children, your hobbies, and your interests. Creating a richer profile of yourself that goes beyond your résumé will let the staff see you as more than just their new boss, and it will give them some insight into what you value. It will also help create a foundation from which you can build later, when you make a personal connection with each staff member in individual meetings.

**Share your goals.** What do you hope to get out of your time in this school? In what ways do you hope to effect change and growth? Talk briefly about your general goals and vision for your time as their leader.

**Have some fun.** If it fits your personality, don't be afraid to introduce yourself to a staff in a lighthearted, interactive way so as to ease any tension or worry the staff may carry. In the past, I have known new principals to play games with facts about the principal—Three Truths and a Lie, Bingo, Jeopardy, and other guessing games. This will present you as someone who is creative, fun, and willing to add laughter to otherwise tense situations.

However, as noted above, it's most important to be yourself. If you are naturally serious and businesslike, be so—just don't take yourself too seriously. Your staff will want to know that you have the ability to relax and find enjoyment in your work.

**Avoid making promises you can't keep.** I once told a staff I hoped I'd be there "as long as you'll have me." Just four years later, though, I was asked to transfer to another school. Many staff felt betrayed and abandoned, and several even quoted my words from that first meeting. The lesson to remember here is that if you make promises about your plans, you'll be held to those promises.

**Wrap up the meeting by welcoming questions.** When you have finished speaking about yourself, ask, "Is there anything you'd like to know about me—as a person, as an educator, or as a leader?" Give your staff time to think—as every educator knows, wait time is important—and then address any questions they have.

A few notes here. If you are asked something for which you have no answer, it is best to simply be honest. Responding with, "I am not sure about that, but I will find out and get back to you" communicates not only that you can admit when you don't know something, but also that you are willing to seek answers and share what you've learned. Make a note of questions like this right after the meeting, when your memory is fresh, and *be sure you follow through*. Further, if you are asked something about a decision you have not yet had time to make, explain that you are still considering all the details. It is perfectly legitimate and fair to say, "Until I have more information, I'm not comfortable answering just yet. I'll make sure to keep you updated."

**End the meeting in a timely manner.** Your first meeting with your staff should not be a long one for several reasons. First, there is not a staff *anywhere* that enjoys long meetings. Second, this initial meeting is an opportunity to show your commitment to honoring their time—and demonstrate your ability to run an efficient meeting. Last, the staff will need time to think about what you've said to them, to process it with one another, and to generate more questions they would like to ask you.

**Explain the next step.** As you wrap up the meeting, finish by telling them you will reach out to them to set up individual meetings in the next several weeks; then, thank them for their time and wish them a good day.

## Step 2: Conduct Individual Meetings

An individual meeting with a staff member will tell you a lot about each person, but it will also expand your understanding of the school in general. You will discover who your leaders are, who brings a positive—or negative—attitude to your school, and what personalities may work well together. Best of all, these meetings will help you piece together the history and culture of your school. In that sense, these meetings are really a unique combination of a jigsaw puzzle and a history book. The staff will have a lot to tell you about what has happened with previous leadership, the nature of the school's culture, and what the staff values as a whole. When you put all the pieces together, you'll get a clearer picture of how to begin as the school's next leader.

**Find a meeting place that will put staff at ease.** Individual meetings with staff members should take place in a comfortable and nonthreatening environment. If your office has a table where you and the staff member can sit across from one another, use that; if not, meet in a conference room or in a lounge area. I find it is best to avoid sitting at my desk with a staff member across from me; the desk serves as a formidable barrier between me and the teacher and can make the teacher feel he or she is "in trouble." After all, no one likes to sit on the other side of a principal's desk, including—or even especially—adults.

**Show as much flexibility as possible—without over-scheduling yourself.** E-mail the staff and offer them several choices for a time to meet with you. Ask them to get back to you—or, in the case of a large staff, get back to your secretary—with a time slot that would work for them. Depending on the size of your staff, you may need to block out several days for these meetings. I find that a 15- to 20-minute meeting is usually sufficient. Remember, though, that after a while, these individual meetings will begin to run together and feel more like a nagging chore than a genuine, authentic, and personal way to connect with your staff. I find that any more than five or six in a day will turn an exciting opportunity into an arduous task.

**Focus on getting to know one another.** After I welcome a staff member with a handshake and a smile, I like to sit down together and begin with a statement of appreciation, such as, "Thank you so much for taking the time to come in today. I have been looking forward to talking with you!" Then, I ask questions to get the staff member to open up a bit. The following questions may serve as a guide.

- Tell me about your role here at the school. Walk me through a typical day in your shoes.
- What other roles have you held before—at this school or in previous schools?
- What other jobs have you held outside of education?
- What brought you to education?
- Tell me about your family, friends, pets—whoever supports you in your life.

- What do you like about this job? What do you dislike?
- What do you think is your biggest challenge on a day-to-day basis?
- Tell me about this school. What are your favorite parts? What do you wish would go away?
- Did you feel good about previous building leadership? Why or why not?
- What do you hope to get out of me as a leader?
- What do you hope I can bring to our school?
- Is there anything else you'd like me to think about as I approach my first year?

I have found that as I work through these questions, the conversation naturally gives me opportunities to talk about myself as well—as a leader, yes, but also as a person with other interests and experiences.

**Find opportunities to share your values.** When talking with teachers, you will find natural places to insert your opinion on instruction and student growth. This is a great way for teachers to get to know what you will value as a leader.

Remember, the main goal of these individual meetings is *connection*. You'll want to look for commonalities and take advantage of any chance to bond with each staff member on a personal level. As you settle into your new role, you can use these connections to build your relationship with each staff member.

## Strategies and Solutions for Meeting Your School Community

Meeting the students who attend your new school and their parents is a very different process from meeting your staff. Fortunately, it is more spread out over time, and it happens naturally, depending on when and where you first interact with students and their families.

## Meeting the Students

Student interactions are the easy ones. Every day, you have the chance to get to know students. You will speak to them as they come into the building, as you visit classrooms, during lunch or unstructured time, at after-school events, and at extracurricular activities. You will also get to know them because of celebrations of success, as well as disciplinary or social issues that require your intervention. Getting to know them well takes time over the course of many different interactions. There are several ways to facilitate meaningful connections with students in your school.

**Take your time.** You don't need to know every student's name and personal story right away. Quite honestly, it takes a lot of time—and, depending on the size of your school, it is entirely feasible that you will never actually know every child well. Give yourself a break on this one. Recognize that it may take several years before you feel like you truly know all your students.

**Set a goal of "Every student, every day."** I'll mention this motto several times in this book, because it is such an important goal that I take extra care to meet in my work. As principal, it is my priority that each student sees me every day. I think it clarifies that I'm the *principal,* and that I am committed to being part of each child's world. "Every student, every day" sounds lofty, but it actually isn't difficult to do; I take advantage of occasions that bring many students together in one place. If I attend bus duty or walk through the lunchroom each day, students see me. I use the time to talk to as many of them as possible in a casual and natural manner, learning their names and a few important things about each one as I go.

**Get personal.** A great way to get to know students is to ask them a lot of questions. Students love to talk about themselves, and when they are asked a lot of questions, they share information that makes them memorable. Ask about their families, their interests, and their background. I like to develop nicknames or inside jokes with students—it helps them feel they've made a genuine and specific connection with me. I learn a great deal about this from my husband, who is an athletic director and football coach. He is masterful at connecting with students on a personal level. When interacting with students, he asks questions like "What are you doing this weekend?" or, "Hey, your mom told me you went to camp this summer. Tell me about it!" He gives them affectionate nicknames that somehow compliment them: "Money" for a quarterback who rarely misthrows; "Butter" for a receiver who moves smoothly and effortlessly through plays; "Slick" for the running back who is great at eluding the defense. His athletes love these special, personal references to their individual talents.

## Meeting the Parents

Meeting parents is also a longer and more natural process than meeting your staff, although your experiences will vary depending on individual parents' philosophies of education. Some parents feel it's imperative that they meet you *immediately*. They will want to talk to you as soon as possible—about their child, of course, but also about a variety of other issues that they value. Conversely, some parents will be perfectly happy if they never interact with you at all. They expect their child to handle the challenges of school without their intervention; they get their kid to school each day and sign a permission slip every now and then, and that's where it ends. Quite frankly, this is how I approach the school experience of my own children. I don't feel a need to connect with the principal unless there is a problem or I have a question. I respect parents who prefer this hands-off approach.

With that said, you will want to make good connections with parents who want to know you. There are several guidelines to consider while forming these connections.

**Meet the bulldogs.** These are the parents that will call you or e-mail you five minutes after your contract is approved by the Board of Education. Typically, it will be because there is something special the parent needs you to know. *My child is gifted, and I want to know how programming will support my child.* Or, *My child has struggled with bullying, and we need to talk about how to avoid it this year.* Perhaps, *I am your PTO president, and we should meet to discuss ways we can support each other.* I call these parents "bulldogs" because they will bark and growl—pleasantly, of course—until they get some face time with you.

It's best to make connecting with these parents a priority—not only to assuage their worry but also because it's practically a guarantee that your bulldogs are the ones who have a very loud voice in the community. If they have a positive interaction with you, it's a good bet that lots of others will hear a positive report on your potential as the building leader.

**Take your time.** After you've met your bulldogs, relax. Don't rush it. If you attempt to connect with all parents right away, you'll undoubtedly forget names and conversations, which will make you seem like a distracted scatterbrain. It is far better to make meaningful connections with parents slowly and over time. Trust me: You will have countless opportunities to meet them. There will be orientation nights, after-school activities, parent teacher organization (PTO) events, extracurricular activities, parent–teacher conferences, and more—and each one will serve to put you in contact with parents.

**Openly acknowledge your limitations.** When taking over a new school, it's a great idea to tell parents that you intend to get to know them personally, but it's also helpful if you are frank in communicating that this will take time. Because I struggle to remember names unless I have met someone several times, I will even say—with a smile and a rueful laugh—"Let me warn you that I need to hear a name three times before it sticks in my memory." Then, when I next see that parent and can't recall the name, I can open with, "Remember, you need to tell me your name again. We aren't up to three yet!" It becomes a lighthearted interaction that buys me some time.

**Watch, listen, and lay the groundwork for a parent web.** When initially meeting parents, I try to ask questions to help me build connections in my mind. A good start is a simple, "Do you have any other children in the district? What are their names, and who are their teachers?" Meanwhile, I make mental notes of parents who are friends with one another, work on PTO committees together, or live close to one another. In doing so, I slowly begin to put together a picture of the school community as a whole.

## Turning Uncertainty into Solidarity: Conversations with a New Staff and School Community

Members of a school staff often feel hesitant and uncertain when they know there is a new principal at the helm. They don't know whether the new leader will stick with the previous administrator's plans, or whether there will be broad changes (which many staff members abhor). Ideally, your initial conversations will dispel any anxiety, allowing you to begin the process of building trust between you and each member of your staff. In the examples that follow, we revisit the scenarios outlined in the beginning of the chapter. Each offers some talking points you may want to use when first meeting your whole staff and your individual teachers.

## Scenario 1: The Staff Meeting

You've been hired to be the principal after several years as a literacy coach. As a coach, you worked with a small portion of the staff; however, the rest of the staff knows very little about you. You want to speak to everyone before summer break, so the retiring principal has called a meeting for you in the school's library. As the staff members enter, you greet each person at the door with a smile. At the appointed meeting time, you walk to the front of the assembled group and begin.

> **You:** *Hello! I am thrilled for the chance to be your leader next school year—and beyond. Some of you already know me, because we've been lucky enough to work as a team for several years. Others probably know very little about me.*
>
> *Let me start by telling you a bit about myself. I was a teacher at the middle school level for eight years. Next, I was given the chance to move down to the elementary level as a literacy coach. I was at Oakstone Elementary for three years and have been here at Rittman Elementary for three additional years.*
>
> *Four years ago, I received my certification in school administration. When I started my career, I didn't think I would ever be a principal; however, when I started working as a coach, I learned how much I loved working with teachers and students in a leadership role. I loved helping teachers learn and grow, and interacting with students in a small-group setting. I also enjoyed working with the principal and learned a great deal about leading a school. I am looking forward to the transition into an official role next year.*

*On a personal level, my husband and I have two children—my daughter is a senior in high school, and my son is a sophomore. I spend a lot of my free time watching them in various theater productions and sporting events. I also love to read—both novels and professional books about instruction and leadership.*

You've gotten off to a good start by sharing information about yourself. You have included personal details, but have also outlined your professional qualifications.

**You:** *As we move into the new school year, I am looking forward to developing some goals together. We'll take a look at our current levels of student achievement; think about our school culture as it relates to students, staff, and parents; and make sure all of you are feeling good about the work you are doing each day. These goals will be collaborative, and we'll work through them together by following detailed action steps. I look forward to our work together!*

*Now, in an effort to respect your time, we'll keep this meeting short. However, I'd love to take a few questions from you. Does anyone have something they'd like to ask?*

**Teacher #1:** *I have a question. Will you be working closely with our current principal as you take over?*

**You:** *Yes. As some of you know, he and I work very well together. We plan to spend a lot of time talking about important issues. He can give me a good perspective on where we've been academically and how successful previous school goals have been.*

**Teacher #2:** *Our current Building Leadership Team is made up of teachers who have been in that role for years. Will you be changing the representatives serving on that team?*

**You:** *I have heard that is a concern for some of you, and I understand why. I also see the value in avoiding big changes at the beginning of my year here. For that reason, I haven't yet made a decision on that. I* *will wait until I speak to all of you individually, weigh all the options, and make a final determination before the year begins. I'm just not comfortable giving a definitive answer until I have more information.*

Here, you're responding honestly to teacher questions, opting for clarity and openness over bland reassurances.

**Teacher #3:** *We heard the district's curriculum director plans to make big changes on the online wiki we use for our main resource. Do you have any information on that?*
**You:** *No, I haven't heard anything about that. I am sure that is a big uncertainty for you, especially because I know many of you access that wiki throughout the summer. I'll ask a few questions and get back to you as soon as possible.*

Here again, you're admitting when you do not know the answer but making a commitment to check in with your district leadership, find that information, and provide it. Remember that it's essential to follow through with promises like this!

**You:** *These are all great questions—thank you! Now, let me tell you about the next step in my transition to this school. My highest priority is getting to know you. To do so, I would like to set up individual meetings to learn more about you. I'll be sending you an e-mail asking for a time that will work for both of us. When we meet, just come prepared to tell me about yourself, your role here at our school, and your personal and professional goals. Until then, though, I'd like to thank you once again for your time and let you get back to your work. I look forward to talking with each of you in the next few weeks!*

The meeting was short and efficient and ended with the message that you value your staff's time.

## Scenario 2: The Individual Teacher Meeting

In this scenario, you are taking over a middle school. You have already had an initial staff meeting in which you introduced yourself and talked briefly about your philosophy as a leader. The meeting went well, although the staff was quiet and reserved as you spoke. You remember your superintendent's warning that the school was a "tricky one." You are now beginning the process of meeting with individual staff members, starting with an 8th grade math teacher, William, who also coaches the track team.

> **You:** *Thank you so much for coming in. Why don't we start with the basics? Tell me about yourself.*
>
> **William:** *Well, as you know, I'm William. I live here in town with my wife and two girls; they are 8 and 11. My wife is a teacher at the high school. We really enjoy living here. It's a great place to raise a family.*
>
> **You:** *And what about here at school? What is your role?*
>
> **William:** *I've been at this school for 20 years. I've taught math at all levels, but I've been teaching 8th grade for 15 years now. I'm also in my 20th year coaching track, which I really love.*
>
> **You:** *That's great. I coached for several years and found it extremely fulfilling; I loved being with kids outside of the classroom. Do you see yourself teaching math and coaching for the foreseeable future?*
>
> **William:** *Funny you should ask. No, I don't think so. I'm considering going back to school to get a certificate to be a guidance counselor; I could use a change, and I think I would be good at that.*
>
> **You:** *I remember deciding I needed a change and seeking my administration certificate. It's been a fun and invigorating experience! What is it about being a guidance counselor that you would enjoy?*

Notice how you begin by picking up on a commonality and making a personal connection.

**William:** *Well, my favorite thing about this job is working closely with students. I'd like to support them with some of the big issues they face. Middle school kids are great—complicated, but great.*

**You:** *What do you mean?*

**William:** *Well, they're just in a really tough part of life. For them, everything seems hard. At this age, kids are in a weird transition with their parents, wanting to be independent but still needing the support; friendships are shaky; confidence is hard to come by; and so on. I love working with kids at this stage in life because I get how hard it is. That's why I coach track; I love just hanging out with kids and helping them find success. I like it when I see them feel good about themselves.*

**You:** *I agree; that's why I'm here, too. What is it you don't like about your job?*

**William:** *Can I be honest?*

**You:** *Of course.*

**William:** *I'm not passionate about the math anymore. I've become a little bit tired of teaching the same thing for so long.*

**You:** *I can see how that would be hard. Although some people are very content doing the same thing for decades, others do really well with occasional change. Let me ask you this: What are your favorite parts about working here, beyond the kids? And what is frustrating for you?*

**William:** *Beyond the students? I'd say working with my colleagues on the 8th grade team. We get along well and work well together. There are some cliques on the staff, though, which I hate. Sometimes it seems like we're all working in isolation with our own grade. I don't know; does that make any sense?*

As illustrated here, a simple question about what a teacher likes and dislikes can reveal information about the overall culture of the building. If you hear the same message from others, you'll know it is a problem that you will need to address.

**You:** *Let me see if I understand: You feel connected to your grade-level team but not to the rest of the staff, right? Why might that be? Is there a history of this here?*

**William:** *Well, our previous principal had favorites. He brought in several teachers from his previous school, and from the very beginning they were "his" people and his favorites; the rest of us felt like outsiders. He also came in and made big changes, empowering his own people and making the rest of us feel left out. That first year, he moved a bunch of us around according to his whims—or, at least, he didn't explain his reasoning to us. I don't think we've ever recovered from that.*

**You:** *I'm glad you shared that perspective. Maybe the threat of sweeping change is what feels so divisive?*

**William:** *Yes. It's what makes me just want to close my classroom door and teach, and then go coach, and avoid everyone. I hate staff politics.*

Here, your questioning uncovers important information about the history of the school leadership and the reasons staff members may feel nervous about you coming in.

**You:** *Well, I hope we can work together to make you feel more connected to all your colleagues. Cohesiveness within a staff is important to me. Can you tell me what you value in a building leader? Or, to put it another way, what do you hope I'll bring to this school?*

**William:** *Like you said, cohesiveness would be nice. I don't know if it's possible, but I miss it. I feel like we had it once.*

**You:** *What else?*

**William:** *I'd just appreciate if you would communicate with us. If you plan to make big changes, make sure you talk with all the people who will be affected so we'll know what you're thinking. I feel like a principal who is honest and transparent is much more trustworthy than someone who's always surprising us with sudden or impulsive ideas.*

**You:** *I will certainly keep that in mind. Communication is something that is crucial in a successful school. I, too, have worked in environments of distrust, and that can be hard. I will say, though, that although I understand your frustrations, I love that the first thing you told me is that you enjoy the students—hanging out with them, helping them, supporting them in this tough part of adolescence. After all, that's why we're really here—for the kids. You'll hear me say that a lot. When I make decisions, I always ask, "How does this help students? Are we making choices or changes for them—or for us?"*
**William:** *Well, that sounds good.*

You are taking advantage of a chance to explain what you value—cohesiveness, communication, putting students first—all while gaining information about this teacher's perspective.

**You:** *Well, I won't keep you any longer. I do appreciate your time and perspective. Please come by anytime you would like to talk. I want to be supportive of you in your work, and I'm here to help you as you work with our students.*

## Scenario 3: The Aggressive Parent

The final scenario in this chapter describes a situation in which you are approached immediately after your welcoming remarks at the beginning-of-year Open House. The parent asks if you have a few moments to talk. You begin by reaching out and shaking her hand.

**You:** *Let's start with introductions. But you already know my name!*
**Parent:** *I'm Seiko Miles. It's nice to meet you in person—I've heard so much about you.*
**You:** *It's nice to meet you, too, Ms. Miles. I'd love to chat with you, but we need to keep this conversation brief. I want to make sure I am*

*available to personally meet as many other parents as possible this evening. Do you think that is possible?*

**Ms. Miles:** *I understand. This won't take long. I just wanted to meet you right away because, quite frankly, you're going to see a lot of me.*

**You:** *Oh?*

## Yes, you have undoubtedly identified one of your "bulldogs."

**Ms. Miles:** *I am very involved in the school. I volunteer all the time. I work in the office whenever they need something, and I am the head of the Athletic Boosters. I'm around a lot!*

**You:** *That's great. Volunteers are incredibly important to a school. Why don't you tell me about your kids?*

**Ms. Miles:** *Well, Shino is a freshman, and Maya is a senior. They are both accomplished athletes in several sports. I know you'll be hearing a lot about them. They are both playing on the volleyball team right now, so you will see them play this fall. They are also extremely successful in school; neither one has ever had anything below an A. And I expect that to continue.*

**You:** *That's terrific. They must be very hard workers. I have watched the volleyball team practice, and I'm extremely impressed by their teamwork and focus. It seems like a great group of girls.*

**Ms. Miles:** *Oh, it is. Maya is the cocaptain of the varsity team. She shares the role with Darisha, who is her best friend. My niece, Audrey, plays on the junior varsity team with Shino. You'll meet their mom—my sister— quite soon. I'm sure she'll find you tonight to introduce herself.*

## Listening carefully to information shared about friends and family helps you build a web of connections among students and parents.

**You:** *I look forward to meeting her! If I don't meet her tonight, I'm sure there will be other opportunities. I think it's probably a long process to get to know everyone in this school, and I want to do it right! I will warn you—and your sister, too—I will need to hear your name several times* *before it will stick in my memory! I have always struggled with names. So the next time I see you, you may need to tell me your name again!*

It's a good choice to acknowledge both your limitations and the fact that it will take time to meet and remember each parent.

**Ms. Miles:** *Oh, I understand. There are a lot of people in this school. Now, I don't want to take up too much of your time, so I'll let you go. I just wanted to make sure I met you right away, since we really will work closely together in several areas.*
**You:** *I'm so glad that you introduced yourself.*
**Ms. Miles:** *And I'm pleased that you took the time to speak with me. I know you're really busy this evening. We'll talk again soon!*

By speaking with this aggressive parent immediately and strategically, you've laid the groundwork for a positive relationship.

Initial meetings with your school community—both as a whole group and with individuals—are the foundation of your success in your new school. With that said, it's important to note that you'll never convince *everyone* to be completely accepting of your new leadership. Some people seem to carry an inherent sense of distrust of leadership, and nothing you can do will change that mindset. It's best to accept and move on; do not waste energy trying to convert someone who simply isn't welcoming. Just move forward with your goals, focusing on the staff, students, and parents who are glad to have you there and glad to follow your vision.

Your relationship with teachers, parents, and students will help you determine the nature of your school's culture. This is an essential step in your first few years.

# Building and Maintaining a Positive School Culture

**2**

### Scenario 1: A Culture of Isolation

*You are in your second month as the principal of a high school. You have determined that the culture of the school is one of quiet isolation. Initial conversations have revealed a history of teachers working largely alone, rarely meeting to plan together or discuss student learning. The school's culture seems like a lonely one. You decide to meet with the head of the English department to determine if you have accurately assessed the situation.*

### Scenario 2: A Culture of Confidence, Understanding, and Teamwork

*When you are hired to take over a middle school, you hear wonderful things about the school from parents, teachers, and staff. The teachers speak openly to you about how they enjoy working closely in teams with their colleagues. There is a strong sense of school spirit, camaraderie, and joy in the building. How can you make sure this type of culture continues to flourish? You turn to the school guidance counselor for perspective.*

### Scenario 3: A Culture of Distrust

*In your first few weeks as an elementary principal, you get a vivid picture of a staff that seems very distrustful of one another. You have even heard comments from staff such as, "Be careful what you tell her. Might as well tell the newspaper, for how fast the world will hear," and "He'll act like he's on board, but he's going to bad-mouth you the minute you turn your back." How can you build trust among your staff? After thinking it through, you develop a plan to address your concerns. Before you move toward implementation, though, you ask to meet with your superintendent to get his approval.*

Being hired as a school principal is a heady, exciting thing. You will feel strong, successful, and eager to take on the challenge of leading a large group of people—students, teachers, and families.

And then the reality hits: Where do you even *begin*?

The truth is, schools are complicated places. They can be full of support, laughter, growth, and fulfillment; they can also be places riddled with distrust, old wounds, and competitiveness. Most often, some combination of all these things makes up a school's culture. I have a loose definition of *school culture*; to me, it is the complicated combination of all the thoughts and feelings that each student, staff member, and parent brings as he or she enters the doors of the school building.

How do you determine where your school lands on the culture spectrum? Is the school culture positive, negative, or ambivalent? Or, more likely, is it a complex mixture of all three?

My first year as an administrator, I was an assistant to a powerful and skilled principal who had been asked to take over leadership of the school and turn around the culture of the building. The school community was struggling for several reasons. Recent redistricting had left the building with reduced enrollment, so the school felt quiet and hollow. Most of our students lived in poverty and were left alone much of the time as their parents struggled to keep the family afloat. The students were unenthusiastic at best; at worst, they were belligerent and disrespectful. The staff felt rejected and weary. Time and again, conversations with students, teachers, and parents revealed a culture of apathy and helplessness. We didn't need conversations to see this; the feeling was practically a physical one, unmistakable to anyone who set foot inside. In fact, even the building had been neglected—furniture was aging, paint was peeling, and everything seemed to be covered with a thin layer of dirt and dust. Overall, there was a dispirited, downtrodden sense to the place.

When I was officially hired, the principal shook my hand and congratulated me. Then, she looked me straight in the eye and said, "Your job is to help me turn this place around. And we have our work cut out for us."

I couldn't even fathom how to begin, but my principal knew. Over the course of the year, I watched and listened as she focused her efforts on building and maintaining a positive school culture.

## Strategies and Solutions for Creating a Positive School Culture

The approach I learned from my principal, and the one I advocate still, is a three-step process.

### Step 1: Gauge the Past

Past decisions, even those made years ago, can still have an effect on your current school culture.

**Research the school's history.** Every school has a history. Whether the school has been open one year or 100 years, a *lot* has happened. It's easy to cobble together a thorough picture of your school's history simply by asking, "Why are things this way? What happened to get us where we are today?" I put special focus on the input from veteran staff members; they know the most, of course, and I usually find they are quite eager to share their perspective.

**Stay impartial when gathering information.** As you learn about the journey your staff has traveled, remember that *there is no real truth*—only a whole lot of different perspectives. For example, staffing decisions may have been made previously that hurt some teachers while simultaneously helping others; as a result, some teachers will have a negative point of view, while others are thrilled with the way things have been managed. Gather as much input as you can, and don't make up your mind until you feel you have heard the perspective of as many people as possible.

## Step 2: Build from the Ground Up

After you have determined what has happened in the past to form the current culture of your school, it will be time to think about moving it in the direction you'd like it to go. There are several ways you can make this happen.

**Establish trust.** You are the model for a culture of trust in the building, so you should be trustworthy yourself. Your integrity will be constantly scrutinized in this role, but each time you do the right thing, you will be building trust between yourself and others. For example, if you are told something in confidence, keep the secret. If you say you will do something, do it. Avoid gossip at all costs. Stay committed to your basic philosophies about students and revisit those philosophies often on a personal level and when working with staff.

**Show appreciation.** When I speak with members of my school community, I try to find a way to thank them for their work. There is an adage that applies perfectly to educational leadership: No matter how much you think you are showing your appreciation, it's not enough. So I try to give constant positive feedback; I find my gratefulness translates into a stronger school environment.

**Stay positive.** It's best to bring an optimistic, upbeat, and can-do attitude to work each day. This seems obvious, but it is harder than it appears. When a staff member is feeling frustrated or downtrodden, it is easy for sympathy and support to turn into commiseration. There is a distinct difference between the two; be aware of when you have crossed over, and pull yourself back to your role as a positive, problem-solving leader.

**Don't ask someone to do something you wouldn't do yourself.** You will garner immense respect if you jump in and complete tasks no one expects you to take on—like the lousy jobs no one in a school wants to do. Don't think you are above those jobs. For example, when I see a spill in the cafeteria, I hustle to grab the mop bucket to clean it up. I cover bus duty—especially in the rain or snow. I change the laminator film and fill the copier with paper when I see it is low. Doing these small tasks will show your staff that although you are their leader, you are one of them, and you recognize that everyone is working toward the same goal.

**Ask questions as a way to seek solutions.** When you see indications of poor morale or recognize areas of frustration, focus on what you might do to improve the situation. Try simple questions: *I can see you are upset; what can I do to help you? How are you feeling? What can we do together to improve this situation? What would solve this problem for you?* Recognizing trouble and seeking solutions will help you show your genuine interest in the well-being of your staff, students, and school.

**Take it one step at a time.** Building a strong school culture doesn't happen in the first few weeks of school. It takes time, energy, focus, and dogged determination. At times, it will feel like you'll never reach your goals. Stick with it, one conversation and one decision at a time. Eventually you'll get your building where you want to be.

**Understand ebbs and flows.** As the school year progresses, there are times that are more difficult for parents, teachers, and students. I find that the most challenges come right before major holidays, during high-stakes testing, and during the dark, cold months of the year. These are the times when your school culture will feel weak and wobbly. Power through—things will improve in time.

**Don't expect perfection.** Schools are filled with human beings, and as such, you will never have a perfectly positive, joyful, model school culture like the one you wish you could have. There will always be negative people; there will always be grumbling and complaining in some capacity. When you hear nay-saying, ask yourself if it is an accurate representation of the building as a whole. If, after some reflection, you decide that it is not, let it go and move on.

## Step 3: Keep the Momentum

Once you feel that your school's culture is in a good place, what can you do to make sure it stays there? Here are some strategies I recommend.

**Relentlessly take stock.** Ask questions. Ask them constantly. In your conversations with staff, students, and parents, seek to determine if your school's culture is staying strong. *How are you feeling about the work we are doing here at school? Is there anything you need from me? What are some things you wish we were working on?* Of course, asking is the easy part—listening carefully is the challenge. Focus on what people say to determine if they are happy when they are in the building, if they are proud to be part of the school, and if they are eager to give time, energy, and focus to making your school an excellent one. It will also guide your decision making if you sense that the school's positive culture may be slipping.

**Be visible.** Check in often with teachers, students, and parents. There is nothing worse than a school leader who disappears into an office and rarely emerges. Make sure you are out and about, actively solving problems and making decisions.

**"Every kid, every teacher, every day."** As mentioned in Chapter 1, I have a personal goal to see every student every day. I try to see every *teacher* every day as well. This sounds daunting, but I can usually do it if I make myself available during transition times such as lunch duty, bus duty, and class changes. Being visible helps establish that you are the leader and that you are fully engaged in the day-to-day work of being a building principal. It isn't always possible to see every person every day—the realities of meetings, emergency situations, and times you are not in the building will prohibit you sometimes—but it can still be a goal.

**Get personal.** Get to know members of your school community on a personal level. Ask them about things they care about, things that may worry them, and things they are celebrating. Get to know the names of their family members and what is happening in their lives. They will appreciate that you care, and they will be glad for the personal connection you build with them.

**Be personable.** I like to invite my staff to get to know me as a person beyond the walls of the school building. I invite them to my home for gatherings; I introduce them to my family; and I talk with them as a person struggling to balance the same kinds of things they struggle to balance. My particular approach may not be right for you, but remember that when the members of your staff get to know you, you increase the odds that they'll be able to trust you and your leadership.

**Look beyond the classroom.** Teaching may be occurring in the classroom and students may be achieving academically, but school culture goes far beyond the classroom. Be mindful of the success and spirit connected to extracurricular activities such as athletics, theater, music, journalism, and community events. Keep an eye on both teachers and students to make sure there has not been a decline in attendance, attitude, engagement, and behavior choices.

**Get people together.** Get your staff together often to connect with one another. Providing a staff lunch, organizing a potluck, or planning after-school gatherings are all ways that your staff can come together. A school culture in which the grown-ups like and enjoy one another's company will infiltrate all aspects of your school culture. After all, when people know one another on a personal level, they will grow close and want to take care of one another, and this strengthens your whole school community.

**Seek ideas and input from everyone in your school.** Make sure you have set up a structure in which you can get feedback about your school's culture. Whether it is a formal survey or simply a well-established open-door policy, make sure members of your school community have a way to connect with you and share ideas about ways to maintain a positive school environment.

**Build an advisory team focused on culture.** Beyond getting regular input from members of the school community, I like to seek allies who care as much about having a positive school culture as I do, and I ask them to serve on an official team. We meet monthly; our meetings follow a loose agenda and cover anything from the practical (key points we need to share with parents at our Open House) to the fun (planning a year-end staff party). This team makes up a core group of people who are deeply invested in keeping our school culture strong. Together, we openly discuss how people are feeling: Are things going well? Are there any indications of discord? Is there something we can do to lift morale or bring us closer together as a staff?

**Reward evidence of positive culture.** When I see a member of our school community doing something that enhances the school's culture, I make the time to express appreciation. For example, I keep a box of school stationery on hand, and whenever I can, I write a quick note of thanks when I see that something positive is happening. As I walk around the halls, I frequently search for evidence of positive culture and verbally acknowledge what I see, expressing my appreciation. Actively rewarding positive school culture will ensure that it sustains itself.

## Making It Positive: Conversations That Build, Promote, and Maintain Your School's Positive Culture

As with many parts of a principal's job, effective communication is the key to determining the current state of your school's culture. It will help you build and maintain a strong school culture in your beginning years as a principal. Here we will revisit the scenarios outlined in the beginning of the chapter, giving you conversational starting points to help you.

### Scenario 1: A Culture of Isolation

You are getting an uneasy feeling about the high school you have just been hired to lead. Initial conversations with staff seem to indicate that many work alone. You don't get a sense that there is collaboration between teachers, either about students or about curriculum. You decide to meet individually with several teachers you know are leaders. In this case, you are talking with Sarah, who is the head of the English department.

> **You:** *Thank you for taking time to meet with me today, Sarah. I was hoping to get some perspective from you about how the staff here works together.*
>
> **Sarah:** *I'm happy to help. What specifically were you wondering about?*
>
> **You:** *Well, can you tell me about the collaboration and teamwork here? I am not getting a sense that there is a lot of that type of thing going on.*
>
> **Sarah:** *Well, I would agree with you on that one. Some people seem repelled by the idea of working with others.*
>
> **You:** *Do you feel that way?*
>
> **Sarah:** *I don't—not at all. I'd love to collaborate with other teachers! We could have some great conversations about students that could help us know them better. For example, if I have noticed a student struggling in class, or starting to make poor behavior choices, it would be great if I could walk down the hall and ask this child's other teachers if they are experiencing the same thing. Then we could team up with, say, a guidance counselor or an assistant principal to figure out what's going on and help the kid out. But that just doesn't happen here.*
>
> **You:** *Is there collaboration on the curricular level?*

You are asking a lot of questions to gain understanding.

> **Sarah:** *Not at all. But that one is a little easier to understand; a lot of us are teaching courses that no one else teaches, so there really isn't anyone to collaborate with. But even when we could collaborate about instruction, a lot of people here just feel really passionate about their subject area and have very set ideas on how they want to teach it. They don't want to think about changing the way they teach.*
>
> **You:** *Yes, I can understand that, too. Can you tell me why you think things are this way?*

**Sarah:** *When I was first hired 10 years ago, there was a lot more collaboration. Then we went through a really tough time because the district had to make budget cuts. All of us lost some planning time, and we all had courses added to our teaching load. It was very divisive, because a lot of people didn't think the allocation of increased teaching load was fair.*

Based on this teacher's answers, you can build a snapshot of the school's history and begin to see how past decisions are affecting your current school culture.

**You:** *I can understand that. How do you feel?*

**Sarah:** *Well, can this be just between you and me?*

**You:** *Absolutely. One of the things you will learn about me as a leader is that I will keep confidential conversations private. You will find I value trust above most all else.*

Here, you've clearly articulated that trust is one of your core values, and you have begun to establish it by reassuring the teacher you will not share anything about the conversation with others. The next step is to honor that promise.

**Sarah:** *I am still angry about what happened. They cut two teachers from the English department, so we all had to take on a sixth class period. Meanwhile, the science department actually added a staff member—the science teachers are only teaching five classes, and the department head teaches four. He was tight with the previous principal, and he was the head baseball coach, so he—and his department—got everything they wanted. The principal justified it by saying since he was the coach of an important athletic program, he needed less of a class load. But that's not fair because he earns extra money coaching—why should he have less to do during the day if he's making more than we are? It didn't make any sense then, and quite frankly, it doesn't make sense now.*

**You:** *It sounds like something that would have been difficult for everyone in your department. That is something I will definitely look into.*

You are staying impartial—acknowledging Sarah's perspective but not promising a change. The only thing you're promising is something you know you can deliver, which is further inquiry into an apparent inequity.

> **You:** *Is there anything else you'd like to share with me?*
> **Sarah:** *No, I think that covers it.*
> **You:** *Again, I'd like to thank you for coming in. Your time is valuable, and I'm grateful that you set some of it aside for us to talk. This conversation has been helpful! Let's continue to communicate as we begin our year. I know you are a leader in this building, and I truly appreciate your perspective.*

By expressing genuine gratitude, you've laid the foundation for a positive relationship with key instructional leaders.

### Scenario 2: A Culture of Confidence, Understanding, and Teamwork

In this scenario, you are pleased to find that the school culture is obviously a positive one. Teachers, parents, and students are eager to tell you all the wonderful things about the building, and you definitely get the sense that there is collaboration, appreciation, and trust amongst the members of the school community. You want to make sure things continue in this way. You know the school's guidance counselor has worked in the building for many years, and you decide to meet with her to get her perspective.

> **You:** *I'm glad we could meet today. I wanted to talk with you about the culture in our building. From everything I've heard, and from the general feeling in the building, I am so impressed by the culture here—it seems so positive! There is a genuine feeling of collaboration and trust.*
> **Suzanne:** *I'm glad you feel it! It's definitely a special place.*

**You:** *And I want to make sure it stays that way! You've worked here for a long time, so I know you will know what went into making such a wonderful school culture. Can you help me brainstorm ideas for how I can ensure the school continues like this?*

**Suzanne:** *One thing I can tell you is that the teachers really like it when the principal is visible. Our previous leaders were great at stopping in and talking to teachers every day, checking on them and getting to know them as people.*

**You:** *I agree with that. My plan is to try to see every teacher and student—even if I just say hello—every day. It's a lofty goal, I know, but I am going to try to be there for every arrival, lunch period, and dismissal whenever I can.*

You are sharing your plan to do everything you can to be visible and see every teacher and student every day.

**Suzanne:** *That's great. Another thing that makes our school special is the staff's commitment to showing appreciation to one another. We all know everyone is working really hard, and it helps when our efforts are acknowledged.*

**You:** *I agree. I will make it a priority to do that. I would like to start staff meetings with a list of things I appreciate, and I like to send notes to thank a staff member who has gone above and beyond expectations. I am also looking into businesses that might donate lunch to staff members on a monthly basis as a way to thank them for their hard work.*

Showing appreciation for staff and getting them together in an informal setting reinforces positive working relationships.

**Suzanne:** *Well, we'd love that! Everyone likes to eat!*

**You:** *I also think it's important that we continue to have such strong school spirit. It seems like everyone here is really into extracurricular programs.*

**Suzanne:** *Oh, yes! We all take a lot of pride in our athletic programs. Many students attend the games and matches, and our athletes typically win several championships every year. We also have many kids involved in our music program. When there are concerts or performances, the gym is packed with people.*

**You:** *I'm committed to doing whatever is needed to keep that spirit strong. I love how many of our students are wearing school colors on any given day. It really is a great feeling.*

You are looking beyond academics to gauge the culture of the school.

**You:** *So I feel like I have some ideas to make sure the positive environment here will continue under my leadership. I hope you'll help me monitor things so that we can maintain this great school culture.*

**Suzanne:** *Absolutely! I talked frequently with the previous principal to share ideas to keep our school such a special place; I'd love to continue that with you.*

**You:** *I look forward to that. We'll make a good team. Thank you so much for talking this through and for being willing to continue these conversations going forward. I appreciate your time and perspective.*

Once again, this is an example of how showing gratitude, one person at a time, is a way to build a positive school culture.

## Scenario 3: A Culture of Distrust

You have barely settled into your new office at an elementary school, and you are already hearing comments that trouble you. Staff members speak openly about one another in negative ways, warning you about colleagues who cannot be trusted and will not be loyal to you. You make a plan to address this problem, but before you put your plan into place, you reach out to your superintendent.

**You:** *Thank you for meeting with me today. I wanted to make sure I got your perspective and approval before going forward with my plan to address the culture of distrust at school.*

**Superintendent:** *Thank you for sharing your thoughts with me. I'm eager to hear your plan.*

**You:** *The first thing I'm going to do is meet with each teacher and talk to them about trust. I'll ask them why they feel they can't trust their colleagues and piece together the reasons things have become so bad. I will also ask some difficult questions, such as "Do you think you are trustworthy? Would your colleagues agree with that?" I am hoping to get some really good conversations started in which the staff can reflect on their role in this culture of mistrust. I also feel that doing this will show that I am not afraid to have open, honest, difficult conversations.*

This part of your plan involves figuring out why the culture is what it is—the historical perspective you need to begin your work. You are also taking advantage of an opportunity to show yourself as an honest and trustworthy leader.

**Superintendent:** *That sounds challenging, but I think it's a great place to start. What will you do next? Will you tell them you expect a change in how they treat one another?*

**You:** *I don't think that would be effective. I'd rather encourage a change than command one. So my next step will be to talk about my belief that trust is an integral part of having an effective school. I'll talk about the positive things that can happen with a foundation of trust— strong working relationships based on collaboration and communication, of course, but also a work environment that can be fun, inspiring, and uplifting.*

**Superintendent:** *I think these individual conversations will be very beneficial. What will you do to ensure there is a positive result from them?*

**You:** *I am planning a staff get-together at my house in a few weeks. I will be providing dinner and music, and I am going to encourage everyone to come just to have fun. I'm going to set up the area so everyone mingles, getting to know one another on a personal level. Then I'm going to continue to encourage frequent get-togethers, rotating among the homes of staff members who are willing to host. It will help us see into one another's worlds and foster more understanding and trust. It will also help the staff get to know one another well, which is the most important part of trusting relationships.*

You are providing an opportunity for staff members to get to know you and each other on a personal level.

**Superintendent:** *I like this plan. Any other ideas?*
**You:** *As the year goes on, I'm going to talk a lot about trust. I'll address it at staff meetings and in individual conversations. I'll reiterate that I value trust among our staff, ask people if they have done anything trustworthy lately, and praise any moments when I can see trusting relationships in action. At the end of the year, I will do a staff survey and find out if they feel there has been an improvement in our culture of trust, and I will seek their ideas for further growth and improvement.*

You are setting up a structure that will allow your staff to contribute ideas and share feedback.

**Superintendent:** *I like that you plan to continue articulating that trust is a priority for you, and that you will seek their ideas for next steps. They will like having a voice in the process. I'm eager to hear how things work out for you. Keep me posted, OK?*
**You:** *I will. Thanks again for your time. I'm eager to get started!*

Working to build and maintain a strong school culture is always a challenge for a principal; it can feel like an exhausting and never-ending battle. But it is also, hands down, one of the most rewarding parts of being a principal. It feels good to lead a school to a place where everyone feels valued, where everyone is working together toward the same goal, and where people feel fulfilled and happy to be a part of it. It is absolutely worth the time and energy you invest.

### 3

# Establishing Good Habits for Balancing Priorities

### Scenario 1: Making a Plan

*After you are hired to be the principal of a middle school, you know there will be many things to do to prepare for the start of school. You place a call to the outgoing principal, who is taking a job at your district's central office, to ask for perspective and support in building a thoughtful plan for managing your priorities at the start of the year.*

### Scenario 2: Managing High-Intensity Times

*Your first year as principal has been a good one, but as the end of the school year approaches, everything seems to be spinning out of control. There are countless things you need to do, and you're convinced you're going to forget some of them. Worse, you don't know what you don't know—what if there are tasks that need to be completed that you haven't even thought of? You ask your administrative assistant to sit down with you and review your to-do list and make a plan for completion.*

### Scenario 3: Using Downtime

*In your first year, you have fallen into the habit of working at a frantic pace. But then, in mid-November, your calendar seems to open up a bit—the building schedule is running smoothly, there are not many discipline issues, and everyone in the school community seems focused on the building goals. While you are thrilled to find these pockets of extra time, you feel you can't slow down. There must be something you have to be handling at all times, right? You call a colleague who has been a principal for several years to ask him about this uneasy feeling that comes with actually having some free time throughout the day.*

A principal manages so many tasks. We are asked to meet the needs of scores of people, adhere to a long list of policies, and make our way through a seemingly endless to-do list. Over time, juggling it all becomes easier; you'll develop a system for keeping track of your responsibilities and prioritizing tasks, and you'll handle it all with a matter-of-fact calm. But it's not like that at first.

I barely remember my first months as a principal. I was in survival mode, making decisions and solving problems at a pace that felt rapid and panicky. I was working like a woman possessed, yet I felt like I wasn't keeping up. I stayed up late managing paperwork, spent my days racing from place to place, and devoted my weekends to planning and preparing for the new week. All of this took a physical toll, but the emotional toll was my true struggle. *Every* problem seemed dire. *Every* decision felt significant. *Everything* felt like an emergency, as though my instant and active involvement was imperative to the very *existence* of the school.

On one particular day late in the fall, it all became too much. I had five voice mails from parents I needed to return, upwards of 50 e-mails to answer, and three sticky notes on my office door with queries from staff members. My secretary had just cornered me to ask for a few minutes to discuss a problem with a recent purchase order. I knew I had to find some time to update my "Weekly Update" on the website and social media, because our community counted on frequent communication from me. My desk was a disheveled mess, and—catching a glance at myself in the mirror—I realized *I* was a disheveled mess, too. I stood there in my office, overcome with this thought: *I will never, ever, ever get this all done.* Just then, a teacher marched in the office with a student in tow. "This young man needs a conversation with you," she snapped. She turned and pointed to the chair reserved for students sent to the office for discipline problems. "Sit there," she hissed, before turning on her heel and marching out of the room.

I felt *that* feeling—the one I get when I am about to burst into tears—and I knew I had to find a moment alone. I gritted my teeth and told my secretary, very calmly, "I will be back in a moment." I left the office, walked down the hall to the boiler room, unlocked the door, and went inside. It smelled of cleanser, machinery, and musty tools. I moved to the back of the room, behind the electrical panel, behind the HVAC coolers, *way* back where no one would ever think to look for me. I sank into a cross-legged seated position on the concrete floor.

I spent several long, hard moments there, lamenting, pouting, and cursing the day. Then, as my senses returned, I had a clear and simple realization: *None of this is as important as it seems.* I mulled that thought over for a while. Yes, the things that I faced each day mattered, but not nearly as much as I felt they did. Perhaps I could loosen my grip a little bit and relax. Perhaps all I could do . . . *was all I could do.* I stood up and took several deep breaths, and then headed back toward the office.

That day was the first time I realized I didn't need to let a long list of tasks bring me to despair. With time, I came to know that some issues don't need to be addressed right away; in fact, some do not need my involvement at all. And I learned how to be mindful about what needs to happen first—as in, *right now*—and what can wait until later.

## Strategies and Solutions for Balancing Your Priorities

Here are some basic guidelines to follow. Good habits, once established, will serve you well for years.

**Be honest about your limitations.** I have learned to admit when I can't address a problem right away. I'll say, "I understand this is a priority for you, but I am not sure I will get to this in the next few days. Can we talk about alternative solutions? Or can we table this until I can make it a priority?" In other words, if I am not able to address a problem in a timely manner, I am just open about it. I avoid promising I'll get to something when I simply can't; unfulfilled promises make me appear scattered and unable to manage my job.

**Don't be a martyr.** No one likes a martyr, especially not one who has been hired to lead, make tough decisions, and represent the school's vision. It's best to avoid saying things like "I'm just so busy and overwhelmed with everything I need to handle; I can't possibly take on one more thing." The students, parents, and staff don't expect you to have an easy, stress-free job. So when it gets difficult, don't complain about it.

**Be strong—and watch your attitude.** Although you need to admit your limitations, it's important to keep in mind that you were hired to be the strong one—the leader who can handle a large list of tasks without faltering, pouting, or complaining. When you feel frustrated or overwhelmed, you can manage it by taking a moment *to yourself* to lament and then get back to work with a positive, can-do attitude.

**Stay organized.** I am most successful when I begin each day with a clear sense of my schedule. Rarely does it unfold exactly as

I'd planned, but having a rough idea of how to distribute my time and energy makes me focused, which makes me more efficient, which makes me appear to others as if I am in control. There are several components to this level of planning:

- *Creating a scheduling system that works for you.* I've known principals who manage their schedules on their smartphones, and I've known principals who work with paper calendars and sticky notes. We are all unique in what works for us. Use whatever system fits your style and professional personality; it doesn't matter what it looks like, just so it is effective in keeping your responsibilities organized and manageable.

- *Taking time to prioritize.* At the beginning of each week, and again at the beginning of each day, review your to-do list and your calendar. Pinpoint items that can be "flexed." There is no question that you'll have to find time to deal with multiple events for which you cannot plan—a facilities crisis; a medical emergency; a sudden visit by your superintendent; or a significant discipline issue that will require hours of investigation, conversations, and paperwork. It helps to have a general idea of what can be cancelled, postponed, or delegated to someone else, should the need arise.

- *Keeping track of tasks and crossing them off as they are completed.* Whether you work on a mobile device or with a small notebook, keep track of items that come up throughout your day that will need your attention, and when you have completed them, mark them clearly off your list. I keep a simple stenographer's pad with me at all times and add to it as I go through the day. It includes all the things I need to get to, including items related to things outside work. A recent glance at my notebook showed me this:

» Call Mr. Chavez re: teacher placement
» Plan initial staff meeting
» Order supplies
» Finalize schoolwide calendar—check with PTO?
» Payroll training
» Bookshelves? Any extra? (!!!!)
» Ask Jill about kindergarten training
» Ask 3rd grade team about placing new enrollees—class sizes high!
» Special Ed meeting/norms
» Make dr. appointment for Jack
» Meet w middle school re: IEP students moving up
» Call bus garage—specific routes

OK, I admit it—there were a lot more things on my real list, but this illustrates how a running list provides me with a quick look at what I needed to accomplish. Note my simple code for urgency: !!!! Again, we're all different, but this is a fluid, easy-to-manage, portable system that works well for me.

**Lean on your support.** Beyond staying organized and managing tasks, it's important to have some help. As my 5-year-old daughter once said to me of my then–administrative assistant, "Mommy? Ms. Quinn is *really* the principal, isn't she?" My daughter was exactly right; Susie Quinn was my right arm. She managed my schedule, reminded me about upcoming events, filtered through my mail and screened phone calls, and tactfully "mentioned" things I ought to be prioritizing. Without her help, I literally could not have been successful as a school leader. Working with her taught me that an effective principal needs a support system to help manage the pace and scope of the job. It doesn't always have to be an administrative assistant; it might be an assistant principal, a guidance counselor, a custodian, or even a lead teacher. It doesn't matter what official "title" your biggest supporters hold; what matters is that they align themselves with you and keep you focused on your work.

**Connect with colleagues.** Whenever I feel the gloom of having too much to do but too little time to actually do it, I pick up the phone and call one of my "principal friends." Often, they are feeling just as I am. I will no sooner get out my opening lament—"Aaahhhh!"—before we're both laughing and poking fun at ourselves. *It'll all get done,* we remind one another. *We always feel this way at this time of year.* Together we talk about what is challenging and how to manage it. What needs to happen first? What can wait? What can be delegated? The perspective of a colleague who is traveling the same journey, at the same time, with the same perspective, can be an immensely helpful resource.

**Always, always, always put students first.** It has become a bit of a cliché, but it is a fundamental truth: In education, if you make decisions and prioritize your work based on what is best for students, you will never be wrong. I was once on an interview committee in which we presented the following scenario to candidates for an open principal position in my district: *You are standing in the main office holding a stack of forms that need to be signed when a teacher comes in and says she wants to talk about an idea for her afternoon class. The phone rings, and your secretary tells you it's the superintendent—he wants to talk to you right away. At the exact same time, a student walks in and heads toward the clinic; he is crying and red-faced. What do you do?* Candidates that chose *any* option other than helping the child were not considered.

**Learn the cycle of leadership and how to ride it.** In leadership, there are ebbs, flows, and everything in between. There will be times when everything is buzzing along well, giving you time to sit back and think, reflect, and enjoy yourself as a principal. Similarly, there are times that you will feel frantic in your pace. Both experiences are part of the normal cycle of leadership. They will come, and they will go. The wheel keeps turning.

**Embrace unpredictability with humor.** The best thing about being a principal is that no day is the same, and the worst thing about being a principal is that no day is the same. When reflecting on a day's events, I often chuckle with this thought: *Well, I didn't expect* that *to happen today.* I've learned to be at peace with having a job in which each day brings surprises and unexpected changes. A good approach is to embrace it with laughter. Finding humor in the unexpected twists and turns of your day will make you more positive with the challenges of your job—and help you serve as a role model for others.

## Balancing Priorities: Conversations to Guide Decisions About Your Time

The scenarios in this chapter's opening summarize some of the challenges you may encounter managing your workload in your first years as a principal. Here we address each scenario with conversations that may help you learn to identify and manage your priorities.

### Scenario 1: Making a Plan

In this scenario, you have been hired to be the principal of a middle school. The outgoing principal, Tyler, is moving to a new role at your district's central office. He is willing to share some of his experiences and perspective from his time in the building, which you hope will help you make a plan for managing your priorities during the first few weeks of the school year.

**You:** *First, congratulations on your new job. It sounds like an exciting opportunity!*

**Tyler:** *I am looking forward to it. I sure will miss the school, though. It's a really great place; you're going to love it here.*

**You:** *That's what I hear. But that's exactly why I wanted to talk with you. I want to make a plan for the first few weeks, and I'd love your perspective on how to manage all the things that I'll need to pay attention to.*

**Tyler:** *It's a great idea to plan ahead! You might find it helpful to sit down with the school calendar and make a list of everything that is happening. Figure out what events you must attend, what things are probably fine without you, and what things you don't need to worry about.*

**You:** *Can you give me some examples?*

**Tyler:** *Sure. The week before school, you will have Student Orientation, the New Student Breakfast, and an opening PTO meeting. You will definitely need to be at all of those because you'll be meeting students and parents. The calendar will also show a Board of Education meeting, the first cross-country meet, and the team meetings for teachers to begin planning their year. Those are all things you don't have to attend—you can catch them when they come around the next time. And the calendar will have two or three other things on it, such as a meeting scheduled by district nurses to review student health plans. You don't need to worry about that one at all. They will take care of everything and will inform you of any concerns as needed.*

Notice how events can be prioritized, with items relating to students coming first.

**You:** *That's really helpful. It helps to know I don't need to kill myself getting to every single event right away. What about things I should make sure I'm doing?*

**Tyler:** *You will want to make a specific plan for the first two or three days of school. Make it a priority to personally greet teachers and students, and visit each classroom to say hello and welcome students back. You may also want to attend each lunch period and attend some* *after-school athletic practices so kids begin to know you and see how you want to get to know them. I always kept my schedule completely clear for the first few days because I wanted all of my time spent making connections with students.*

## Students always come first.

**Tyler:** *The downside, of course, is that things you've put off by clearing your schedule will still pile up, so you'll start to feel like you're falling behind. I relied heavily on Lesa, my administrative secretary, to help manage my schedule by spacing out meetings and commitments. She is an excellent resource for you; she knows what should be a priority and what can wait. She also screened a lot of things out that I didn't need to deal with. For example, she took all phone calls from salespeople; she forwarded messages to the appropriate person if needed; and she managed my mail. I didn't have to do any of that, which cleared my time up for other things.*

## Notice the importance of relying on others for support.

**You:** *How were you sure your secretary was making the right decisions with your time, your phone calls, your mail, and so on?*
**Tyler:** *Well, the two of us had worked together for many years, so she knows me very well and knows what I value. It might take some time to determine if that system works for you, or if you'd like more control over your schedule and time than I did. I was fine letting her handle it, but that's up to you.*
**You:** *That's helpful. I'll talk with Lesa and get her opinion, too. I'm sure together we can figure out how to work together as a team.*

## You are considering how to create a system that works for you.

**Tyler:** *That's the first step. As you continue with your year, though, I hope you'll contact me whenever you have questions. I'm just a phone call away.*

**You:** *I'll definitely take you up on that. I truly appreciate your time and mentorship!*

## Scenario 2: Managing High-Intensity Times

Our second scenario addresses how you may feel at the end of the year, which is typically a highly intensive time for a principal. In this case, you are feeling a lack of control, and you fear you are forgetting—or worse, not aware of—some tasks you may need to be prioritizing. You get together with your administrative assistant, Sherrie, to talk through the problem.

> **You:** *Phew! As you know, I am feeling nervous about everything right now. Things just seem to move so fast and furious this time of year!*
> **Sherrie:** *Oh, I know! The last few weeks of school always feel like this. We'll get it all done, I promise.*
> **You:** *I am sure you're right, but sometimes it doesn't feel that way! Can we go through the list I have and review it? Then you can tell me which things I have forgotten.*
> **Sherrie:** *Of course!*

You are relying on your support system to consider your priorities.

> **You:** *I have almost completed class lists for next year, and when I'm done, I'll turn them over to you so you can send out letters to parents with each child's teacher assignment. I have wrapped up all of the interviews for the teaching openings we had due to retirements, and I am making a recommendation to the Board of Education this week. That will complete the hiring process, and I'll be able to put the final touches on my staffing plan. I have planned my speech for the "graduation" ceremony for students on the last day, and I recently met with the PTO president to finalize the funding they are offering to support some of our purchases over the summer.*

**Sherrie:** *Check, check, and check.*

**You:** *Other things on my list to complete: Work with the custodian to select paint colors—we are getting all classrooms painted over the summer. Put together a "checkout" list for teachers to complete before they leave. Get out a final newsletter for our families, summarizing this year and wishing them a good summer. Update the website. Send a final tweet on Twitter and post a summer message on our Facebook page. Work with the technology department to update computers over the summer. Those are the things I think of as most important. Do you have anything to add?*

**Sherrie:** *Those definitely are the most pressing. How about closing out all our purchase orders and finalizing staff evaluations?*

**You:** *Yep, those need to be high on the list as well. Thanks. Anything else?*

**Sherrie:** *Do you want to think about any furniture purchases or mainte- nance repairs we need?*

**You:** *I know those are important, but they're not pressing. Could we work on that when things slow down after students and staff leave for the summer?*

You are being honest about your limitations, showing a realistic grasp of priorities, and tabling things that really *can* wait.

**Sherrie:** *Sounds good. You've got quite a list. How are you holding up?*

**You:** *Well, luckily, I don't really have the time to feel sorry for myself! No, I'm doing fine. Busy—but I like being busy. And this is the job, after all!*

A positive attitude is an invaluable ally.

**Sherrie:** *And you have a good plan. I really don't think we're forgetting anything. And if we are, we'll deal with it as it comes!*

**You:** *I'm sure there are things we aren't thinking about or aren't expect- ing. But like you said, we'll handle whatever comes our way!*

The certainty of unpredictability is one of the many challenges of the principalship. By acknowledging this reality, you're preparing yourself for the flexibility the job demands.

## Scenario 3: Using Downtime

This scenario describes the uncomfortable feeling you may have when, after a time of frantic work and a pace that seems impossible to manage, you have some open time in your schedule. Everything seems to have settled in a bit: teachers are teaching, students are learning, parents are quiet, and you have an uncanny sense of *calm*. You can't help but wonder what you should be doing—after all, there *must* be a problem to solve each moment you are working . . . right? You call a trusted and experienced colleague, Heather, for some insight.

> **You:** *Thanks for taking my call. I need to talk to someone who has been through this job for more years than I have. I'm calling with an odd question. After several months of a frantic pace, things seem really quiet right now. I feel like I shouldn't actually have quiet time! Does that make sense?*
>
> **Heather:** *I'm glad you reached out to me. I know exactly what you are feeling right now.*

When uncertainty strikes, seek out the counsel of a colleague who can commiserate and offer perspective.

> **You:** *You do? That makes me feel a little better. Is it normal to feel uncomfortable with downtime?*
>
> **Heather:** *Of course it is. I remember when I first started this job, I felt nervous anytime I had a quiet day. I was sure there was something I was forgetting to handle.*
>
> **You:** *That's exactly how I feel.*

**Heather:** *But it's a sign of good leadership that you don't have constant emergencies. It means you have empowered your staff to manage small problems before they turn into big ones. And it means you have a bit of time to focus on other things—stuff you can't get to when you are smack in the center of your busiest times.*

**You:** *Tell me more about that.*

**Heather:** *Well, your busiest times are at the beginning of the year when you are dealing with problems that come when school just opens; during assessments; before holidays, when discipline issues seem to increase; when staff evaluations are due; and at the end of the year, when you are planning for the next school year and you are fielding countless questions and concerns from—well, everyone.*

Notice the identification of the ebb-and-flow cycle of a principal's job.

**Heather:** *But the beautiful part about this job is that it is nicely balanced with periods when you actually can breathe. That's where you are right now, I presume?*

**You:** *Yes, I guess so.*

**Heather:** *So here is what you do at this point. You get to all the other things you want to do. You touch base with teachers by asking them how their year is going, if there is anything they need to make their instruction more effective, or if there is anything they are concerned about. You spend some time talking with parents when they stop by the school; it's a natural and easy way to build relationships with them. Best of all, you spend time hanging out with students—invite some of them to have lunch with you, or check in with them in class, or make phone calls to parents when you see students doing things that are extraordinary. So, yeah. Just slow down and build relationships.*

The advice here is to refocus on your connections with students. They are your touchstone.

**You:** *Building relationships with kids sounds like a good use of time. I bet it will be something that will pay off in the future.*

**Heather:** *You want people to know how much you care about them—especially students. They'll give you their best if they like and respect you.*

**You:** *Well, I feel a little better. I guess I felt like I needed "permission" to slow down and enjoy this downtime.*

**Heather:** *Permission granted! And call me anytime. Like when things get crazy a few weeks from now and you need me to remind you that there will be downtime again—you just have to wait for it!*

As you begin your work as a principal, it will be very important for you to establish habits to help you balance your priorities. Doing so will help you stay calm, organized, and focused on your main goal—leading a school that provides an excellent educational experience for students.

# Providing Effective Instructional Leadership

### 4

### Scenario 1: The Curriculum

*After several years teaching science at a high school, you have landed a job as a principal of a middle school. You know you have much to learn about the required curriculum that guides the teachers' instruction. You ask a colleague for ideas on how to get up to speed—quickly—so you can evaluate the quality of classroom instruction in your school.*

### Scenario 2: The Classroom

*You've just completed an observation in an elementary math class, and you found yourself impressed by the pace of the lesson, classroom routines and management, and the obvious workshop model framework of the classroom; however, you're unsure of how well the teacher addressed particular aspects of the curriculum. You recognize this may be ignorance on your part, so when you have your post-observation conference with the teacher, you directly address your uncertainties.*

### Scenario 3: Reflection

*With your first year as a principal coming to a close, you want take stock of your effectiveness as an instructional leader—and pinpoint some areas for improvement. You have built a trusting relationship with a fellow principal in your district. You ask if she'll take some time to help you reflect on your year.*

There are many established protocols and systems principals can rely upon while we're establishing ourselves as leaders. The district-approved student handbook provides guidance on disciplinary measures, the central office's background checks support hiring decisions, and the school's maintenance team takes the pressure off when it comes to running the facility. These supports make the job more manageable—not easy, mind you, but manageable.

Instructional leadership is a little different, and it can be a lot more daunting. What constitutes "good instruction" changes with the times and in response to new research. Staying on top of these developments, and cultivating a depth of expertise that inspires confidence from your staff, can be particularly steep hurdles for a new principal.

When I left my secondary teaching position to become an elementary administrator, I had doubts about how well I could outline the best practices of instruction. "I worry a bit about being an instructional leader for this staff," I confessed to my supervisor. "I've never taught elementary school. What do I know about elementary curriculum and instruction?"

She stopped me. "You've told me a few times now that you're not sure what good instruction looks like at this level," she said. "But good instruction is good instruction, no matter what the level."

"But it *looks* really different," I protested. "How do I know if the teachers are implementing good teaching practices in the classroom?"

"I think you're confusing two issues," she told me. "There's curriculum, which is different depending on the grade level, and there's good instruction, which is not."

She went on to point out that I *did* know what good instruction looks like—an organized classroom, solid routines, and lessons that engage students and connect to things related to students' real lives. "And all of that occurs with what you know is the basic premise of good teaching: direct instruction followed by guided practice and independent work," she said.

"Maybe you're right," I admitted. "I feel like I can identify good teaching. Maybe it's the actual curriculum that has me nervous."

"And that's easy to fix," my supervisor replied. "You can learn by utilizing curriculum resources. I can direct you to several excellent ones. And you can learn by asking a lot of questions. Ask me, ask your administrative colleagues, and best of all, ask the teachers. They know the curriculum better than anyone. Over time, you'll grow to understand it like they do."

I appreciated her faith in me—and her advice. I did just as she had suggested: sought resources to read, scoured our district's curriculum wikis, and asked teachers a lot of questions. Eventually I grew more confident, which made me a stronger instructional leader in both areas, teaching and curriculum. I still wouldn't call myself an expert, but I can hold my own, and I can support teachers in their instructional work.

Further, I have become more knowledgeable about current educational best practices. I will briefly define some of those practices here. Each one has been extensively studied, and further resources are readily available.

- *Professional learning communities (PLCs):* To summarize a complicated process in just a few words, a PLC is a group of educators working collaboratively to focus on results and ensure that students are successful in their learning. Probably the leading voice for PLCs is Richard DuFour, who has authored several books and articles describing PLCs and suggesting how to successfully implement them in schools. My favorites of his books are *Revisiting Professional Learning Communities at Work* and *Cultures Built to Last: Systematic PLCs at Work.*

- *Teacher leaders:* Teachers who take on leadership roles in a building, particularly in the areas of curriculum and instruction, are unsung heroes for principals. They are highly skilled educators whose gifts include the ability to encourage, inspire, and challenge their colleagues. For more on teacher leaders, seek out *The Power of Teacher Leaders: Their Roles, Influence, and Impact* by Nathan Bod and Andy Hargreaves and *Never Underestimate Your Teachers: Instructional Leadership for Excellence in Every Classroom* by Robyn Jackson.

- *Coaching:* Many educators today acknowledge that teachers can learn from "coaches" much like athletes do. In the field of education, coaches can be an official "instructional coach" hired by the district, a colleague who possesses the knowledge and patience to guide teachers toward growth, or even a trusted administrator. In this model of professional development, coaches challenge teachers to improve their instructional practice through observation, carefully worded guiding questions, and support throughout change. My favorite resource for this topic is *The Art of Coaching* by Elena Aguilar.

## Strategies and Solutions for Effective Instructional Leadership

Here are several strategies I've adapted over the years that have helped me grow into a capable and confident instructional leader.

**Think like a coach.** My husband is an excellent football and baseball coach, and when I watch him in action, I am always struck by how being an instructional leader is similar to coaching. We must do all the things coaches do—motivate, talk about what should be happening on the field (or in the classroom), model, lead the vision, coach every member of the team (or staff), and be the face of the program (or school) while knowing that everyone is watching. We must keep energy high, focus on the end goal, and continue to help our players (teachers) grow. Just as a coach knows if a game is being played well, I know if a class has been taught well and can offer feedback to help teachers improve. So, when approaching my work as an instructional leader, I think of myself as a coach.

**Use your teacher leaders.** To continue using the sports coaching analogy, consider that even professional coaches are not necessarily the experts on every nuance of the game—in fact, some of them have never even played the game themselves. What they have done, though, is make themselves students of the game. And, even more critically, each of them has a team of assistants to help them. A football coach will have a defensive coordinator, an offensive coordinator, a special teams coach, and a whole pile of other assistants who are the masters of a particular part of the game. Similarly, as principal, you have teachers who naturally take a leadership role and can help you "coach" other teachers on your staff. As a result, you don't need to know every single thing about curriculum. You can rely on these "assistants"—teacher leaders who can help you implement curricular and instructional goals.

**Seek to understand the basics of curriculum.** Although you do not need to be the master of all curricula, it's a good idea to learn the basics. Whether your district and state follows nationally recognized standards such as the Common Core, or whether your state has adopted another list of learning targets, it's important to learn a bit about what should be taught in each grade level. Make it your business to learn what expectations have been set for teachers and students at each grade level. This can be done easily by going to your state's Department of Education website and downloading standards and curriculum guides, and then committing time to reading and memorizing what standards are covered in each year of learning. Reference them often until they become part of your encyclopedia of knowledge about your work.

**Support PLC work.** As mentioned above, it's not your job to master all nuances of the curriculum. That job should fall to the teachers. So, in that sense, a principal can be a good instructional leader by getting teachers together into professional learning communities. As mentioned, PLCs are groups of teachers who share a curriculum, subject area, or particular group of students. Working together as a PLC, these teachers can have an enormous effect on student learning beyond their individual classrooms. When building the schedule or planning for professional development time, I work hard to build time for PLCs to meet and talk about what is expected, brainstorm ideas on how to most effectively teach their content, and plan lessons with similar scope, sequence, and rigor. In addition, teachers within a PLC often find it enormously helpful if they can watch each other teach and then discuss what they saw; finding time or class coverage for them to do this will be extremely helpful for them.

**Talk about instruction constantly.** Keep the focus on instruction by making it a part of conversations on a consistent basis. When talking with teachers about their work, I always try to give them feedback (which will be covered in more depth in the next chapter) and ask questions that will challenge teachers to think about what effect their work has on children. Here are some basic questions to get conversations started:

• Do you feel your students have a good grasp on your intended learning outcomes?

- What did you intentionally do in your lesson to help your students grow?
- What will you need to revisit during your next lesson?
- How did you differentiate for the various learners in your class?
- What did you feel went really well in your lesson? What do you wish you had done differently?
- Are there any students you are worried about?
- How are you challenging your most gifted learners?
- What do you think makes a good teacher?
- How do you know if your instructional approach is effective?
- Is there data to back up what you are doing in the classroom?
- How do you challenge yourself as a teacher?
- How did you become such an expert at what you do?
- What are your favorite resources?
- Whom do you watch when you want to see good teaching?
- What do you do to make sure teaching stays fresh and new, so that the students' learning is fresh and new?

**Set clear expectations.** I make it very clear what my expectations are for instruction. For example, at the first staff meeting of the year, I might outline the following expectations:

I expect every classroom to have the following:

1. *Clear learning goals that the students can articulate* ("I'm learning how to have a controlling idea for my paragraph.") Knowing what they are supposed to be learning will help students succeed.
2. *Time for student practice.* Students will be engaged and challenged by the content of the lesson; they will not simply receive information and reproduce it on demand.

3. *A workshop model of instruction.* Students will work together to achieve common goals and build understanding.
4. *Data collection and awareness.* Ongoing formative assessment will be used to measure student understanding and content mastery, and shed light on instructional approaches that are working and those that need to be revised. Current or recent standardized assessment data will also be consulted.
5. *Conversation to support growth.* Students will know how they are doing and will receive specific feedback that will further their learning.
6. *A growth mindset.* Teachers and students alike will persevere and embrace mistakes as opportunities to learn. Everyone will do their best and will avoid making excuses. The work is challenging, and everyone will rise to that challenge.

**Reflect.** Constant reflection about your work as an instructional leader will help you continue to grow, just as you hope your teachers will do. Here are some questions I have asked myself when I reflect on my work:

1. *What evidence is there to indicate positive change?*
   - Can teachers talk clearly about differentiation?
   - Have I seen evidence of formative assessment in classrooms?
   - Is our Response to Intervention (RTI) program working well?
   - Do teachers collaborate and engage in meaningful collegial discussions?

2. *What did I intentionally do as an instructional leader? What did I not do?*
   - When I got busy, what aspects of the job got away from me? What steps can I take to avoid letting things slip?
   - Did I engage in my own professional development?

- Did I stay committed to walk-throughs and feedback?
- Did I use time effectively at staff meetings and professional development opportunities?
- Did I empower my teacher leaders?
- Did I work to build staffwide instructional capacity?
- Did I support the continued growth of our PLCs?
- Did I work with specialty teachers (gifted specialists, intervention teachers, special education teachers) to support their growth?

3. *What do I need to revisit?*
   - Am I taking advantage of every opportunity to make instruction student-focused? If not, what steps can I take to make sure that happens in the future?
   - Am I staying committed to focusing on the influence we are having on each child?
   - Am I certain that all stakeholders know our instructional goals?
   - What else can I do to keep us energized as we pursue our instructional goals?

**Identify and provide professional resources.** There are many fabulous resources available to help teachers enhance their instructional practice. I try to identify these resources—by doing my own reading and by asking for suggestions from colleagues and teachers—and make them available. A centrally located professional library will help more teachers access these resources and help you establish and maintain a culture of adult learning.

As I've mentioned, being an instructional leader does not mean you are the master of all content and curriculum. It means that you know what good instruction looks like and that you know how to continue to promote a culture of learning and growth. All of these suggestions can help principals be the catalyst for instructional growth and positive change.

## Guiding Good Teaching: Conversations to Help You Become an Effective Instructional Leader

Anyone who has been a principal for more than five minutes knows that the job requires savvy leadership in multiple areas—facility management, professional development, financial decision making, personnel, and on and on. All of these are important, but an effective principal must put particular focus on instructional practices within each classroom.

Here, we revisit the scenarios outlined in this chapter's beginning. You may find yourself in any of these scenarios in your first years as a building leader.

### Scenario 1: The Curriculum

In this scenario, you admit to yourself that you don't know much about the curriculum being taught in your middle school. Your experience as a high school science teacher hasn't prepared you to know what middle school students are learning. You know it's important to figure out what is supposed to be taught, so you turn to a trusted colleague, Beth, for help.

> **You:** *I really appreciate your listening ear, Beth. I feel like I have inadequate knowledge about the instruction and curriculum at the middle school level. I have, quite literally, no experience with it.*
>
> **Beth:** *I completely understand, but this is an easy problem to solve. I've been a middle school principal for several years, and only lately do I finally feel like I've learned most of what I need to know. In the beginning, I was just like you—I didn't know much about the curriculum. But, again, it's easy to learn.*

**You:** *How?*

**Beth:** *Well, for one, there are tons of resources out there. Tons. The curriculum our Board of Education has adopted is aligned with the Common Core standards, so there are resources at the federal, state, and district levels to support us. There was a massive effort to help us all understand how to implement the new standards in the classroom, and most of those efforts are incredibly helpful.*

**You:** *Can you suggest a few websites or books that were particularly helpful to you?*

**Beth:** *Absolutely. I'll send over some of the things that helped me, and I'll e-mail you some helpful website links.*

Colleagues are often the best place to begin when seeking resources.

**You:** *Thank you so much. What other things did you find to be helpful?*

**Beth:** *I talked about instruction all the time and asked questions constantly. I identified the teachers that seemed to emerge time and again as experts in their curricular areas and delivered the best instruction to students. I visited their classrooms often, and I asked them piles of questions about their instruction. I asked how they created their lesson plans, how they incorporated the required curriculum into what they knew about their students as learners, what tricks they had to help students who needed support, and how to push students who mastered the content easily. By asking questions constantly, I learned more about good instruction, and teachers came to know how much I value it.*

Talking about instruction and asking teachers questions not only helps you learn; it also helps communicate your expectations for classroom practice.

**You:** *That sounds like a great plan. I think that's exactly what I'll do! Do you think that should be my highest priority? Learning the curriculum?*

**Beth:** *Absolutely not. I wouldn't suggest burying yourself in memorizing the required curriculum right away. You can be an extremely successful* *instructional leader without knowing the curriculum as well as the content experts teaching it. After all, good instruction is good instruction—it's connecting with kids, at their level, in ways that will challenge them to learn and grow. Just make it a priority to get familiar with the curricula and study them regularly. In time, you'll have a firm grasp of them. Don't worry about being an expert right at the beginning.*

You do not need to be the master—just the leader.

**You:** *I still don't feel confident about that, though. Did you, when you started?*

**Beth:** *Of course not! I was nervous as could be! You will grow into it.*

## Scenario 2: The Classroom

While observing a math lesson, you are impressed by the pace, management, and routine of the classroom, but you are unsure if the teacher, Carli, was addressing a topic aligned to the curriculum. You know you don't have the knowledge to be certain, so when you talk to Carli, you begin asking questions to address your uncertainty.

**You:** *Let me start by telling you how much I enjoyed watching your class. I was impressed with the work you have put into establishing classroom routines; students really knew exactly what to do at each point in the lesson. The lesson was well paced and moved along smoothly.*

**Carli:** *Thank you! I spend a lot of time at the beginning of the year setting up routines so students don't get bogged down with what they are supposed to be doing. They can focus on what they are supposed to be learning.*

**You:** *That's wonderful—your work has definitely paid off.*

**Carli:** *Thank you!*

**You:** *I also noticed how engaged the students were. They were really enjoying the learning, and they were excited about the challenges. Now, let me ask you a couple questions about the content of the lesson.*

**Carli:** *Sounds great.*

**You:** *You were covering the addition of fractions. What led you to that lesson?*

**Carli:** *We have just completed a weeklong study of numerators and denominators. I did some formative assessment and determined the students had a great understanding of both. They were ready to take it to the next step, which is adding fractions together. The lesson you saw was just the beginning of our work; we worked with like denominators, and we'll practice that for the next two days.*

**You:** *And then?*

**Carli:** *And then I'll move to adding fractions with unlike denominators. That is always difficult for students.*

**You:** *Why do you think it is a challenge?*

**Carli:** *Well, before they can add, they need to do some multiplication to set up the adding. It's outside of their comfort zone to do one operation to set up for another.*

**You:** *That makes a lot of sense to me. I am new to the curriculum. Can you talk to me about how this part of it fits into the whole?*

**Carli:** *Absolutely. In the grade level before this one, students learn the basics of fractions—what they mean, where they exist in the real world, how to write them in response to a problem. Then, in my grade level, we dig deeper into the concepts and terms related to fractions—the meaning of numerators, denominators, and improper fractions—and start to manipulate them a bit. We work with making similar denominators and then add or subtract them.*

**You:** *And what happens after that?*

Here, you are using questions to gain a better understanding of curricular decisions.

**Carli:** *The next grade level digs deeper still. They move into multiplying and simplifying fractions, and dividing improper fractions.*

**You:** *That makes complete sense. Thank you for clarifying it for me; I am learning about curriculum, and I need teachers to help me figure it out!*

You are learning the basics of curriculum by relying on your teachers' expertise.

> **You:** *Did you feel your students were successful when they worked independently on fractions?*
>
> **Carli:** *I do—well, most were. There are two students who did not do well on the formative assessment I gave at the end of the class, so I pulled them into a small group the next day and retaught the lesson. They did a much better job grasping the content the second time around.*
>
> **You:** *Would you do anything differently if you were to reteach that lesson?*
>
> **Carli:** *You know, I reflected on that quite a bit. If I could do it differently, I would shorten the instructional time in the mini-lesson, do a quick formative assessment, and then allow the students who grasped it quickly to move to their independent work. Then I could teach more targeted content to a smaller group of students who need more help and support.*

Here's an example of how your questions about instructional practices can be edifying for both you and the teachers you ask.

## Scenario 3: Reflection

With your first year as a principal coming to a close, you want to think about how effective you were as an instructional leader and where you need to improve. You have built a trusting relationship with a colleague, Vanessa, who is an experienced principal in your district. You ask if she'll take some time to help you reflect on your year.

> **Vanessa:** *So you want to talk about your year as an instructional leader. Let's start with the positives—what do you think you did well?*

**You:** *I feel confident in how I focused so much conversation on instruction. I talk about it constantly.*

**Vanessa:** *What do you mean when you say you "talk about it"?*

**You:** *Well, it's a lot more than just talking, of course. I ask a lot of questions. When I do classroom walk-throughs, I have brief feedback conversations with teachers, during which I might ask them about their intention for the lesson, what outcomes they noticed, how they differentiated for various learners, how they want to change their instruction, and so on.*

Regular conversation with teachers allows you to question, think, listen, and learn about curriculum and instruction.

**Vanessa:** *That's definitely a good strategy.*

**You:** *I also felt good about how I focused on formative assessment this year. We really made some strong gains in using daily assessment information to adjust our instruction. I saw lots of evidence of that happening in the classroom.*

**Vanessa:** *Great. Anything else?*

**You:** *One final thing I did when observing classrooms or designing professional development was to keep asking myself, "What's our purpose here? How does this help kids? How will students learn because of this?" I applied those questions to almost all of my instructional work.*

**Vanessa:** *Excellent—again, a great strategy. Now, what do you think you could do differently?*

**You:** *Unfortunately, I didn't feel good about the resources I put into the hands of teachers. I was so busy this year that I didn't do as I'd intended. I wanted to do several book studies and develop a professional library for teachers to explore.*

**Vanessa:** *That's something you can do for next year. And you will get busy—which is why you need to rely on others to help you. Who could you use to build some capacity in your instructional leadership?*

**You:** *I need to rely more on my master teachers. They are such experts—when I see them teach, I'm so impressed with what they know.*

*I should tap into their knowledge and ideas more, and use their favorite resources to build the library. I should also rely more on support staff—those teachers who may be experts in a particular area, like special education and gifted education.*

Notice the reliance on a team of master teachers and "assistants" to support the instructional leadership.

**Vanessa:** *I like that idea. What else would you like to focus on as you move into next year?*

**You:** *I need to work on knowing the curriculum better. My understanding of it is very, very basic.*

**Vanessa:** *That will take time, though. And remember, you don't need to be the master of all things curriculum; you should rely on your teachers for that. So work toward a solid, but not necessarily expert, understanding of what should be happening each year in each class, but beyond that, keep your focus on what the instruction looks like.*

A basic understanding of the curriculum is valuable, but a focus on leading is essential.

**You:** *That's what I'll do. I am going to make some specific goals for myself for next year—the curriculum study, establishing the professional library with the help of master teachers, and calling on support staff and specialty teachers more—and then, again, I'll reflect on how it all went.*

**Vanessa:** *I'll be glad to think it through with you next year.*

Self-reflection leads to new insight. Through this process, you set yourself on a course for more effective leadership next year, the year after, and for years to come.

Being an instructional leader is one of a principal's primary jobs—yet, paradoxically, principals are rarely absolute experts in all curriculum and instructional practice. In spite of this, though, a principal can be successful by approaching instructional leadership in a systematic and pragmatic manner. By putting systems in place to foster best instructional practices, relying on teacher leaders to discuss important curricular decisions, and mindfully reflecting on the work, a principal can be an effective instructional leader even without an extensive tool kit of knowledge.

### 5

# Conducting Staff Evaluations and Delivering Feedback

### Scenario 1: The Pre-observation Conference

*After just a month as the principal of a middle school, you set up a pre-observation conference with a teacher about whom you know very little beyond the fact that he teaches 7th grade science and coaches several sports. You have met him and spoken to him casually; he seems very likeable and clearly enjoys his work. You also know that he's popular with students and parents. You are eager to talk to him to gain a sense of his instructional skill, talent, and philosophy. Your main goal in your initial meeting is simple: To get to know him as a teacher.*

### Scenario 2: The Written Evaluation

*In a classroom observation as part of a teacher evaluation, you found very few concerns. The teacher seemed to have a firm grasp on classroom management, instructional practices, and knowledge of her students. Before meeting with her for the post-observation conference, you summarize your thoughts into a narrative that will be the foundation for your conversation.*

### Scenario 3: The Improvement Plan

*After talking with the previous principal, receiving unsolicited input from parents, overhearing passing comments from staff, and reflecting on what you've seen so far, you conclude that one of your teachers is, quite frankly, ineffective. You met with her in a pre-observation conference and found her comments to be shallow and dismissive. You observed her classroom several times, and each time, you noticed her lack of classroom management and her disorganized approach to her lessons. You realize the students on her roster are receiving a subpar education. As you prepare for your post-observation meeting, you know it is time to have a difficult conversation with her—and place her on a specific plan for improvement.*

Evaluating and providing feedback to staff members is important for many reasons. For one thing, it can be the catalyst for a strong school culture. Talking with staff members about their work— where they feel they are effective, where they struggle, what challenges them—is a way to build powerful, trusting relationships with your staff. Second, these conversations are an opportunity to clarify that you value good teaching and are willing to do the work necessary to support every teacher's quest for excellence. The time investment you put into meeting with them will pay off immeasurably in how it affects classroom instruction. Third, the feedback you offer can push teachers to think about their instruction with renewed energy and focus. Teachers tend to have long careers, spanning more than 30 years in most cases, and good teachers will evolve over that time. They do not teach exactly the same way in their last year as they did in their first, because their knowledge of the subject has changed, best instructional practices have changed, technology has changed, and students have changed. As the principal, the evaluations and feedback you offer have the power to shape a teacher's evolution in positive, meaningful ways. Fourth, and finally, when you offer strong evaluations and engage in thoughtful conversations with your staff, you, too, will continue to evolve. You will learn to recognize good teaching while gaining new ideas about how students learn. You'll be growing your teachers—and yourself.

When I was a beginning administrator, I dreaded doing observations and evaluations. I can still remember the slightly sick feeling I had in my stomach each time I went into a classroom in an evaluation capacity, or each time I talked through what I'd seen in an observation. It wasn't that I didn't feel confident in my knowledge of good instruction or what a high-quality learning environment looked like. I did. The problem was that I was young, insecure, and nervous. I was unsure of how to offer feedback, ask questions, or offer suggestions without causing teachers to get angry or defensive. I always had the teachers bargaining union on my mind; I had heard horror stories of evaluations gone wrong and how union representatives were called in to mediate between the teacher and the principal. I got anxious thinking I might say something wrong and all of a sudden find myself in a grievance situation. I feared that the most experienced teachers would scoff at my input as worthless, thinking I was—and I *was!*—an inexperienced administrator.

Because of this sense of trepidation, I spent my first several years as an evaluating administrator simply telling teachers that they were doing everything exactly right. They were fabulous. Perfect. *Masters.* All my feedback was thoroughly complimentary and supportive. "You're doing a great job," I said, over and over, to each teacher, even to those I *knew* could stand to improve their teaching practices.

Over time, as my confidence grew and my mentors' advice sank in, I learned that offering constructive feedback didn't have to cause unease or apprehension—not for me, and not for the teacher in question. Instead, it could spark incredibly interesting conversations and serve as a gateway for teachers to confide in me about things they knew they could and should improve. It could also be a means for me to learn about each teacher's professional practice. In fact, far from breaking down relationships, as I'd feared they would, evaluations could be used to build a relationship with each individual teacher.

## Strategies and Solutions for Conducting Evaluations and Delivering Feedback

There are several things to keep in mind when planning, implementing, and completing staff evaluations. For the purpose of simplicity, I will refer only to evaluations of teachers, but all these tips apply to evaluations of office, kitchen, custodial, and support staff as well.

**Know the contract.** Most teachers work on a contract that has been negotiated between their bargaining unit and a school district's administrative team. This contract will clearly outline the number of evaluations you must complete each year for each staff member. The requirements may vary, depending on the teacher's experience or contract cycle. Take the time to read the negotiated agreement carefully and make sure you understand exactly what is expected of you. If you are ever in a disciplinary situation with a teacher, or if you want to write an improvement plan for a teacher who is struggling, the surest way to encounter a roadblock is for you to not have completed evaluations as required by the teachers union.

**Know your state and district mandates, and use their resources.** Does your state require you to complete evaluations on a particular template? Is there an online evaluation tool available to help you manage the process? Are you required to submit evaluations to your district or state—and, if so, is there an efficient, streamlined way for you to do so? Seek out information about any supportive technology or systems that may help you as you complete your evaluations.

**Make a plan.** I have a system to help me plan my evaluations. First, I create a spreadsheet and enter in each staff member's name. I add columns titled *pre-observation conference, observation,* and *post-observation conference*; additionally, I add several columns labeled *walk-through* or *classroom visit*. Then I add a targeted date for each, spreading out the dates throughout the year and adding them to my calendar. I reference this plan to help me keep up with the work. In my experience, the effort it takes to stay on track with evaluations is far less depleting than the sinking feeling of realizing I'm way behind and might not catch up.

**Get to work.** Using your planning sheet as a guide, begin by visiting classrooms and taking brief notes on what you see there. Look for specific evidence of strong instructional practices, high student engagement, effective use of technology, differentiation, and formative assessment. Don't wait to start this work; walk-throughs can begin within the first few weeks of school. Starting early will emphasize that you are making staff evaluations a priority, and it will make you visible to teachers and staff.

**Use your plan as a progress-monitoring tool.** When you complete each conference, observation, and walk-through, update your planning spreadsheet with the date. It can also help to take it a step further and color-code cells or give them some other at-a-glance visual indicator that the task is complete. For example, when I complete an evaluation, I change the color of the cell to yellow, because they look so delightfully *complete* when I use a cheerful, bright color. As the year proceeds, my spreadsheet will look less white and more yellow. All yellow = all done.

**When meeting with teachers before the observation, lead the discussion with targeted, specific questions.** Often referred to as the "pre-observation conference," this meeting allows you and the teacher to talk about what you'll be looking for and what you'll see. It gives the teacher an opportunity to talk to you about all of the components of the classroom you may not otherwise know—the complexities of the student population, the concerns and celebrations, and how instructional decisions have been made. The conversation will cover things a standardized evaluation cannot capture. I recommend structuring the conversation around questions such as these:

- How is the school year going so far?
- What are some things you feel really good about in your planning and instruction?
- What things are you concerned about?
- What is the personality of the class as a whole group?
- Do you have specific celebrations or concerns about any individual students—academically, behaviorally, or socially?
- How supportive is your parent group?
- What technology do you consistently use in the classroom?
- What resources do you depend on? What resources do you wish you had?
- When I come to observe, is there anything in particular you would like me to concentrate on? These will be our specific "look-fors" that we agree upon, so we both have an understanding of what you're trying to accomplish in your classroom.
- Is there anything you would like to ask me before the observation?

**Be sensitive to how teachers are feeling.** Take some time to reassure nervous teachers that your evaluations are meant to be supportive of their work, not retributive or punitive. (New teachers, in particular, tend to be anxious about the meeting and the ensuing observation and post-observation conference—this is, after all, their first experience with someone evaluating their work as a teacher.) You might say, "I look at observations as a way for you to showcase all the wonderful things you are doing in your classroom each day. I'm here to give you positive feedback, and together we will talk about areas of growth. We are a team with the same goal—providing a great learning experience for your students." Words like this will go a long way toward building trusting relationships with new and experienced teachers alike.

**When observing, be completely present.** I take exhaustive notes when observing a teacher and am careful to focus on all the aspects of the classroom. What is the teacher doing? What are the students doing? Is it evident that a classroom routine has been established—and are the students held accountable for following that routine? Are the students very clear on the lesson's intended outcomes? Is the teacher actively engaged in consistent formative instruction and assessment? Is the classroom environment one in which student learning can flourish? Have I taken note of all of the agreed-upon look-fors?

Focus all your thinking and energy on *this* classroom at *this* moment. By doing so, and by taking in-depth notes to back up what you see, you will be able to provide authentic, helpful feedback during the post-observation conference.

**Be efficient.** The number of responsibilities that you carry makes it imperative that you be efficient in how you complete your evaluations. My first few years, I took exhaustive notes, and then I went home each night and spent hours rewriting them onto the official evaluation template my district required. Now, I save myself time by taking notes in bullet-point form directly on the evaluation template on my laptop or tablet. When my observation is over, I stay in the classroom long enough to carefully proofread my work, and then I save the evaluation as a "final version" and send two copies to the printer in my office. By the time I walk out of the classroom, the paperwork is done. I return to my office, slip the completed observation write-ups into a folder labeled

"Post-observation Conferences," and send an immediate e-mail to the teacher suggesting potential dates for a follow-up meeting. Then, when I meet with the teacher, I pull out the copies of the write-ups—one for the teacher, one for me—and we go through the bullet points together. If our conversation results in me needing to adjust the evaluation in some way, I do it right there during the post-observation conference and print the teacher a new copy.

**Conduct a post-observation meeting as promptly as possible.** Just as students benefit from timely feedback from teachers, your teachers will benefit from timely feedback from you. It's best to have a post-observation conference within a day or two of the observation. The lesson will still be fresh in your mind and the teacher's, so you will be able to have a more detailed and impactful discussion. Holding the meeting within a few days is also a sign of respect—it indicates to teachers that they are a priority for you and cuts down on the amount of time they have to worry about what kind of feedback you might have.

**Think about the setting of the post-observation meeting.** The tone of the meeting will be vastly different depending on where you meet. A conference in your office with the teacher sitting across from you will feel "official" and formal. One held in the teacher's classroom during a planning period, with the two of you side by side at a work table, will feel more casual and informal. There is a time and place for both types of meetings. Be mindful of your intentions and plan accordingly.

**Structure the post-observation conference so that both you and the teacher have an equal voice in the conversation.** I follow—very loosely—a five-step process:

1. *Begin with questions.* I want the teacher to have the first opportunity to express an opinion. I start by asking, "What did

*you* think of the lesson? Did it proceed as you'd planned and expected? Did you make any changes as you proceeded with your instruction?"

2. *Share observations.* I share my observation notes with the teacher, working through my bullet points and weaving my takeaways together with the teacher's self-assessment. I offer positive feedback whenever possible, complimenting the teacher on specific areas of strength and pointing out things that went particularly well.

3. *Ask more questions.* As a way to offer suggestions for areas of change, or to spark a conversation about improvement, I ask a lot of questions. After all, any feedback can be constructed into a question. Since questions require answers, you and the teacher will have a two-way conversation rather than going through a one-sided list of recommendations.

4. *Share the "official" information.* If your state or district requires a final summative "rating"—typical ratings range from *ineffective* or *developing* all the way through *effective* or *skilled* and top out at *most effective* or *accomplished*—this is the time to talk to the teacher about the rating you have chosen. If you have had ongoing conversation with the teacher, and if your post-observation meeting is thorough and clear, the teacher should not be surprised at the final rating.

5. *Solicit suggestions and close with positives.* I wrap up the post-observation meeting by asking the teacher what I can do to be helpful or supportive, and I conclude with several additional positive comments about the observation. I conclude by saying, "I really enjoyed spending time in your classroom. I already look forward to the next time I get to see you teach." A smile, a handshake, and a final reassurance will end the meeting well.

**Prepare yourself for tough conversations.** It's inevitable: at times, you will have to have some tough conversations. As much as we would like to think we will always be leading a staff chock-full of highly talented, driven, and energetic teaching experts, there will be teachers who need improvement, and there may even be times when you have to discuss disciplinary action or even dismissal procedures.

The best way to handle tough conversations is with a mix of compassion and resolve. I always begin by acknowledging the feelings in the room: "I know this is very difficult for you; I understand you may be feeling angry or concerned for your job. I want everyone on our staff to feel successful, and I don't like that the things I am going to tell you today will be upsetting." I repeat this same message—using different words, perhaps, but communicating the same meaning—over and over again throughout the meeting. I let teachers know that I believe they can improve, that I will provide the support needed for them to grow, and that I want them to remain part of our team on the condition they commit to growth and change.

**Make official improvement plans manageable and specific.** Depending on your district's policy, you may have a formal improvement plan template, or you may need to create your own system to document the areas in which you expect improvement. When you develop the plan, it is wise to identify no more than three specific areas of improvement focus. The last thing you want is for a teacher to feel overwhelmed or that it is impossible to meet your expectations. Always include specific action steps you expect teachers to complete and a clear time line for completing those steps.

**Gather your own evidence, and make up your own mind.** If you hear concerns about a teacher's performance, that's a cue for you to do some investigation. I once worked in a building in which the outgoing principal and several teacher leaders spoke disdainfully of a particular teacher. They felt she was aloof, unqualified, disorganized—and, therefore, ineffective. But I heard no complaints about her from parents or students, and when I took a look at her students' state assessment scores, they were consistently solid and in line with those of her colleagues.

I made a commitment to figure out what was happening in the classroom. I visited often, seeking an understanding of the classroom environment, teaching strategies, and relationships with students. I found the teacher to be extremely dedicated to her class; she was constantly meeting with students, differentiating her instruction, helping them individually when they didn't understand a concept, and connecting with her class on a deep and personal level. The only thing she was doing "wrong," actually, was staying intensely private. Teamwork and collaboration did not come naturally for her; she liked to work alone and focus intensely on her students. Since she seemed to be successful with this approach, I let it be.

**Don't fight every battle.** A wise mentor once said to me, "We all have our own frailties." There is no perfect teacher out there. Some overthink their work; some underthink it. Some are disorganized; some are so organized they lose the ability to loosen up with their students. Some are tough; some are soft. Some improve with time; some falter. Teachers are people, and they will bring their complex personalities and complicated lives to the job each day. It is best to look at a teacher's overall effectiveness, relationships with students, and commitment to learning—and let the little things go, like I had to do with my teacher who was fantastic with her students but antisocial with her colleagues. If students are happy, safe, and growing, you have an effective teacher on your hands.

**Don't back down from important battles.** You will encounter certain situations in which you think, "This cannot happen under my watch." I've felt this when I've seen teachers being unkind to students; when I've noted fractured, uneven collegial relationships; when students who were successful the previous year began to flounder in their next teacher's classroom; or when a staff member was blatantly ignoring contractual rules. When you feel this type of concern, trust your gut. Step up and have those difficult conversations. Help the individuals involved map out a change and insist upon improvement.

## Managing Staff Effectiveness and Growth: Conversations to Provide Feedback and Support

Evaluating teachers and offering them meaningful feedback can feel like a monstrous job. It's a constant balancing act between supporting them, pushing them to improve, rewarding their hard work, and letting them be the experts of their instructional practices. Yet this clear and honest communication can be the key to success. It *is* possible to simultaneously celebrate excellent teaching, guide teachers toward growth, and develop relationships of trust that will serve you for years to come. In the following conversations, we revisit the scenarios from the beginning of the chapter, turning the tips I've outlined into practical, authentic conversations with staff.

### Scenario 1: The Pre-observation Conference

You plan to meet with Joe, a well-liked middle school science teacher and coach, in preparation for your upcoming observation with him. From your conversation, you hope to get to know Joe as a teacher—to gain an understanding of his particular skills, talents, and instructional philosophies.

> **You:** *Thank you so much for meeting with me, Joe. I have heard really nice things about you from the parents of your students.*
> **Joe:** *I appreciate hearing that.*
> **You:** *It seems like they really appreciate the relationship you have with their kids. And you are really respected as a coach, too.*
> **Joe:** *I feel like coaching makes me a better teacher. I am lucky enough to have a lot of the students in my class try out for my teams, and they are really successful because they work really hard at both.*
> **You:** *I agree that the connection between the two can be very powerful. As you know, this meeting will help me prepare to observe you teach. I'm looking forward to seeing what's happening in your classroom! What are some of the things you'd like me to look for when I visit?*

Here, you are explaining the objective for this pre-observation meeting: you want the teacher's perspective on what you will see during your visit.

> **Joe:** *Over the past few years, I have spent a lot of time mastering our new content standards. As you know, they have changed significantly because of federal mandates. I'm looking forward to showing you all I have learned and how I'm delivering the instruction to my students.*
> **You:** *That's great. I'll make sure I focus on that. Are there any aspects of your teaching practice that you're working to improve? I like to observe those areas, too, so I can provide some suggestions and feedback.*
> **Joe:** *I don't know. I feel good about my instruction right now.*
> **You:** *That's great. You'll learn, though, that I'm always asking teachers to reflect on their teaching and think about ways they can get better—after all, we can all learn and grow, right? For example, as a leader, I'm working on organizing my time so I'm able to spend more of it in classrooms.*

**Joe:** *OK, sure. Well, when I think about it, I'd like to spend more time working individually with students. Science is a class where there is a lot of whole-group instruction; I very rarely work with students in a one-on-one situation.*

**You:** *How would you go about that?*

**Joe:** *I don't know. Maybe I could continue to deliver full-class instruction, but when the students go off for independent work or to complete some of the lab requirements, I could pull some aside and help them.*

**You:** *What specific areas might you target with them?*

Notice how your targeted, specific questions push the teacher to think more deeply about his instruction.

**Joe:** *Probably their writing. I have several students who grasp the science concepts, but when I ask them to respond to a question in writing, they really can't seem to get their thoughts down. They ramble and get off topic.*

**You:** *I am willing to bet that you're onto something there. Science can be tricky when you're trying to write about it; I can relate to that because science concepts are easily understandable to me, but I couldn't begin to articulate the facts behind them.*

**Joe:** *Yeah, so maybe I could work on that.*

**You:** *Why don't you work on that a few times before my observation? Then I can observe your whole-class instruction and your time with a small group of struggling writers. I'd love to see how it goes and offer feedback—positive and constructive feedback—based on what I notice.*

**Joe:** *That sounds OK. It's different, though—our previous principal didn't focus much on evaluations.*

**You:** *This must feel strange, then. I get the sense that you're hesitating, and I don't blame you; if your previous experiences with evaluations didn't have as much principal involvement, I bet you're wondering why I am making them such a priority. But remember, I'm not here to be*

*critical; I'm here to help. And I admire that you've identified a way you*
*can provide more targeted instruction for some of your kids; I want to*
*help you make that a success.*

It's so important to reiterate the intention to be supportive, not punitive. Here, you are acknowledging the teacher's feelings and offering reassurance.

> **Joe:** *That would be good. It's a new thing for me, so hearing what you*
> *have to say would help.*
> **You:** *That's great. I love this type of thing—brainstorming different teach-*
> *ing techniques and then seeing them play out in action. I really look*
> *forward to visiting your classroom!*

## Scenario 2: The Written Evaluation

Scenario 2 describes a situation in which you have observed a teacher's classroom and found much to admire. The teacher, Kathy Miller, seemed to have a firm grasp on her classroom management and her instructional practices, and it was apparent that she knew her students well. You fill out a standards-guided document provided by the district, summarizing your observations into a narrative that will be the foundation for your post-observation meeting. After Kathy adds her thoughts, this document will serve as the formal evaluation in her personnel file.

| Teacher: Kathy Miller<br>Evaluating Administrator: Jen Schwanke<br>Date: 2/23/16<br>Time of evaluation: 10:30 a.m.–11:20 a.m. | |
|---|---|
| **Standard 1:**<br>Teachers understand student learning and development, and respect the diversity of the students they teach. | **Ranking: D (Distinguished)** |
| | **Standards observed: 1.3, 1.4, 1.5** |
| | *Evidence:* Mrs. Miller made it clear that all students would reach their full potential. In a small-group setting, she said, "We are all going to set some goals for today's lesson. I will talk you through this, because I want to make sure I challenge you!" There was also evidence of Mrs. Miller modeling respect for students' diverse cultures, language skills, and experiences; she took time out of her planned lesson to allow one student to explain a particular ritual in his native country. Finally, Mrs. Miller did an excellent job modifying her formative assessment for her highest-achieving students and special education students. She spoke with each student individually to assess their understanding, and it was clear she used different language and questioning based upon their baseline data.<br><br>*Comments:* Mrs. Miller understands student learning and development. She works hard to meet the needs of each individual student. She models respect for all students and fosters an environment in which individual differences are respected. She believes all students can learn, establishes positive relationships, and encourages students to achieve their full potential. |

| Standard 2: Teachers know and understand the content area for which they have instructional responsibility. | Ranking: A (Accomplished) |
| --- | --- |
| | Standards observed: 2.1, 2.5 |
| | *Evidence:* In working through her word-study lesson, Mrs. Miller's knowledge of content was evident; she knew how to adjust her instruction based upon student level of understanding. At one point, she told a small group, "You have mastered the vowel-consonant-vowel sounds more quickly than I'd thought. I am going to skip right into our next concept—I think you can do it!" She then proceeded to move into longer words with VCV patterns. In addition, she made easy connections to life experiences—"Let's take a moment and think about advertisements, billboards, or restaurant names we may have seen that have these patterns." |
| | *Comments:* Evidence of Mrs. Miller's knowledge of curriculum and content is displayed in each lesson she develops. She explicitly teaches concepts and models strategies, and uses a variety of materials for instruction. |
| Standard 3: Teachers understand and use varied assessments to inform instruction, evaluate, and ensure student learning. | Ranking: P (Proficient) |
| | Standards observed: 3.3 |
| | *Evidence:* Mrs. Miller had analyzed data to determine her students' learning. She had grouped her students based upon an earlier assessment; she had determined a group needed further interventions on a previous lesson and pulled them together for focused work while the rest of the class completed independent practice. |
| | *Comments:* Mrs. Miller has a solid understanding of formative and summative assessment within the classroom. I wonder if she has involved her students in self-assessment and long-term goal setting to address gaps between performance and potential; additionally, I look forward to discussing other assessment types, their purposes, and the data they generate; I would like to touch upon state and local standardized assessments and the effect—if any—their data have on Mrs. Miller's instructional practices. |

| Standard 4: Teachers plan and deliver effective instruction that advances the learning of each individual student. | Ranking: A (Accomplished) |
| --- | --- |
| | Standards observed: 4.3, 4.6, 4.7 |
| | *Evidence:* Mrs. Miller's lesson involved a workshop model approach of explicit, direct instruction, then guided practice, then independent activities (with her support for a select small group). She began the lesson by clearly outlining learning goals: "Today we will study how letter patterns exist in many different words, and we will learn how to recognize and use them in many different situations." The activities she had designed for students during independent work time helped students develop as complex problem solvers. Mrs. Miller also used several different resources, including her projection system and a document camera, which allowed her to show students multiple examples of strong student work. |
| | *Comments:* Mrs. Miller plans for and delivers effective instruction in support of our state's standards. She clearly articulates the intention of the lesson and circles back to it multiple times in the lesson, which helps students have a stronger understanding of their learning. |
| Standard 5: Teachers create learning environments that promote high levels of learning and achievement for all students. | Ranking: A (Accomplished) |
| | Standards observed: 5.1, 5.2 |
| | *Evidence:* The classroom is set up in such a way that students feel safe, heard, and able to work at a pace that fits their ability. In one brief incident with a particularly challenging student, Mrs. Miller pulled her aside and talked quietly and gently with her; the situation de-escalated quickly, and no other students seemed to notice the problem at all. In each observed interaction, students were treating one another kindly and respectfully. |
| | *Comments:* Mrs. Miller's classroom is inviting, calm, and welcoming; there is clear evidence of well-established routines. Students work cooperatively; they are kind and helpful to one another, and they have the confidence to successfully work both together and independently. There is consistent positive acknowledgment of student success. |

| Standard 6: Teachers collaborate and communicate with students, parents, other educators, administrators, and the community to support student learning. | Ranking: A (Accomplished) |
|---|---|
| | Standards observed: 6.1, 6.3 |
| | *Evidence:* Although it was not observed directly in this lesson, Mrs. Miller has proved to be an excellent communicator who often collaborates effectively with others. She serves on the Principals' Leadership Council, organizes her team's parent-teacher conference nights, and is a member of our district's Communication Committee. She is well liked and respected by colleagues, parents, and students. *Comments:* Mrs. Miller communicates and collaborates with stakeholders involved in her classroom, our school, and our district as a whole. She naturally forms strong partnerships with parents and colleagues while working to support her students. |
| Standard 7: Teachers assume responsibility for professional growth, performance, and involvement as an individual and as a member of a learning community. | Ranking: P (Proficient) |
| | Standards observed: 7.1 |
| | *Evidence:* In this lesson and in other interactions with Mrs. Miller, I have found her to have a clear understanding of and commitment to upholding her professional responsibilities. *Comments:* Mrs. Miller is known for her commitment to and passion for education; she takes her job very seriously, and she holds the teaching profession in the highest regard. I look forward to discussing her plans to engage in continuous, purposeful professional development—not only this year, but for the next several years. I am eager to support her in her plans for growth and change. |

Date of post-observation conference:

Reflection from teacher:

Teacher signature:

Principal signature:

## Scenario 3: The Improvement Plan

The third scenario involves a teacher about whom you have some serious concerns. You've heard from parents and colleagues that the teacher, Nicole, is ineffective, and through your experiences—walk-throughs, observations, and an exasperating pre-observation conference—you've reached the same conclusion. To address the problem, you have developed a formal improvement plan for Nicole. You sit down with her for the post-observation conference to share the plan and discuss specific action steps.

> **You:** *Thank you for coming in today to discuss my recent observation. Let's start by getting your perspective. How do you think the lesson went?*
>
> **Nicole:** *I don't know. OK, I guess.*
>
> **You:** *Which parts of it do you feel went well?*
>
> **Nicole:** *Well, the students seemed to enjoy the lesson. They seemed to get it.*
>
> **You:** *How did you know?*
>
> **Nicole:** *I guess they just seemed happy enough, afterward.*
>
> **You:** *That's one of the things I wanted to talk to you about. When I observed, I didn't see evidence of any kind of assessment—formative or summative—that would give you an indication as to whether the students were grasping the content.*
>
> **Nicole:** *OK. I'm giving a test at the end of the unit, though. I could show it to you if you want. I already have it written from last year.*
>
> **You:** *But there were some other concerns I'd like to address. I want to prepare you that this is not going to be an easy conversation; I'm going to challenge you on some of the things I've seen happening in your classroom, and I'm going to hold you accountable for some specific points of improvement I'll need to see from you.*
>
> **Nicole:** *"Hold me accountable." What does that mean? Are you putting me on an improvement plan?*

**You:** *Actually, yes, I am. And I can tell that upsets you—which is completely understandable. This is difficult for me, too; the last thing I want is for a teacher on my staff to feel defensive or anxious. I just want you to join me in an effort to improve your instructional practices. I will be here to help you with whatever you need.*

You are acknowledging this teacher's feelings, identifying your own vested interest in the situation, and trying to connect with her as someone who is there to provide support.

**Nicole:** *What is it you think I need to improve on?*

**You:** *Let's talk through that. I've written two specific goals on your plan. I'll show it to you now so you can see my thinking in writing. First, I'd like to see improvement in the structure of your classes. In my observation, I noticed you lose a lot of instructional time to transitions. At the beginning of class, there was almost a full 10 minutes wasted while students fiddled around, chatted with you and with one another, and slowly made their way to their seats. Then, after you had delivered direct instruction to the class, you asked them to begin practicing independently. Some students never really got on task, while others struggled to concentrate because of other unrelated activity in the classroom. For that reason, I'd like to help you put some structures in place so students are maximizing opportunities for learning every moment they are in your care.*

**Nicole:** *My class has always been a little unstructured. I hate to have kids be so focused and restricted all the time. And I was talking with them because I think building relationships with them is really important.*

**You:** *It is—it certainly is. We'll want to talk about how to do that relationship work without losing so much instructional time. Perhaps you can look for ways to do it before and after school, before and after class, in casual settings, and so on.*

**Nicole:** *What's my second goal?*

**You:** *I have noticed you struggling to stay organized. After seeing you miss several important meetings, I have begun to wonder if you have a system in place for checking your calendar. I have also observed that sometimes it takes you several weeks to get papers graded and put into our online grading system. At times, you have even lost papers. A quick look at your work area shows stacks and stacks of folders and papers; I would like to help you manage that type of thing so you can be more organized—and, thus, more calm and confident as a teacher.*

**Nicole:** *Ha! I've always been disorganized. Good luck trying to change that.*

**You:** *I have some ideas that might help. Are you willing to try? I would like to include you in developing the specific action steps we will follow, and determine an appropriate time line for completion.*

**Nicole:** *I guess. Sure.*

Prepared with detailed notes and evidence, you have gone through two specific areas of concern, and you have made it clear that you expect to have input on action steps and dates for completion.

**You:** *Great. Now I'd love to hear your thoughts. How are you feeling about this?*

**Nicole:** *Well, it seems like a lot. I didn't think I had that much I needed to work on.*

**You:** *Based on my observations, I feel strongly that there is room for growth, and I feel we can easily meet these goals throughout this year. I'm prepared to provide you with professional learning opportunities, time to observe other teachers, or any other resources you need to meet these goals.*

You are refusing to "back down" and showing that you are committed to seeing improvement.

**Nicole:** *That will help. I guess I have no choice, right?*

**You:** *I'd rather you think about it as an opportunity. I want you to feel successful and happy as a teacher, and I don't sense that's how you feel now.*

**Nicole:** *I don't, that's for sure.*

**You:** *I know you're feeling upset and are frustrated with me, but I hope you'll try to separate me from the issue at hand. I hope you will be able to approach this with a positive attitude and a willingness to try some new things.*

Once again, you are acknowledging the teacher's feelings and presenting yourself as an ally rather than an adversary.

**Nicole:** *OK, I'm in. I'll try.*

**You:** *Thank you. Let's talk about action steps. What are a couple things you can do to address our first goal—bringing more structure to your classroom?*

**Nicole:** *Well, honestly, I don't even know what that looks like, really.*

**You:** *So maybe a first step would be to observe someone who is an expert in running a structured classroom?*

**Nicole:** *Sure. That would be good.*

**You:** *Why don't I arrange for two days outside of the classroom to observe a teacher in another building in our district? I can work with the principal to connect you with a teacher who will be helpful. Then, perhaps that teacher can visit your classroom and help you implement a plan.*

**Nicole:** *OK. What steps would you like me to take for the second goal? Like I said, I've always been disorganized. I can't imagine how that will ever change.*

**You:** *In the short time I have had working with Mr. Ramirez, our assistant principal, I have found him to be one of the most organized people I've ever met. Somehow he manages to respond to all e-mails within 24 hours, completes all paperwork on time, and keeps ahead of every item on his to-do list. He has offered to come to your room and help you work through some of the stacks on your desk.*

**Nicole:** *Then what?*

**You:** *Well, then, your second action step—after weeding through things you don't need—will be to develop a tight plan for managing your work in the future. Mr. Ramirez will help you develop a checklist of things that must be done immediately, things that can be postponed, and things that you can discard from your list.*

**Nicole:** *OK. That sounds good.*

**You:** *I'd like to add a third action step to this goal. As you know, we have transitioned to a Google system for e-mails and calendars. I'd like you to "share" your calendar with me, so I can keep an eye on things you have scheduled, such as staff meetings and parent meetings. I'll make sure any schoolwide commitments are on that calendar. All I ask is that you consult it daily and work to keep it updated.*

**Nicole:** *Well, it's worth a try.*

**You:** *Do you think it might work?*

**Nicole:** *It might. You may not believe this, but I really do want to be more organized. I want to be a good teacher.*

**You:** *I know you do. That's why I want to help. And that's why I'll touch base with you often to talk through your progress and see if you need anything from me. I'll also stop by your classroom to offer frequent feedback. Remember—I want you to think of me as someone here to help you, not someone who is punitive or evaluative each time.*

Throughout this tough conversation, you have been focused, professional, and compassionate. You have communicated to this teacher multiple times that you are eager to help her succeed.

**Nicole:** *OK. Let me know when you'd like me to observe that other teacher.*

**You:** *And I'll have Mr. Ramirez reach out to you to start the organization work. Until then, I'll write up a copy of these goals and action steps, and I'll slip a copy into your mailbox so you have it for reference. Good luck! I'll be in touch!*

In each of this chapter's scenarios, the principal was able to connect with a teacher by asking questions and offering support and suggestions for growth. In the end, the evaluations you provide for teachers should always be the basis for meaningful and useful feedback—which will improve the teachers' experience in the classroom and the quality of instruction provided for the students in your school.

# Providing Focused and Budget-Friendly Professional Development

### 6

### Scenario 1: Making a Plan for Professional Development

*In initial meetings with your staff, you asked every teacher to identify the kinds of professional growth they were interested in pursuing. Based on their answers, you conducted a survey to whittle down the possibilities to a single focus, and with the results in hand, you develop this year's plan for schoolwide professional development.*

### Scenario 2: Utilizing the Expertise of Colleagues

*Your school district schedules two professional development days each year— one in the fall and one in the spring. No students report to school on these two days, but teachers report to work for training. Several teachers tell you the days aren't very helpful because they are simply "one and done," with no follow-up support and no actual changes in instructional practices. Looking at your budget, you realize you can't really afford to have an expensive "expert" come in anyway. You decide to ask the staff to plan a professional development day in which they will share an area of their own expertise with their colleagues. You begin your planning by contacting the previous principal, who now works in the curriculum department at your district's central office.*

### Scenario 3: Professional Learning Communities

*When the superintendent described your new school to you, he made it a point to let you know about the PLC work happening in the building.*

*"They are fully up and running with professional learning communities," he said. "It's important that you support them in any way possible so that the momentum they've built can continue." When meeting with your school leadership team, made up of four teachers from each grade level, you ask them to help you figure out how best to do this.*

Amid the countless management tasks of a principal, it is easy to let professional development (PD) fall to a lower spot on your list of priorities—especially in the first few years, when it can feel like you're barely keeping your head above water. But it is a mistake to let this happen, because one of your most important responsibilities is ensuring that each teacher is providing all students with the best instruction possible. Providing access to engaging and energizing professional learning is one of the best ways to do this.

Fortunately, developing and executing a high-quality, sustainable professional development plan does not have to be an all-consuming task. With the right approach, it requires only a modest investment of time and minimal oversight. I learned this firsthand. When I took over as principal of an elementary school, I had no experience teaching at that level, so I felt uncertain about how to approach PD. Although I valued ongoing professional learning as a way for teachers to refine their craft and expand their expertise, I was worried about my ability to support the growth of *these* teachers. But since I knew enough to know I didn't know enough, I made it my business to learn how to build a PD model that was inexpensive, efficient, and self-sustaining.

There were several steps to the process. I started by reaching out to other principals and asking questions about their own PD models. Next, I identified strong instructional leaders within the building and asked them to teach some of their most effective strategies to their colleagues. I asked teachers what supports they needed—what training they would find beneficial in their teaching, what professional books I could provide for them, and what other resources would help them. I sent several teachers to outside conferences and training sessions; afterward, I scheduled time for them to share what they learned with their colleagues. Over time, these experts expanded my knowledge of best instructional practices at the elementary level, and I grew more confident in my ability to oversee truly effective—and cost-effective—professional learning.

## Strategies and Solutions for Developing a Professional Development Plan

The truth is that there are all kinds of ways to provide quality professional development. Let's begin by looking at some of the many factors to consider when determining the best approach to PD with your staff:

- *The size of the school.* Is it a large school with departments, in which teachers can work together in small groups? Is it a small school with only one teacher in each grade or subject area? Or somewhere in between?

- *The size of the district.* Large districts often have someone—or several people—in charge of providing professional development to staff. Teachers may be pulled from the classroom on a regular basis for learning, or there may be a push-in model in which other teachers—a coach, a department leader, or a teacher designated an "expert" by district leaders—come into the school or classroom to work with teachers. On the other hand, there may be virtually no support on the district level.

- *Previous professional development.* If teachers have been engaged in thoughtful, meaningful professional development for years, you will need to approach PD much differently than if the staff has been receiving little to no PD.

- *The level of your learners.* Depending on whether you are leading an elementary, middle, or high school, teachers' professional development needs will be different. For instance, elementary teachers will need PD that is focused on young learners—how their bodies and brains develop, what early interventions may be most effective, and how to challenge high-achieving students. Although these topics are valuable at the secondary level, their PD might have a more curricular focus and present a very different slant on, say, technology integration and meeting students' social-emotional needs.

- *What the data say.* By studying the data trends from your school, you will gather a sense of where to focus your professional development efforts. The data will tell you what specific content areas need the most attention.

- *The resources available.* If your budget allows for it, you may be able to bring in experts to provide professional development; you may even be able to send some of your teachers to professional conferences, trusting that they will bring back learning to share with their colleagues. In some situations, though, there is little to no money for professional development—which means it will be up to you, as the building leader, to provide it for your staff.

- *District priorities.* You may work for a school district that establishes professional development goals for the district as a whole. In these cases, the district's main office has identified a specific growth area for all teachers. Examples might be improving literacy or English language instruction, refining special education services, incorporating Makerspaces or creativity summits into all classrooms, or implementing new standards into all classrooms. It's wise to be clear on PD initiatives that come from your district leaders so you can align your building's PD with that of your district.

As the principal, it is your job to assess how best to support your teachers in their own learning. I have some recommendations for going about this.

**Gather some history.** Talk to veteran staff members and study previous building schedules to find out how much value your school has previously placed on professional development. Factor these findings into your decisions. For example, if you make professional development a priority in your first few years, will that be an abrupt change for teachers? Are they used to consistent and structured programs? What approaches and emphases might have been employed and abandoned in years past?

**Ask, "What do you need?"** Whether by conducting a survey, meeting with small groups, or gathering the perspective of your school's leadership team, find out areas in which teachers would like additional training. Here's an example of a survey to gauge professional development needs.

## PROFESSIONAL DEVELOPMENT: WHAT DO YOU NEED?

Indicate with numbers 1–5, with 1 being "most interested," your interest in learning more about the following topics:

___ Behavior management in the classroom
___ Using tablets in instruction
___ Flexible grouping
___ Differentiation
___ Communicating with parents
___ Formative assessment techniques
___ Using formative assessment data
___ Using social media in the classroom
___ The workshop model of instruction
___ Instructional efficiency
___ Instructional planning

By asking what your staff members want to learn about, you will be able to begin developing a plan for providing professional development that will have the greatest effect in the classroom. You also show respect for your staff by giving them a voice in decisions about their own professional learning.

**Find time.** While you may be lucky enough to be in a school where there is already time blocked off for PD—be it daily, weekly, monthly, or even biannually—that is not always the case. If it has not been a priority in the past, there may be very little specific time for teachers to gather together and work on professional growth, so you may need to adjust the school's schedule to allow for it. I remember having to get very creative in order to do this in my school, and it involved finding coverage for classes, switching teacher planning periods and duty schedules, and providing substitute support and release time. If you think outside the box and look to uncover hidden resources, you can usually make it work.

If the teacher's negotiated contract prohibits the changes you would like to make for professional development purposes, reach out to your district leaders and brainstorm ways to make professional learning time a priority in the next contract negotiations. Obviously, you won't get the changes you're looking for immediately, but you can be the one to lead or at least advocate for a long-term change that will be beneficial for teachers and students alike.

**Make a plan.** Once you know areas of focus and when you can fit PD into the school schedule, make a plan for the year—and, ideally, for a few years. Determine what your priorities are, based on teacher feedback and your own assessment of the situation. Keep your priority list small—just one or two initiatives are plenty!—so you can truly focus on them. Make a specific plan for a progression of learning, just as you'd plan for a classroom of students. I call my plan a "Year at a Glance," and I include all topics we will be covering throughout the year, broken down by month. I also try to sketch a larger vision for future years. For example, if we focus on "establishing learning goals" this year, teachers can use the knowledge they gain as a springboard to focus on "differentiation practices" the next year and "assessment practices" the year after that. Each year's focus should build on the work from previous years.

**Spread out the work.** It's tough for a principal to be effective at all the other management tasks the job requires *and* lead an excellent professional development program that supports true growth and change. When it comes to PD, it's best to look for help and delegate, delegate, delegate. Have your administrative secretary help you with clerical work. Tap your assistant principal or your school leadership team to determine who can help organize, present, and evaluate professional development throughout the year. Reach out to master teachers for their ideas and support, and contact other principals to talk about the best ways to be efficient and effective in delivering PD.

**Consider available resources.** Much has changed in recent years in terms of what is available for teachers to improve their instructional practices. Online classes, webinars, districtwide and statewide trainings, online and community colleges, and offerings from educational service organizations are widely available in what seems like a nonstop array of excellent learning opportunities for teachers. Assuming they really do apply to your areas of focus, tap into these resources as a way to supplement your PD plan.

**Look for internal experts.** Every day, an entire staff of teachers walks into your school. Each of them is an expert at something—or several somethings. Don't let these hidden assets go to waste! Ask teachers what their particular areas of strength are, and go into their classroom to observe them at a time when they will be showcasing these skills. Then set up knowledge and strategy exchanges, and invite your vetted experts to take the lead.

This strategy is a particular favorite of mine. Last year, for example, two of my principal colleagues and I asked all our teachers to create a two-session PD class focused on an aspect of their practice they felt particularly strong in and passionate about. They submitted session descriptions, which we compiled into a brochure and distributed to the teachers in each building. Throughout the year, teachers from all three buildings could attend any or all of these sessions, which were all held early in the morning before the start of school (determined to be the best time slot for the majority of our teachers). The sessions were held at the home school of each respective presenter, and we built in travel time for teachers to get back to their classrooms before students arrived. It was one of the most powerful professional development programs I'd ever been part of—and our teachers gathered countless ideas from one another. Best of all? It cost us nothing.

**Know when to outsource.** There are times when only an outside expert will do—especially when there is something particularly new your staff needs to learn. In those cases, there are three ways to approach the PD: You can send some teachers to a state or national conference with the expectation that they will come back and share their learning with colleagues; you can seek experts who can come in and train your staff directly; or you can seek online classes, workshops, and webinars offered by reputable experts in the particular area of need. Although these options may come with a considerable cost, it is worth it to ensure your staff receive the necessary training from a master in that particular area.

**Vet your PD.** There are a lot of excellent PD providers out there, but there are also lousy ones. If you are outsourcing your staff's PD, you'll want to make sure it is worth the money you spend and that it aligns with your goals. For example, before sending a teacher to a professional conference, make sure you peruse the conference brochure to see if the presenter expertise and topics really meet your building's needs. Before purchasing resources or having teachers sign up for a class, research the content and intent of the PD. And be wary of flashy advertisements for "quick and easy" PD. Each year, I get hundreds of e-mails from individuals or start-up organizations offering PD. Often it is offered by "consultants" who have little to no experience as educators but are aggressively seeking ways to "get into" the schools. These individuals and organizations tend to be more interested in your money than in genuinely bringing positive change to your school.

**Work closely with your principal colleagues.** Other principals in your district or in your area may have excellent professional development models that would work for your school, and they may be happy to share some of their ideas for implementation in your school. They also may be willing to team with you to share the expertise of current staff members; for example, some of your teachers could provide PD for another school and vice versa.

**Follow through.** As every teacher and principal knows, the most frustrating PD experience is the "one and done" type. We've all seen it: an all-knowing expert comes in, scatters some well-meaning advice, and wishes luck to everyone on the way out the door. After that, there's nothing. No one talks about it, no one changes anything, and instruction does not improve. Being hyper-aware of how ineffective this type of PD is, I try to make professional development a constant conversation. I refer often to the written plan—referenced above—that is meant to encapsulate our vision for the entire year and beyond. I speak about it individually, at team or department meetings, and at staff meetings; in each conversation, I am seeking to determine what teachers have adjusted in their instructional practices as a result of what they have learned. These conversations help me communicate that I expect new learning to truly be applied to the work—and help me evaluate the effectiveness and value of the PD.

**Make professional reading an expectation and model its use.** There are countless publications available that provide excellent information to teachers—new ideas, strategies, and ways to approach instruction—and they are all available at virtually any time. Teachers can learn and grow on an ongoing basis or during down times such as holiday breaks, summer break, and long weekends. I make sure I am constantly tapping into professional reading and sharing what I have learned, and I offer to purchase reading for teachers whenever they request a particular publication, whether it be a periodical or a professional book.

## Teachers as Learners: Conversations to Develop a Solid Professional Development Plan

The scenarios in this chapter's opening are all examples of situations you may encounter when developing a plan for professional development for your staff. We will now revisit those scenarios in the form of a sample plan and conversation.

### Scenario 1: Making a Plan for Professional Development

The first scenario describes a situation in which you survey staff to determine their professional development needs and use their feedback to focus on a specific area of growth. The sample PD plan shown offers a way you might choose to put your ideas into action. This plan assumes your district has two professional development release days but no regular time (i.e., weekly or monthly) allotted for PD.

## SAMPLE PROFESSIONAL DEVELOPMENT PLAN FOR YEAR 1

Goal: Improve and refine our use of a classroom workshop model

- *September–October:* Meet with all teachers to discuss their comfort and knowledge about the workshop model. Group staff based on their level of expertise.
- *November:* Provide each teacher with a text that addresses the workshop model. Set a time line for staff to complete the book and be prepared to discuss it with colleagues.
- *December:* On your district's PD release day, group teachers based on their expertise area to discuss their book study. Appoint someone to be the leader of each group, and provide guided discussion questions for the group. Capture their thinking on a Google Doc that can be shared with the rest of the staff.
- *January–February:* Film several "experts" teaching using the workshop model, followed by a conversation with you during which they reflect upon their work. Compile the best video examples that highlight good use of the workshop model.
- *March:* During your second district PD release day, have teachers work in small groups to watch the strong examples. Have teachers talk about what they felt went well and how they could apply what they saw in their own classrooms.
- *April:* Ask teachers to reflect upon their learning and document changes they are considering for their classrooms in the next school year.
- *May:* Survey teachers to determine what was most successful about the year's work and get their ideas for future PD.
- *June:* Using data from the survey, develop a plan for the next school year and outline a plan for subsequent years.

## Scenario 2: Utilizing the Expertise of Colleagues

In the second scenario, you are exploring the idea of asking staff members who are recognized experts in certain pedagogical areas to lead a professional development day. To determine how best to proceed, you call the building's previous principal, John, at his new office in your district's curriculum department.

**You:** *Thank you so much for taking my call, John. I wanted to get some ideas for a professional development day I'd like to plan.*

**John:** *I'm happy to help!*

**You:** *My initial idea is to ask teachers who have a particularly successful instructional practice, or a specific knowledge base, to share their expertise with colleagues.*

**John:** *There are some outstanding teachers in the building; that shouldn't be hard to do.*

**You:** *Can you tell me where you would begin, if you were planning something similar? In my initial planning, I am thinking we will focus on just two areas—teaching using the workshop model is one, and the other is communicating learning outcomes to students.*

You have settled on a narrow and specific focus for your staff's formal professional learning. Now you're seeking expert guidance on how you might deliver it.

**John:** *Absolutely. And I think those are two areas where the teachers really could use some support. Let me tell you where I would start, if I were you; I'd definitely look to Katie to have her share how she structures the workshop model in her math classroom. I'm sure you've seen it—that class runs like a well-oiled machine, with kids working independently at levels matching their understanding of each particular concept. She also teams with Connie and Lucas, who have an excellent grasp of the workshop model. The three of them could get together and create a powerful professional development presentation.*

**You:** *That sounds perfect! I'll start with the three of them.*

**John:** *Remember, though, you won't want it to be just one "session" or "training." It should be more like a series. They could have an initial session in which they define the workshop model, a second session where they review the important components of workshop and give suggestions for implementation, a third session where they model each components, and so on. Then you'll want to make sure you follow through.*

**You:** *What do you mean by that?*

**John:** *I suggest making time to see what happened after each session. Either by observation or by asking pointed questions, you'll want to determine if teachers have adjusted their thinking or changed how they deliver classroom discussion as a result of what they've learned. Don't just assume it's happening; look for it.*

**You:** *That makes sense. What about communicating learning outcomes? Whom do you suggest I seek out as experts in that area?*

**John:** *That's an easy one—ask the teachers in the science department. Several years ago, they all attended a conference that focused on how we communicate with students, and learning goals was their primary focus. They all came back from the conference intent on mastering the best way to ensure students know the end goal in each lesson.*

John has pointed out several internal experts who would be a perfect fit for your plan. You have also gained some insight into your staff's past professional development activities, and these can be factored into your approach.

**You:** *Thank you so much. You saved me a whole year of watching and listening to determine who my experts are. Hopefully by next year at this time, I'll know who my experts are for our next professional development plan!*

**John:** *I am happy to help. Also, in the next few months, I would be glad to show you some of the newest online resources that are available in areas of curriculum. There's some good stuff out there now, and teachers could use it on their own time.*

**You:** *That would be fabulous. I'll be in touch to schedule some times to get together.*

**John:** *I just want to say once again, though, that I believe follow-through is the most important component of professional development. In the past, I've made the mistake of providing PD and then doing nothing beyond it. If I were you, I'd make sure every single PD is followed by an* *observation or conversation to determine what changes have occurred. If you see no change, you'll need to reevaluate your plan.*

Even well-chosen content delivered by illuminating experts is likely to have minimal impact without conscientious follow-through.

**You:** *Thank you for the advice. It's easy to assume PD will lead to change, but I see that it's my job to make sure that happens.*
**John:** *Absolutely.*
**You:** *I am so grateful, John; thank you for your expertise!*

## Scenario 3: Professional Learning Communities

In this scenario, your superintendent has made it clear that he expects the strong work of your school's professional learning communities to continue as it had with the previous principal. Knowing how powerful PLCs can be, you wholeheartedly agree, but you need some help figuring out how you can best support the PLC work. Your school leadership team gathers to help guide your approach to this challenge.

**You:** *I am so glad you were able to come meet with me today. You are all leaders in this building, and you play a leadership role in your PLCs. I'd love to hear your thinking on how I can make sure PLC work continues in the way it has in the past. I know your previous principal led some very powerful PLC work.*
**Teacher 1:** *We went through some extensive training several years ago, and we all read various books and publications about PLC work. That helped us develop a strong initial understanding of how PLCs should be structured and how they will work best. Those resources are all still in our professional library, and I think it might be good to revisit them as a staff every now and then. New teachers should read them, too.*
**You:** *I have also read a lot about PLCs, but I'd like to make sure I have read the same materials you have. I'll make it a priority to go to the*

*professional library and catch up, and I'll have our new teachers do the same. Great point.*

Here, you are confirming that professional reading is an expectation, and you are modeling its use and value.

**Teacher 2:** *Another thing that has been instrumental in our PLC success is our commitment to regular meetings. It's easy to get caught up in all the things we need to get done in the course of a day, a week, and a school year—but we never miss our weekly PLC meeting.*

**Teacher 3:** *I agree, and it's not easy. But our previous principal made it clear that she expected PLCs to be one of our highest priorities, and she held us accountable for that.*

**You:** *How did she hold you accountable?*

**Teacher 4:** *She attended our PLC meetings whenever possible, and even when she couldn't stay for the whole meeting because of another commitment, she made sure to check in. If for some reason we had cancelled the meeting or weren't staying focused on our professional development during the meetings, she asked us to explain why, and she redirected us to get us back on track.*

**You:** *Can you tell me, specifically, how she achieved that?*

**Teacher 4:** *Each PLC developed an agenda for each meeting, which was stored as a shared Google Doc. Then, during our meetings, we all took notes within that document, so the principal could quickly reference our discussion topics and our progress. She would add comments, and mostly they were complimentary and encouraging; if she had a question, though, she wasn't afraid to comment with something like "Does this line up with your goals?" or, "I have it on my schedule to attend your next meeting—let's plan to talk more about this." It was a great way to keep us accountable and moving forward.*

**You:** *That's fantastic. What else helped make your PLC work successful?*

**Teacher 1:** *We were accountable not just for holding the meetings but for doing something with the meeting's content. Our principal looked* *for evidence of our PLC work during her walkthroughs and evaluations. She would make sure we were making real changes in our teaching.*

This exchange is a reminder that successful PLC work requires follow-through from the principal.

**Teacher 2:** *She also asked us what additional training we needed, if there was a particular topic we wanted to learn more about, or if we needed access to different resources.*
**Teacher 4:** *It showed that she really supported our work.*

Here's an example of how the question "What do you need?" can help teachers feel supported and motivated to continue learning.

**You:** *That's really helpful. I'll make it a point to get input from teachers on what areas they would like to work on. Now, there's something I'm wondering about. Can I ask a really honest question? It sounds like your previous principal made PD a priority and invested lots of time into it. Did she struggle to manage it all?*
**Teacher 3:** *She was really good at delegating. For example, if there was something we needed to do, she asked the office staff to help us—placing orders for professional reading, scheduling an observation, contacting experts if needed, and so on. She looked to the leadership team to help with surveying staff and suggesting changes. She really delegated a lot of the tasks to others.*

Managing an effective professional development program requires you to find ways to share the workload.

**You:** *This has been extremely helpful. I will work hard to be as effective a leader as your previous principal, and I'll do all I can to help you stay focused on PLC work as you have in the past. I'm really excited to be part of a building with such a strong PLC foundation. I feel very lucky!*
**Teacher 1:** *We are looking forward to it, too. Just let us know how we can help.*

In this chapter's scenarios and conversations, you can see the value of committing time and energy to building a strong plan for professional development. Although it is easy to get lost in management tasks as a principal, it is a mistake to let PD fall down on the list of priorities. After all, every teacher—even the most masterful, experienced, and devoted—can find some room for growth, and all students benefit when teachers continue to explore their craft and evolve and refine their instructional practices.

# Approaching Student and Schoolwide Data

### Scenario 1: Data Reports

*You and your family attend the Board of Education meeting to celebrate your official hiring. As you are leaving, the district's director of data and assessment pulls you aside. "I'd like to talk to you about the assessment data coming from your new school. There is a lot to celebrate, but there is also an area of concern." You agree to meet in her office to talk about what assessment data say about your school.*

### Scenario 2: Standardized Assessments

*Soon after being hired as principal, you check your new voice mail account for the first time. There is a message from a parent who is concerned because she believes her daughter is gifted, yet results from a standardized school ability test the previous spring indicate that her child is "only average." She believes the results from the test indicate poor teaching at school. You realize that she needs an explanation about the difference between a standardized achievement test and a school ability test.*

### Scenario 3: Monitoring Progress Through Data

*At your new school, there is a Response to Intervention (RTI) coach who works closely with teachers to develop plans for students who are struggling academically; she also coordinates input from parents and support staff. This coach serves as the step between typical classroom interventions and the decision to move a student toward a special education evaluation. You meet with her to talk about her process and how she uses data to monitor student growth.*

There is power in data. Used wisely, assessment data can help teachers see patterns in their students' performance and address students' specific intervention and enrichment needs through mindful and targeted instruction. Data can also help school psychologists, classroom teachers, and intervention specialists share detailed information about student growth, which creates a team of informed, collaborative, and focused adults working together to meet student needs.

But data can also be misunderstood and overused. Unless teachers and support staff understand that data make up just one part of a student's full profile, data may do more harm than good.

Several years ago, when data began to grow in importance for educators and I was just beginning my work as an administrator, I was quite intimidated by the whole concept. I didn't understand how data could be used to guide instruction or inform professional conversations about individual student growth. In fact, I didn't even know how to read a schoolwide or individual student data report—all the acronyms and "data words" were nonsensical to me. Stanines? Standard deviations? Norm-referenced? I hadn't a clue about any of them.

I'll never forget the day, late in spring my first year as a principal, when a parent called me about her child's results from a recent achievement test. She had received the data report in the mail, and was understandably upset; not just that her child's results were abysmal, which they were, but that prior to this report there had been no indication that there was cause for concern. Her daughter had been receiving *A*s and *B*s in all subject areas. The parent demanded to know what could possibly have happened for her daughter to receive a "Basic" designation on this achievement test. She wanted to know if her daughter's grades had been inflated in the classroom, what kind of tutoring or support we planned to offer to bring her daughter back up to a high level of achievement, and what kind of discipline would be given to the teacher who had failed to teach her daughter what she needed to know for the test.

As this parent spoke, I grew more and more uneasy; I felt the possibility of a serious, undiagnosed deficiency in one of my teacher's instructional or grading practices rising before me. What other students might be affected? How would I find out? What would I say to the teacher? Then, a thought: Could this parent be misinterpreting her daughter's data report? Even I—I, who was supposed to know this stuff—often found it to be confusing. Perhaps this parent was looking at the report incorrectly? I took a deep breath to gather my composure before telling the parent, "I understand why you are concerned and upset. Why don't you come in to meet with me and we'll take a closer look at the report?" I also asked if I could invite our school psychologist to sit in. "He has extensive knowledge about how to interpret assessment reports. I'd love to have his perspective as we look at your daughter's results." She agreed to this plan.

When I called the psychologist to invite him to our meeting, he provided some reassurance. "Those data reports are very hard to understand," he said. "Sometimes there are short explanations that accompany them, but they are usually in small print, hidden carefully on the back. And even if someone reads them, they don't make sense unless there is a basic understanding of data terms."

When we met the next day, the parent handed over the report to the psychologist. He stared at it for a just a few moments before looking up. "I know exactly what happened," he said. "See that column of numbers labeled 'DNA'? Do you know what it means?"

Collective head shaking.

"It means 'Did Not Attempt,'" he said. "For some reason, on a large part of this test, your daughter did not complete questions that were required."

"But that's not like her," the parent protested. "She would *never* just *skip* whole parts."

"Maybe there were questions on the back of the test that she didn't see," the psychologist offered. "Maybe she ran out of time. Maybe the directions weren't clear to her as to when she should stop. It could be any number of things, but it's not that she got answers wrong. This report shows that she didn't even try them."

I don't know who felt more relieved, the parent or me. Both of us pledged to investigate reasons for the many "DNAs" (she with her daughter, me with the assessment's proctor), and I was left to reflect on a powerful lesson: how easy it is to interpret a simple "score" on a standardized assessment in the wrong way and how close I came to chasing an instructional problem that didn't really exist.

## Strategies and Solutions for Approaching Student and Schoolwide Data

As the principal, it's essential that you learn enough about data interpretation to support sound instructional decision making—and that you are wise enough to ask for help when you need it. Here's how I recommend going about it.

**Get a firm grip on the basics right away.** Find a way to educate yourself on the basics of data reports by learning the meaning of terms that are most widely used. This isn't difficult to do; there are countless resources to help. For example, a quick search on Amazon will reveal innumerable publications about using assessment data in various ways—to communicate with parents, to drive professional development, to make educational decisions about students, to guide instructional decisions, and so on—and most of them are extremely informative. There are also excellent online resources that offer a range of support—from quick point-by-point summaries to full courses—that are designed to help you gain a basic understanding of all things related to data.

**Learn the difference between achievement data and ability data—and how to use both.** There are two specific types of data, and they mean very different things. Achievement data give information about a student's understanding of content at any given point in time. Ability data tell what a student should be able to achieve throughout an entire educational journey. It is important that you have a clear understanding of the differences between these two and that you educate teachers and parents as well. Having both data points on a student is valuable because it allows you to compare the way a child *is* achieving in school with the way the child *should* be achieving. If the two aren't in line with one another, you may need to make some intervention or enrichment decisions.

**Identify your resources.** There are educators who enjoy delving into data. They find it great fun. Although that is mind-boggling to me (Really? *Fun*?), I am appreciative of those people. They are usually eager to share their knowledge and expertise with others. It is a good idea to seek out these experts and make a connection with them; they can serve as support when you encounter something you don't understand about data.

**Break it down.** After the administration of a standardized test, data will come back to you in a tiered report; there will be summaries by full school, grade level, teacher, and student. (If it is a districtwide assessment, the superintendent or designee will also receive a report summarizing the results of all students in the district.) When you get the data reports, you will want to look at them from a schoolwide lens and then break them down by grade level, teacher, and student. Each data subset will tell you something different, from whole-school trends to specific student achievement. I pay particular attention to subsets such as our ELL population, our special education population, our economically disadvan-taged students, and our growing subset of minority students. It is important that I keep a sharp focus on these subgroups to ensure we are moving all students forward in their achievement at a rate comparable with that of their peers.

**Look for trends and communicate them to teachers.** By the time standardized assessment data are reported, often months after the test is administered, the snapshots of individual student achievement provided might not be an accurate picture of what the students can do now. Standardized test data are actually more useful when looked at through a wider lens.

I like to study whole-class or whole-school data from the past several years in search of trends—not only trends in specific instructional areas but also trends that are specific to teachers, grade levels, and departments. When I see patterns emerge, I make it a point to share them with teachers. They want to know what I am seeing and what should guide conversations about the causes and implications of particular data trends. For example, not long ago, I studied our trend data and noticed that for three years in a row, our school had very poor results on the measurement portion of a standardized math assessment. To study a cause, we gathered the teachers together for a discussion. We all brought our ideas as we carefully studied the trend data. After much discussion, it dawned on us—our students were not scoring well on measure-ment because no one was really digging deep into instruction of measurement. The science department had been assuming that the math teachers were covering the topic, and the math teachers were relying on the science teachers to take care of it. A simple realignment of our plans ensured all students would get full expo-sure to measurement—in both math and science—and we saw a noticeable uptick in our scores the next year.

**If you have any doubts, seek multiple data points.** When looking at data reports, there are always outliers—points that are extremely high or extremely low. Typically, these should be disregarded because there may have been something unusual that happened during the administration of the test. Unless you have reason to think an extreme score is possible, proceed with caution; don't swoop in with intervention or enrichment plans until you have a way to gather multiple data points that support the accuracy of your suspicions. Looking at many different types of data—not only instructional data but behavioral and social-emotional data—will give you a clear, accurate picture of a student as a learner. The bigger the picture, the better any instructional decisions will be.

**Study data as a team.** When seeking to understand what student or school data are telling you, it is helpful to talk about it with a team. Data teams can be made up of a group of people who are interested in what data tell them, passionate about student achievement results, and willing to lead their colleagues to meaningful, provocative conversations about data. I have worked with data teams made up of teachers, data experts, school counselors and psychologists, and central office administrators. Each person brings a different perspective, which ensures we all have a thorough, accurate picture of what the data really say. It's best for the data team to meet regularly, four or five times a year, to evaluate both standardized summative assessment results and common formative assessment results.

## Knowing How to Use Assessment Results: Conversations to Guide Data-Driven Decisions

This chapter opened with three very different scenarios in which data might be used to make a decision or offer an explanation.

We now revisit those scenarios in conversation for a look at how a principal's basic understanding of data can drive the decision-making process.

## Scenario 1: Data Reports

This scenario describes a situation in which you have just taken over an elementary school, and your district's data and assessment director, Jill, wants to share some concerns she has about the data she has seen coming from your new school. You sit down to talk it through.

> **You:** *I'm glad we are able to talk about some of the trends you're seeing from the data at my building. Hopefully it will give me some specific areas for focus as I begin my new role as the principal.*
>
> **Jill:** *That's why I wanted to meet with you. I've noticed some things that I want you to be aware of. I have one concern, but I also have some really good news, too. I'll start with the things that are worth celebrating. In looking at the data, I notice that for the past five years, data trends in your 3rd grade are excellent. Students are consistently scoring above the state average in achievement, and the value-added reports indicate that most students are making above one year's growth in both reading and math. That's in every classroom.*
>
> **You:** *That's amazing. I'll make sure to share that information with all teachers who have worked with the 3rd graders. They all deserve the credit.*

Analyzing trend data helps you zero in on the impact your teachers are making on their students' learning—and allows you to celebrate this excellent work.

> **Jill:** *As with any data report, it could mean two things: It could mean that your 3rd grade team has done an excellent job planning their*

*instruction and working together to push students to achieve. And it could just mean that the 3rd graders are very well prepared from the instruction they've received from kindergarten through 3rd grade; since 3rd grade is the first year students are given a statewide achievement test, we can't really say which of these two possibilities most accurately reflects what's going on. And perhaps it's both.*

**You:** *Does their achievement line up with their ability scores?*

**Jill:** *For the most part, yes. That's why I am so pleased with this trend. Many students are achieving higher than their ability score would indicate.*

**You:** *Regardless, it's great news!*

Here is an example of the distinction between achievement and ability, and how comparing the two can show the value of classroom instruction.

**Jill:** *All the other data look really solid, with the exception of one area of concern—6th grade math. For the past three years, the scores there have been lower than we would expect. I noticed this trend last year, and this year's data show it again.*

**You:** *OK, a question to clarify: What do you mean the numbers are "lower than we would expect"?*

**Jill:** *I have compared your school's 6th grade math scores to those of other schools in the district and in surrounding districts, and it is definitely lower than what these other schools are showing. Several years ago, our district enacted a specific math program in 5th and 6th grades; most students are putting up very high achievement numbers, but at your school, the numbers fall around the state average. I have a hunch we may need to go back and retrain the teachers in your school on this math program to make sure they are using all the things the program has to offer.*

**You:** *I'd love to get the perspective of the teachers on this, too; they may have insight that would help us figure out if they are missing some specifics of the program.*

**Jill:** *That's an excellent idea. They may have other ideas, and I'm sure they will be eager to seek a cause. And they know the students better than we do, so they can speak to the specific student results when we break it down to that level.*

Studying data as a team allows you to gather multiple perspectives, and you'll be able to break the data down from a full grade level to specific students.

**You:** *I'd love for you to work with us on that if possible; you have a deeper understanding of all this data stuff than I do! I know the basics, but I will rely on you throughout the year to help me learn more— especially how to use data to make good instructional decisions.*
**Jill:** *I'd be happy to. It's my job to help you with this! Let's make sure to communicate often.*

Even if you know the basics of data interpretation, arranging for guidance from an expert will allow you to make better leadership decisions.

## Scenario 2: Standardized Assessments

In the second scenario, Mrs. Bower, a parent of an 8th grader, has contacted you after receiving results from a standardized assessment that measures a student's school ability. She is convinced her child is gifted, but the report she has received indicates her child is "only average." You realize she is confused about the difference between achievement and ability. You call her to talk it through.

**You:** *Mrs. Bower, I'm returning your call regarding your daughter's results from an assessment that was given in the spring. I understand you are concerned because the results indicate that Sophie is an average learner, but you feel her results should indicate something else.*

**Mrs. Bower:** *Absolutely. I believe my daughter is a gifted learner, so I think her results should be higher than they are. Sophie has always been so successful at school. She's taking the highest level of classes that you offer, and she has always received straight As.*

**You:** *Well, that's wonderful news. Let me guess—she's a very hard worker, isn't she?*

**Mrs. Bower:** *Yes. She spends hours working hard to get those grades. That's another reason I think she is above average. Her commitment and love for school show me that she's very smart. So I want to know what the teachers aren't doing to help her get higher results on tests like this.*

**You:** *Well, let me explain a little more to you. Schools give two types of assessments: one type is a school ability assessment, and another is an achievement test. Achievement tests will tell us how much a child can do or what a child understands at any given point in time. It shows us what they are achieving in school in comparison with other students of that grade and age. A school ability test, though, is sort of like an IQ test, except it applies only to a child's ability in a school setting. It gives us a picture of what a child should be able to do.*

Here, you are making the distinction between ability and achievement assessments.

**Mrs. Bower:** *Which type of test is this one?*

**You:** *This was a school ability test. And it indicates that your daughter has an average school ability.*

**Mrs. Bower:** *Well, that's not at all what I think.*

**You:** *But look at it this way. What it does tell us is very important. Her work ethic and her commitment to school have her achieving higher than many other students with an average school ability. That's actually great news. She's a high achiever—which will serve her well throughout her life.*

**Mrs. Bower:** *I guess that makes sense.*

**You:** *It's much better than the reverse. If she had an above-average ability and wasn't achieving well, you'd have a problem on your hands. But I think this is cause for celebration!*

Here, you are using the two types of data together to shed light on the reasons behind the student's performance at school.

**Mrs. Bower:** *Well, I guess I'm going to have to think a little more about this.*

**You:** *And remember, this is just one test. It measures school ability only. She very well could be gifted, as you suspected, in other areas.*

**Mrs. Bower:** *How can I find out?*

**You:** *You could always seek a full outside evaluation if that information is important to you. I don't know that it should be, though. I think it would be best to focus on all the wonderful things Sophie does in school rather than on a single test's ability score.*

**Mrs. Bower:** *Yes, I can agree with that. I just don't want her to think she's only average.*

**You:** *I'd continue to support her and encourage her hard work. It doesn't matter what her school ability is if she continues to achieve at this level!*

**Mrs. Bower:** *That's true. OK, I'll think on it some more. Can I call you if I have other questions?*

**You:** *Absolutely. And if I do not know the answer, I'll find out for you.*

You're willing to seek help from experts when it's needed.

## Scenario 3: Monitoring Progress Through Data

In the third scenario for this chapter, you meet with a teacher, Michelle, who serves your building as an RTI coach. She helps teachers, parents, and students through the Response to Intervention process, and you hope to learn more about how this works and how to use data to make decisions.

**You:** *Thank you for agreeing to talk with me! When I first heard that this school has an RTI coach, I was thrilled. It sounds like a really important job.*

**Michelle:** *I feel like it is important. Our district added this position because we had many, many students who were struggling at school, but in many cases, we didn't feel like there was an unidentified learning disability. Often, we thought students just needed some specific targeted interventions to catch them up with their classmates. I applied for the job because I love helping kids, but I am also really interested in student data and what they tell us about the need for classroom support.*

**You:** *I'm glad I have you, then; interpreting data is not a passion area for me. I know the basics, but I will rely heavily on you to help me interpret these numbers! Why don't we start with you talking me through a typical RTI process?*

**Michelle:** *I would be happy to. It starts when teachers come to me with a specific concern about a student. They may have taught a concept to the class, and, when they proceed with building on the concept or moving on to more complex practice, they see that a student just can't seem to master the skills needed. Of course, the teachers have intervened with some more focused and small-group instruction, but have found even that doesn't help. That's when they come to me.*

**You:** *And what do you do?*

**Michelle:** *I brainstorm ideas with the teacher to see how we can help the student. I also ask the teacher what communication has already occurred with the parent, and together we make a plan for communicating our ongoing concerns. I work together with the teacher to implement our plan, and I keep specific data on the student. I keep many different types of data: I use classroom assessments, standardized assessments through progress-monitoring tools, and anecdotal data. I also gather from many different situations, including the regular education classroom, related arts classes, and even unstructured time such as the lunchroom. It all helps give me a solid picture of the student as a learner.*

Notice how the use of multiple data points creates a comprehensive picture of the student as a learner.

> **You:** *What do the data tell you?*
>
> **Michelle:** *They tell us if our interventions are effective. Sometimes, it doesn't take long at all to see success, at which point I'll pull back some of my support. But if we see a student doesn't seem to be responding to our interventions, we meet again to discuss options. At that point, we have the parent join us for the conversation so they are in the loop about it all.*
>
> **You:** *What happens when everything you try doesn't seem to work?*

You are relying on your data expert, and you are asking a lot of questions to help you learn the basics of data use.

> **Michelle:** *That's when I call a meeting with the teacher, the parent, the school psychologist, and you—the principal. We review all the interventions we have implemented, we discuss each data point, and we talk about whether we suspect the student may have a specific learning disability that may be hindering his or her path to success. If we do suspect a disability, we fill out the paperwork for a multifactored evaluation.*

Note how the data will be studied as a team, with input from many different individuals, so that multiple perspectives will be considered.

> **You:** *And depending on the results of that full evaluation, you will know whether the student can receive supplemental educational services through an IEP.*
>
> **Michelle:** *That's correct. If the student doesn't qualify for services, I continue with the supports I've put in place through the initial plan, continuing to determine what instructional skills and approaches might work with the student. We keep trying things, keep studying the data,*

*and keep trying things. It's a really good system that ensures we don't let any student fall through the cracks.*

**You:** *I really appreciate your explanations. At this point, I will continue to watch you work and ask a lot of questions. I have a lot to learn, but I'm glad there seems to be a good system in place. And I like how you use data to monitor progress and guide your planning.*

As mentioned in the beginning of the chapter, assessment data can be a valuable tool in instructional decision making; however, these numbers are easily misunderstood, and that can lead us astray. The best way to approach educational data is with caution. Carefully and deliberately consider what the data are telling you—and may *not* be telling you—about your school, your teachers, and your students.

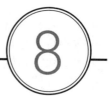

# Supporting the Social-Emotional Needs of All Learners

**Scenario 1: Special Education Students**

*Soon after beginning the school year, one of your special education teach-ers sends you an e-mail with concerns about two students who recently moved into the district. The students are twins, and both have significant learning disabilities. The teacher explains that the twins are struggling aca-demically, even with the significant accommodations that are in place; they also have very few friends and virtually no support at home. The teacher asks for suggestions and ideas for supporting the students.*

**Scenario 2: A Gifted Learner**

*You check your voice mail and find a message from a parent who wants to discuss her 4th grade daughter, Amy, who has been identified as a gifted learner. She explains that Amy is an extremely bright child, but it is hard for her to make friends. She often feels isolated at school. The parent wants to know what you plan to do to ensure her daughter receives appropriate social and emotional support. She asks you to return her phone call at your earliest convenience so you can make a plan for the upcoming year.*

**Scenario 3: Students Dealing with Trauma**

*As you prepare to take over leadership of a large elementary school, you are contacted by a county social worker. She tells you about a family of*

*sisters and brothers whose parents were recently deported; the children
are separated from one another, with some staying with relatives and others
in foster homes. The youngest, a 1st grade boy enrolled in your school, has
been struggling the most; he is displaying violent behaviors and lashing
out at his caregivers. She asks if you can get together to make a plan to
support him.*

Each student in your school is a unique individual, yet they are all grappling with similar challenges: building and maintaining friendships, pursuing social and academic goals, successfully interacting with adults, and establishing themselves as individuals. Even the most fortunate and well-adjusted children will face obstacles as they navigate their way into young adulthood. Unfortunately, though, many students will have to contend with family trauma, bullying, violence, peer pressure, drug and alcohol use, mental illness, and other serious threats to their social and emotional well-being.

I think most of us would agree that a student's life today is generally more complicated than it was even just a few years ago. The rapid spread of social media and students' access to online resources and interactions diminishes the control that parents and school officials previously took for granted. As such, it has grown increasingly important to equip school staff with the tools necessary to support today's students.

## Strategies and Solutions for Establishing Whole-School Support

Later in this chapter, we will discuss strategies for providing targeted support to specific subpopulations of students, but first, we will take a look at four simple, high-level ways to equip your school to meet the social and emotional needs of *all* learners.

**Be aware of what students face each day.** Consult your experts—parents, counselors, and teachers—to determine what social and emotional issues are the biggest challenges to your students. This can be done through conducting formal or informal conversations, a thorough survey of all members of a school community, engaging in collecting data related to discipline or guidance services, or seeking historical perspectives from former students or school leaders. You can use this information to narrow your priorities and focus. It will also help you stay abreast of the latest trends in risk behavior for students. Whether you work with young students or full-fledged adolescents, you should be personally aware of the things to which they are exposed. Research anything that seems concerning to you; find out the origins of the risk behavior, how it manifests itself with students, and how it can be prevented. By doing so, you will make yourself your best expert.

**Equip your guidance professionals with the right tools.** Your guidance counselor—or, in large schools, a guidance team—will naturally lead the social-emotional education of your students. I involve our counselor in virtually all planning and decision making related to students. I check in often to make sure he feels confident in providing developmentally appropriate instruction in social and emotional topics. I encourage him to take advantage of professional development opportunities, including an annual state conference, so he stays up-to-date on standards and expectations for counselors. Like most schools, we only have one counselor for hundreds of students, so I try to give him time to connect with his colleagues to share ideas, talk about solutions to tricky situations, and learn about the best practices related to school counseling.

**Provide adequate staff professional development.** Our world grows more connected and global by the minute. As a result, our students have increased exposure to all sorts of things—and not necessarily positive things, either. On the contrary, this exposure can lead to poor decisions and choices with far-reaching consequences. To support students as they grow into young adults, educators need to have the most current information possible about challenges facing our young learners. We cannot rely on our own school-age experiences, or even on experiences we had when we were beginning our work as educators. For that reason, it's important that teachers and staff receive frequent, timely, up-to-date professional development so they know how to best support every student in their care.

As an example, the police department in our city offers a biennial training for school district officials. My colleagues and I make it a point to attend. We learn about specific behaviors the department is seeing in adolescents and young adults—recent trends in alcohol and drug use, evolutions in social media, risky relationship choices, and ways students hide dangerous or illegal activities. The training sessions always leave us shocked, dismayed, and even a bit depressed, but they also make us much more knowledgeable about specific risks and challenges faced by our students.

**Work to get to know your students on a personal level.** You want them to think of you as someone who will advocate for them if they need it. This does not mean prying into their lives or asking questions that are not relevant to their education; it simply means you should seek to become a trustworthy, dependable adult that they can count on. Here are a few ways to make personal connections with students:

- *Make sure students feel known.* For a child or teenager, what is the worst feeling *ever*? Thinking no one knows who you are. I make it my business to make sure all students feels that someone knows their name and something about them. It takes work, but it's worth it if every student goes home at the end of each day feeling seen and valued. I've picked up tips from colleagues along the way that help me manage this task, including studying the school yearbook, repeating a student's name quietly in my mind after a conversation, and using simple memory boosters to connect names with faces, personalities, and interests (Reading Rena, Brittney Blue Eyes, Sassy Sydney, Dancing Diaski). And I'm sure to always give students time to answer when I ask questions like "How was your weekend?" and "Any fun plans over the holiday break?"

- *Ask questions.* While being tactful and keeping a healthy respect for privacy, I ask students about their families or other people who play prominent roles in their lives. What do they like to do outside of school? How do they spend their time? What are they interested in and passionate about? Again, I don't prod or pry; I just open myself up to get to know students as the people they are.

- *Attend extracurricular activities, and be attentive while you do.* Watch for specific things you can tuck away and reference later: "That was an incredible kick at the end of the game on Saturday. I was so proud of you!" or, "You played your part so well in this weekend's musical. You really love the theater, don't you?"

- *Ask questions that don't sound "interview-y."* For example, "How was your weekend?" sounds canned and impersonal; a comment like "That's an awesome backpack! Did you go shopping over the weekend?" will open up a more genuine conversation.

- *Find unique ways to connect.* I once sat next to a student during a long bus ride and learned that he, like me, was a big fan of a particular TV show. After that, whenever I saw him, I asked him to tell me his thoughts about recent episodes. It was easy to connect with the student because of our shared interest in the show's plot and characters.

# Strategies and Solutions for Supporting the Social-Emotional Health of Specific Student Populations

While the ideal school environment is set up to support the social-emotional needs of all students, some will need particular attention. These groups include students receiving special education (SPED) services, gifted learners, students who are English language learners, students who are economically disadvantaged, and students who are facing trauma. Let's delve into some strategies designed to provide each of these groups with more targeted social-emotional support.

## Students Receiving Special Education Services

Here in the United States, the past decade has brought enormous progress in how public schools provide special education services. Not long ago, students who struggled to learn were pulled out of the general education classroom and taken to a classroom in the far corner of the school, where they were sequestered away with other struggling students. The approach was isolating and embarrassing for the most vulnerable students—the ones for whom school was already difficult enough.

Fortunately, we now recognize that students with special learning needs—those identified as having a learning disability—are best served in an environment with few restrictions; they should be taught alongside their peers whenever possible. In addition, the adoption of the Individuals with Disabilities Education Act (IDEA) ensures that districts are all held to the same expectations. Schools must identify disabilities using a multifactored evaluation administered by a trained school psychologist, determine what services are appropriate and document those services on an individualized education program (IEP), and implement the specialized instruction or accommodations efficiently and effectively.

Although IDEA presents significant challenges to school districts, it has certainly forced educators to rise to the challenge of providing for students with disabilities. Dealing with conditions that range from simple working memory problems to significant cognitive or physical challenges, special education learners finally have the supports in place to be successful in public education.

But putting the appropriate academic supports in place is only one component of supporting SPED students. There's another really important piece—social and emotional growth. After all, when a student has to work extra hard to grasp concepts or complete tasks at school, the effort can become frustrating and depressing. There is a temptation to retreat emotionally, which can lead to isolation and resentment. It is important to consider these risks when thinking about students in the SPED program. Here are some strategies that can help.

**Work very closely with parents of special education students.** Parents are your best resource in determining how to meet the social and emotional needs of students. They know their child the best, after all; they know what makes their child happy, scared, angry, and lonely and how that child acts in these times of vulnerability. Parents also have the highest "stake" in raising a child who is confident and successful. Because of this, parents should have a significant voice when planning what social and emotional supports their child needs.

I used to get extremely nervous when meeting with parents of special education students, especially when they were upset or angry about services the school was providing. I was never sure what requests (or, in some cases, demands) would be made or how we could meet those requests. Over time, I have learned how powerful it is to really listen to parents when they talk about their child's social and emotional needs and factor this information into how we deliver SPED services.

In a recent example, I received a phone call from a parent who was unhappy about her child's "lack of support at school" and "failing grades." As we talked, the parent described how her child was struggling to organize and prioritize homework. Evenings were fraught with anxiety and frustration, assignments were overwhelming and confusing, and the student was turning in work that was not acceptable to the teacher, which meant lower grades. This parent told me her son had begun shouting angrily, "I *hate* school!" and hiding in his room. It had grown increasingly difficult to get him up in time to catch the bus in the morning. The parent felt helpless and alone, which manifested itself as anger and a demand that we "do something."

So we did. We convened as an IEP team to discuss how to reduce or modify the student's assignments and developed a specific plan to alleviate the pressure at home. His grades started improving immediately, and the parent reported a marked decrease in anxiety. Had we not addressed the parent's demands for action, the student would have needlessly continued to struggle academically and emotionally.

**Include input from a whole team.** While parents should have significant input when developing a student's IEP, there are many other experts to consult as well. The IEP team—composed of the child's intervention teacher, general education teachers, parents, support staff, and the administrator in charge of special education services—serves a child with a disability, and they will all have input when planning for and writing an IEP. Every person on this team will serve the child in some capacity, and every one of them should be mindful of the child's social and emotional needs and growth. Further, I try to think outside of the traditional IEP team when we find a student needs more social and emotional support. In the past I have turned to guidance counselors, coaches, extracurricular activity leaders, librarians, paraprofessionals, and any number of other experts who may be able to step in and provide support.

**Frequently revisit your ultimate goal.** In spite of the challenges of paperwork, documentation, data-gathering, and frequent communication required of a special education team, it helps to consistently revisit the end goal—to help struggling learners succeed both academically and socially. During IEP meetings or team meetings about a particular child, I will often reiterate, "We all want this child to be a happy, healthy, and successful student who grows into a happy, healthy, and successful adult. Are we doing what is necessary to achieve that goal?"

## Gifted Learners

When I refer to gifted learners, I am not talking about high-achieving students. Many students do well in school; they get good grades, they get into good colleges, and they have futures that look bright and full. They work hard, use their natural talents and skills, and frequently exceed expectations.

High-achieving students are not necessarily "gifted," though. Students who are truly gifted have cognitive abilities far beyond the norm. They think differently than most of us. They process information at a speed we can't understand. Often, they think in ways that the rest of us consider odd. Quirky. *Different.* As such, they can be at a particular risk for social and emotional difficulties. So how can we make sure that gifted learners throughout the school are as supported socially as they are challenged academically? Here are some strategies to try.

**Involve the parents of gifted learners.** Again, parents are an invaluable resource. Teachers of gifted learners should actively seek the perspective of parents when getting to know their students. They can ask questions such as these:

- What are your child's interests, passions, and strengths?
- Are there things that particularly upset or frustrate your child at school?
- Does your child have a tendency toward some typical personality traits of gifted learners (perfectionism, anxiousness, procrastination, difficulty collaborating with others)?
- How do you support your child at home?

Additionally, it is helpful for teachers of gifted learners to provide regular updates to these students' parents to share specific measures being employed to provide challenge and engagement. Regular communication will ensure everyone is working toward the same goal and in complementary ways.

**Equip teachers with the right tools and background information on their gifted students.** To truly meet the needs of gifted learners, teachers must be prepared to teach beyond academics and look also at helping these students develop solid friendships, make strong connections with teachers and other gifted peers, and have a positive school experience. A good first step is connecting current and future teachers with the student's former teachers to get an understanding of the student's unique challenges and interests. This perspective of experience can provide great insight into how to best work with a child. Many excellent

resources—publications, periodicals, online resources, and professional development conferences—are available to support teachers
as they work to challenge and support cognitively gifted students.

As an example, each year the gifted intervention specialists in
my district attend a state conference that specifically addresses
the unique social and emotional needs of gifted learners. They
share their new knowledge with general education teachers, guiding them through concerns or questions they have developed about
specific students.

**Be mindful with how you create your building schedule.**
Often, gifted learners naturally grasp concepts without the explicit
instruction their classmates require. While this seems to be a
lovely problem to have, it can leave gifted learners feeling bored,
demotivated, and isolated—a recipe for disaster. Thus, it may be
necessary to provide gifted learners with alternate learning environments. Examples include advancement to a more appropriately leveled class or opportunities to choose an elective related to
a particular interest level, further explore related arts, or engage
in supervised independent study. A colleague recently challenged
one of his gifted students to develop a course based on literature
that the student found fascinating—namely, the lives and writing
of early 20th-century American authors—and present his "course"
as a future elective at the school. The student was released from
his schedule early each day to design the course. The result was an
appropriately challenged and enthusiastic student and a "product"
that had a positive effect on other students.

**Connect gifted learners with one another.** Because truly
gifted students make up such a small percentage of all learners,
they can feel lonely and overlooked when in class with their "typical" peers. For that reason, I try to put gifted learners together
when placing students in classes. Even if there are just one or two

other like-minded students together, such placement allows for cognitive and social connections that may not otherwise occur. Additionally, I find that pulling gifted learners together for projects and programs can be successful. This may take different forms—an occasional pull-out instruction with a gifted specialist; extracurricular activities that cater to gifted learners; or focused programs in art, music, and technology that can provide additional challenge to gifted students.

**Arrange for outside mentors.** Gifted learners have a particular need to make a connection to real-life learning. After all, they are the most apt to ask a teacher, "Why do I have to know this?" For that reason, they benefit significantly from a mentor working in a field they find particularly interesting. In these situations, it helps if the school or district has a program to connect outside professionals with gifted learners; those experts can expose students to real-life and work scenarios. If an official program doesn't exist, you can encourage teachers to seek these connections on their own. I saw this happen recently when a teacher arranged for a student to intern with her friend's husband—a well-known marketing guru—and observe some of the inside tricks to channeling intelligence and energy into thoughts and products. It gave the student a vision of how his own thought processes could someday guide his career choices.

## English Language Learners

Unless you have experienced being in a situation in which you do not understand the language being spoken or read around you, it is difficult to relate to the experiences of an English language learner. So many aspects of the school experience that most students take for granted—reading homework directions, asking a question, engaging in casual conversation in the hallway or lunchroom, and even reading the posters on the classroom wall—present real hurdles that ELLs must navigate. It can be draining and very, very lonely. Fortunately, most ELL teachers understand this feeling and work to advocate for these students. Your job is to make sure *all* staff know how to provide ELLs with a positive, successful school experience.

**Work to secure the appropriate staff support.** When developing your staffing plan, make sure you have enough ELL teachers and bilingual aides to support students. Often, ELLs feel as if they don't fit in or are being overlooked; having the appropriate amount of staff members to support them will ensure this doesn't happen.

**Develop a staff of experts.** ELL teachers and bilingual aides specifically sought a special certification to work with ELLs, so they tend to have a unique passion for the work. When hiring ELL teachers, look for candidates who display a deep understanding of how best to meet the needs of their students. A strong ELL teacher will recognize and appreciate the unique learning journey of an ELL; they will also have the empathy and knowledge required to guide students to success.

Once you have developed a staff of ELL experts, you can support their work in several ways:

- Include them in hiring decisions for general education staff.
- Provide opportunities for targeted professional development.
- Develop a schedule that provides time for them to collaborate with counselors, general education teachers, and other staff that also work with their students.
- Purchase resources and supplemental materials unique to the needs of ELLs.
- Offer continuous gestures of appreciation and encouragement.

**Expect an optimal learning environment.** Regardless of whether ELL services are provided in a resource room setting or a general education classroom, the space should be full of visual aids, labels, and clearly marked resources. When evaluating a classroom environment's effectiveness, I look for evidence of a workshop model, with "centers" or "stations" set up for students to focus their thinking. Students should be moving about freely to different spaces in the room, based upon interest and instructional levels. While this is an effective instructional model for all students, it is particularly effective for ELLs because it provides a minilesson with pointed, targeted instruction; experience exploring further independently or in a small group; and time to process learning with their peers. Each component of the workshop model provides opportunities for ELLs to practice speaking and listening in an environment that is based on routine acceptable risk taking.

**Encourage collaboration focused on ELL support.** The same kind of team support that benefits SPED students can be extremely value to English language learners. All teachers who work with ELLs should come together and plan instruction, modify assignments and assessments as needed, and discuss the social and emotional status of ELLs. If done well, this collaboration will enrich the child's school experience because all teachers will have a consistent instructional and emotional approach. Rather than having to figure out expectations and routines of every teacher they see throughout the day, ELLs should instead be able to focus on improving their language, grasping academic content, and building relationships with peers.

**Involve parents as part of the team.** Again, much like an effective SPED program, a strong ELL program is built on a partnership between school and home. You may wish to develop an outreach program specifically designed to establish relationships with the parents of ELL students, perhaps providing translated versions of school communications, assignment guidelines, extra-curricular information, and so on. A solid picture of the parents' level of English proficiency and the amount of structured support available at home can help teachers provide more effective instruction at school.

**Celebrate students' cultures.** Clarify for teachers that you want them to encourage students to use their native language at school—not exclusively, of course, but when it is appropriate to do so, such as when doing so will deepen students' understanding of English vocabulary and concepts, and enrich their learning experience and that of others. Further, it is helpful if teachers educate themselves about the cultures and languages represented in their classroom and seek ways to celebrate this diversity.

## Economically Disadvantaged Students

In almost every community, there are students whose families struggle to make ends meet. Some have virtually nothing—no money to provide food, school supplies, or clean clothes for their children. It's difficult to know how to help economically disadvantaged children, especially if you are in a school where the majority of students come with a low socioeconomic status (SES). It can feel like an upward battle to make a difference when the occupation, income, education level, and place of residence for the families are so limiting.

It's no secret that students with a low SES tend to struggle in school, in terms of both academic achievement and social relationships. While I certainly do not want to promote stereotypes, there are some predictable reasons for this. Low-SES students sometimes do not have the materials and supplies they need. They may have erratic attendance. They may be unable or ill-prepared to join extracurricular activities. And they often live in areas where their neighbors and friends are transient, leading to a lack of long-term, deep, trusting relationships with peers. However, with the right supports, these students can and do achieve on par with their peers or beyond. They can be, and often are, well-adjusted, motivated, engaged, and secure learners. Again, a comprehensive outreach program that connects school to home is a key tool for helping low-SES students succeed in school. Such a program may incorporate some or all of the following strategies.

**Provide supports for parents.** Sometimes, low-SES students come from single-parent homes, with the custodial parent working alone to make ends meet. Other times, there are dual incomes, but the hours and energy put into maintaining two or more low-paying jobs leave little left to support learners. Regardless, schools can support parents in the following ways:

- *Survey parents to determine what support resources they need.* It might be books to read aloud, supplies, tips on helping their child at home, or even the chance to connect with their child at school.
- *Open the school to parents.* Whether it is a morning breakfast, a midday celebration of learning, or evening "open house" events, inviting parents to school helps them feel empowered to be participants in their child's education. Something as simple as retooling your traditional open house display of student work to run in three separate sessions—one on a weekday morning, a second in the evening, and a third on a Saturday morning—can have an enormous positive impact.
- *Spread the word about resources that support children's health and wellness.* Schools are a natural resource for parents to learn about social service supports, free health clinics, and affordable options for visits to the dentist, optometrist, and pediatrician.

It's best to make this information available through multiple channels—the school website, school social media accounts, e-mail "blasts," notes home, and old-fashioned paper newsletters. I once heard my district's director of communications say, "When they tell me I communicate *too* much, I'll know I've done my job." I agree with him; if we want to support our low-SES families, we must do go above and beyond to communicate sources of help and support.

**Ensure economically disadvantaged students have what they need to learn.** In some way, most of us have experienced feeling different and alone. For students who don't have the resources of their peers, that is how it feels—all day, every day, all the time. As a school leader, you can work to make sure that students living in poverty do not feel different from their peers—and that certain basic needs are met. You can do this by using district resources and your guidance counselors to investigate community resources and partnerships. Here are three goals to work toward:

- *All students have proper clothing and materials.* Try collaborating with local service or donation organizations. In the past, we have worked with a local Girl Scout troop who collected coats for students who needed warm clothing in the winter; a neighborhood's Books and Backpacks program, which gathers and distributes school supplies and materials for students; and an organization called Welcome Warehouse, which accepts donations and gives them freely to anyone who needs them.
- *All students have access to well-balanced, nutritious meals.* Community resources such as food pantries or soup kitchens can be helpful for students and families, but your school itself can be a predictable and solid source for all students to have at least two

good meals a day by using the National School Lunch Program. Many schools are able to offer free breakfast and lunch to all qualifying students; if needed, these programs can even extend to evening or summer hours.

- *All students have a group of peers to whom they can connect.* I try to set a culture in our school in which "everyone needs a friend, and everyone can be a friend." Guidance counselors and classroom teachers talk frequently about students and their peer relationships. If they notice a child is alone or seems lonely, they find a "peer buddy" to pair the student with and provide opportunities for the two to develop a friendship—sitting at lunch together, joining similar after-school activities, or connecting the students' parents with one another to create social opportunities.

**Provide full access to extracurricular activities.** Whether it is an athletic team, an art or music performance, or a service club, students with low SES should feel welcomed and unrestricted in their participation. If there are costs connected to joining an extracurricular activity, find a way to waive them—through a scholarship program, donations from school community members, or an exemption program. Students with low SES stand to gain tremendously from participation in such activities. Just this season, my husband coached several students on his football team who would not have been able to participate without the help of scholarships set up to cover the "pay to participate" fee and the cost of practice gear and equipment. Throughout the season, all three boys gained confidence, leadership skills, and a sense of community and "belonging" that comes with being part of a team.

**Use community resources.** I've alluded to this already: many individuals and organizations in your community or neighboring communities are eager to help you meet the needs of students with limited resources. Community centers, police and fire departments, counseling centers, health care professionals, recreation organizations, and even local businesses may wish to develop a partnership with your school. A colleague of mine, the principal of a Title I school, has built a very strong partnership with a local hotel that is part of the Embassy Suites chain. The hotel manager asks her staff to give community service time to the school. In the past year, the hotel staff created—and now maintains—an outdoor classroom area, they volunteer as "guest readers" regularly, and they offer hotel space for the school's Real-Life Problem Solving program. The partnership began simply—with a single phone call the principal made to the hotel's manager. Their partnership has directly benefited students with low SES. With minimal effort, you can empower your guidance counselor and teachers to search for these types of resources along with you.

## Students Experiencing Trauma

It is a heartbreaking truth that so many of students enter our schools carrying the burden of trauma. It originates from many sources—a nasty custody fight or violence in the home, bankruptcy, illness, death, homelessness, abandonment, or immigration issues such as exile or deportation. Many of the suggestions offered earlier in this chapter also apply to students facing trauma. As with the other situations, using guidance counselors and outside resources is a sound approach for helping students in crisis. Here are a few additional things to keep in mind.

**Keep your emotions at bay.** I struggle mightily with this, because I can't bear to watch a child suffer. If I had my way, I'd adopt any number of traumatized children and bring them home with me. Intellectually, I know this is impossible; emotionally, I can't help but want to give everything I have to help a child who is in pain. To manage the emotions involved, I remind myself often that my responsibility is to help equip children to be safe, healthy, well supported, and well adjusted. That means I can't be a hero to one—I need to be a resource for all.

**Use your network and your experts.** Over time, you will develop connections to help you support students in trauma. You will learn the names of social workers, guardians ad litem, independent counselors, law enforcement officials, truancy officers, and immigration officials. Keep the phone numbers of these people close by so you can call them in an emergency or when you simply need some insight in solving a problem. I recently called our school resource officer to discuss a student who had talked with the guidance counselor about some disturbing things happening at home. The officer was able to visit the home and gather more information, which helped us decide to involve Child Protective Services to offer support for the child.

Your school counselor will be a key player in helping students in need, because the counselor will have connections to experts who know best how to help these students. Given all the responsibilities you have as a building principal, you will need to entrust and empower these experts to make contacts and decisions that are best for the children in crisis.

**Know your legal obligations.** There are times you will be in the uncomfortable position of learning that a child's situation requires intervention and will have to decide how to react. For example, you may need to call law enforcement, a caseworker, or Child Protective Services. It's important not to let your knowledge of the case—or a soft heart—get in the way of your legal obligations.

All these strategies can help you navigate the tricky waters of students struggling with trauma. These are some of the most difficult times you will have as a principal, but if you handle them well, you will know you have truly helped a child who needs you.

## Supporting Students: Conversations to Help the Growth of All Learners

The scenarios in this chapter's opening are all examples of challenges you may face as you seek to support the various social-emotional needs of your students. Sometimes it can seem an insurmountable task to make sure each learner in your school is provided the best possible education; however, with the right team of teachers and by partnering with parents and support staff, you truly can "do right" by each and every student. Here we revisit each of the scenarios, putting advice into practice through calm, open-minded, collaborative communication.

### Scenario 1: Special Education Students

This scenario describes a teacher who is worried about two of her students. They are twins, and together they are struggling academically and socially. She e-mails you to ask for suggestions and ideas. After thinking awhile and seeking additional support, you respond to her e-mail.

To: Miss White
From: Principal Pratt
Re: Special Education Caseload

Good morning, Miss White,

Thank you for taking the time to write such a thoughtful and insightful e-mail. It is wonderful how deeply you care for the twins. I can tell how eager you are to help them succeed here at school.

First, I think we should set up an IEP meeting with the twins' parents so we can get a full picture of how things look at home.

Further, we can fully explain our support services and accommodations to the parents. I will have the special education secretary set that up for later this week.

Here, you are communicating your intention to work collaboratively with these students' parents.

Before we meet with parents, though, let's get together to brainstorm ways to use the whole special education team—teachers, therapists, and psychologists—in supporting the twins. With the help of others on the team, we may be able to pull them from the classroom for targeted interventions when needed, or find some support within the classroom setting.

You are emphasizing how much you value a team approach to special education and laying the foundation for positive collaboration.

Another idea is taking a look at your schedule. I'm wondering if we could redistribute some of your responsibilities—such as your morning bus duty—to give you a small pocket of time to work with the twins on specific goals. We could also think about some after-school support for them; there are some community service groups that offer free homework and instructional support after school.

Your comments here show creative thinking and a willingness to consider nontraditional ways to lessen the burden on the special education staff.

Regardless of how it looks in the end, I'm confident we can work together to figure out how to help the twins. After all, that's why we're here, right? We'll make sure they feel right at home here, and we'll make sure they see success.

Wisely, you circle back to the ultimate goal—providing the best possible educational environment for your students.

Again, I appreciate you reaching out to me to start this conversation. I am really looking forward to working with you and the entire special education staff. The students are lucky to have you in their corner!

See you soon,

Principal Pratt

## Scenario 2: A Gifted Learner

This scenario describes a voice mail message you have received from a parent we'll call Mrs. Gupji. In her message, she tells you her daughter, Amy, is a gifted learner, but school has grown increasingly problematic because Amy seems to be struggling to develop and maintain meaningful friendships with peers. Amy's mother wants you to return her phone call to discuss ways that Amy will be supported socially and emotionally in the year to come.

The first step in this situation is to do some research. You start by looking in Amy's cumulative folder or in your district's gifted database to determine if, in fact, she has been identified as "gifted" based on cognitive ability scores or the results from applicable standardized assessments. She has.

Next, you reach out to Amy's previous teachers and to your guidance counselor to gain their perspective and insight about Amy's educational journey thus far. With this information in hand, you're ready to return the phone call.

> **You:** *Hello, Mrs. Gupji. I received your voice message today, and I wanted to return your call so we could talk through your concerns about Amy's upcoming school year.*
> **Mrs. Gupji:** *Thank you so much for your return call. I truly appreciate it.*

**You:** *Before calling you, I looked through Amy's file, and confirmed that she has been identified as a gifted learner according to our state's identification criteria. As you know, being identified as gifted does not necessarily mean that students receive specific services or programs; however, I want to work together to come to a solution so we're sure Amy has the support that she needs. First, why don't you start by telling me a little about your previous experiences?*

You've clarified for this parent that you're aware of the identification criteria of gifted learners and established yourself as an ally in her efforts.

**Mrs. Gupji:** *I'll be honest. It's been frustrating. Early last summer—before Amy went into 3rd grade—we received a letter from the district saying Amy was "gifted" based upon the results of some test she'd taken that spring. It didn't surprise me, because she has always been a bright child, if a bit quirky. Following that letter, I assumed that there would be a program to provide her some kind of alternate enrichment experience, but nothing really seemed to happen. She was lumped in with all the other kids and didn't have a chance to really use all her strengths. And I really worry about her socially; she seems to keep herself isolated. She doesn't really have any friends.*

**You:** *That must be very difficult for Amy—and for you. I spoke with the teachers Amy has had since she began attending school here, and they were very open and honest with me regarding Amy's experiences in the past. To summarize, they felt they were able to challenge her academically, but they did feel she needed more support with the social-emotional part.*

**Mrs. Gupji:** *Exactly. Please know I have no complaints about previous teachers. Amy has loved them all, and she is doing fine academically. But there is a real disconnect between Amy and other kids her age. That's why I am so worried.*

**You:** *As you know, sometimes extremely bright children have a very hard time socially. They think in different ways than their peers, which can leave them feeling that isolation we've been talking about.*

**Mrs. Gupji:** *Exactly. That's why I called—I want to know specifically what you will do in your role as the building principal to help her be supported so she can be successful socially as well as academically.*

**You:** *I absolutely understand. I have done a lot of thinking about this, and I think you will feel better about this situation if I share some of my planning with you. First of all, after talking with Amy's teachers, I learned how eager they are to learn more about the social needs of gifted learners. I have been seeking out professional development opportunities for our staff that specifically address the needs of students like Amy. In fact, two of our lead teachers will be attending a conference on gifted learners and will share their learning with colleagues. I have also subscribed each teacher to a publication that routinely offers tips on how to support gifted learners in the classroom.*

You have a solid plan in place to make sure teachers have the specific training needed to work effectively with gifted leaners.

**You:** *I have also created a list of all gifted learners in our school—Amy included—and I plan to meet with teachers so they know which students may need some additional social support in the classroom. Additionally, since the first day of school is still a week away, I have some time to tweak class schedules to make sure students with the highest cognitive ability are grouped together in the same classrooms, where they can engage more with one another. I have found that when gifted learners are surrounded by like-minded peers, they tend to feel more comfortable and included.*

Your plan includes identifying your gifted students and ensuring that staff have the information they need to support gifted learners. You are also looking at how you schedule students so you can cluster gifted students together, helping them feel connected to and supported by one another.

> **Mrs. Gupji:** *That all sounds great. I do worry, though, that current staff are stretched so thin with the needs of other children. Are there other resources we could think about?*
>
> **You:** *I will be asking the guidance counselor to develop a support group made up of other gifted learners. They will meet regularly to talk about how they are feeling at school. And I'm sure we could think about other options—maybe mentors within the community? I'd like to have a conversation with our district-level leaders to determine what resources are available outside our school. We might think long-term about getting the district's support for developing mentor relationships with business professionals, connecting with local arts or science organizations, or creating a partnership with adults who know how to best challenge gifted learners.*

Here you are committing to a new means of in-school support for gifted learners and beginning to make ambitious plans for the future.

> **You:** *I want you to feel reassured that Amy is in good hands with her teachers and that they are aware of her needs. Please let me know if you have additional concerns as we begin the school year.*

## Scenario 3: Students Dealing with Trauma

This scenario discusses a situation in which you meet with a local social worker to discuss a 1st grader who has just been enrolled in your school—a boy whose parents have been deported, leaving him living in a foster home, separated from his siblings. This little boy, Carlos, has been displaying violent behaviors and lashing out at his caregivers. Working together, you write the following step-by-step plan to help him transition to your school:

**Step 1: Careful class placement**
- Assign Carlos to a class in which the teacher understands the challenges he is facing; outline the teacher's responsibility to provide the appropriate structure and nurturing support.
- Set up a meeting with social worker, school psychologist, school counselor, and teacher.
- Begin writing a transition plan; include past interventions and ideas for current transition.

**Step 2: Meet the teacher and prepare for school**
- Social worker will bring Carlos to school to meet the teacher, experience the classroom, and tour the school.
- Create visual calendar for Carlos to keep on hand.
- Ensure he has all supplies and materials needed:
  - School supplies provided by PTO supply surplus
  - Meal account designated for free breakfast and lunch
  - Transportation arranged to and from school
  - Foster parent access to student online resources (e.g., grading program, student handbook, academic support materials)

**Step 3: Complete record release paperwork, giving permission for school officials to speak to the following:**
- Private counselor(s)
- Foster parents
- Pediatrician
- Previous teachers/schools

**Step 4: Build a supportive network**
- Schedule a recurring formal weekly meeting with Carlos and the guidance counselor.
- Conduct informal check-ins daily.
- Hold monthly meeting with Carlos's foster parents.

**Step 5: Collect data and document**
- Document behaviors and work to identify causes or instigating events.
- Communicate daily with foster parents using a home/school folder.
- Put rewards in place for decreases in unacceptable behaviors.

**Step 6: Connect student with two or three trustworthy peers**
- Seek peers who can support Carlos at school.
- Gain permission from the identified peers' parents.
- Provide unstructured social opportunities for free play with peers.
- Depending on success with peers, help Carlos seek out extracurricular activities of interest.

This plan draws on the support of your guidance counselor as well as a team of experts—teacher, private counselor, foster parents, and pediatrician—as a network of support for Carlos. It also makes use of visual aids for him, ensures that you have satisfied all of his material needs, and provides him with opportunities to connect with peers.

Keeping up with varying student needs will always be a challenge for you as a principal—especially because those needs will be constantly changing. However, staying student-focused and flexible in your thinking will ensure it becomes one of the things you are most proud of in your work.

# Working Through Behavior and Discipline Issues

### 9

## Scenario 1: The Fight

*As a principal of an elementary school, you feel lucky that you have relatively few discipline referrals. One day, though, you learn that two students were in a fight on the bus on the way to school. You bring the students into your office separately to hear their account of what happened, and you take statements from the bus driver and students who saw the fight. You call both parents to tell them about the incident, explain that both boys were equally at fault, and inform them of the disciplinary action you've decided on: in-school suspension and revoked bus privileges for two weeks. That evening, you check your e-mail to find a rebuttal from one of the parents. The content of the e-mail is aggressive and accusatory, clearly meant to upset you. You decide to wait until the morning to respond.*

## Scenario 2: Sticky Fingers

*A middle school student is sent to the office midway through a Friday. She is not a student who is a frequent visitor, so you are a bit surprised to see her sitting there. When you ask her why she was sent to see you, she shrugs and says, "I didn't do anything." Her answer is frustrating, because you are certain that she knows why she is sitting there. You have some investigating to do.*

## Scenario 3: The Plan

*One of the students in your high school has begun making consistently poor behavior decisions. You have meted out the standard consequences, but there's been no change or improvement; in fact, he seems unable to avoid getting in trouble. You reach out to your district's behavior specialist, who performs a Functional Behavior Assessment on the student. Using the results, you get together with the student's team of teachers to come up with a Behavior Intervention Plan to support him in turning his behavior around.*

If there is a school free of behavior and discipline issues, I have yet to find it. I'd love to work there; handling discipline issues is what I like least about being a principal. Still, it is part of the job. As I tell myself, children and adolescents are developing every day, and that process includes making poor choices and learning from them. Sometimes, those choices result in students taking a seat outside your office and waiting for you to come in and manage the problem. The emotions these students bring with them run the spectrum from remorse to nonchalance to confusion to defiance. Your role is to figure out why each student is sitting there and what to do about it.

As a beginning administrator, discipline was a large part of my job; my principal essentially turned all but the most serious issues over to me. And I *hated* it. I hated the investigations, the fact that I was always the bad guy, the very real likelihood that I would somehow bungle a discipline investigation, and the looming phone call to a student's parents. Ah, yes—the phone calls. They were what I hated the most. I *dreaded* calling parents. It always unfolded the same way: the awkward greeting, the suspicious reply, the explanation of why I was calling, the description of consequences, and the inevitable challenging quiz I'd get from parents who seemed eager to find *any* alternative explanation of events than the one I'd provided.

One particular middle school student's behavior choices kept me up at night for months. Brandon was a rascal—he got *tons* of attention by breaking rules, and there wasn't much he wouldn't do. He talked back to teachers. He didn't turn in assignments. He came to class in T-shirts advertising beer and weapons. He walked down the hall shouting suggestive sexual innuendos and waving his middle finger to anyone in his way. Brandon picked fights with peers, clogged up toilets, and wrote filthy words on the locker room walls. He was a handsome and talented young man with bright eyes and a wide smile, but he used up all his energy finding ways to break rules. Brandon had worn out all of his teachers and either annoyed or frightened most of his classmates, so he was constantly being sent to me for incident after incident of insubordination or bullying.

Depending on Brandon's latest infraction, I'd have to spend anywhere from one hour to a half day figuring out what had happened and how to react. The truth was, I had no idea what to do with him. I'd offer a stern lecture, consider consequences, and send him to in-school suspension. Calls to his mother meant listening to long, angry rants. She was "sick and tired" of these calls and didn't understand why "the school" couldn't just "handle" her son. As I held the phone to my ear, Brandon sat across from me, smirking. He knew his mother had no more control over him than we did.

I won't twist the truth and say that I finally had a breakthrough that changed Brandon's life. The reality is that I just hung on each day, trying to do my best, constantly thinking of how I could motivate him to stay out of trouble. And in time, probably just because of the inevitable maturing that comes to most students, Brandon made an uneasy truce with his teachers, with his peers, and with me. In the end, he was just fine. But he put me through the wringer in the process.

In the years since, I have grown quite a bit more confident in handling discipline. It doesn't bother me one little bit now. I know how to do a thorough investigation and how to land at fair, reasonable, and defensible consequences. I know how to communicate with teachers, parents, and students involved in the situation. And I am able to stand by my decisions with confidence. You'll get there, too.

## Strategies and Solutions for Handling Behavior Problems and Discipline

It can take some time to make peace with being your school's top disciplinarian. Here are some ways to speed up the process.

**Empower your teachers.** Even if students think highly of you, they're unlikely to follow behavior expectations just to please their principal. Teachers generally have more pull in this area. For that reason, teachers should have the authority to manage student behavior, to a certain point. When there are discipline problems, I encourage teachers to communicate frequently with parents, develop a specific behavior plan, reward positive behavior choices, and divvy out appropriate classroom discipline when necessary (loss of free time, before- and after-school detention, or loss of privileges). Teachers are the ones who build the most meaningful relationships with students; they know their students best and can provide the best incentives for following behavior expectations at school.

**Clarify that when problems reach you, you will take the lead.** Even when your teachers manage classroom discipline, there will be times students are sent to you for more significant and formidable consequences. When that happens, ownership transfers to you. You will investigate, you will make the decisions, and you will determine consequences.

This isn't always easy for teachers to understand. I have had teachers who referred students to me with a specific consequence in mind get very upset when I chose a different course of action. I don't let this bother me. I simply respond by telling them I understand their perspective and appreciate that they care enough to feel strongly about the child's consequences. Then I explain the thinking that led to my decision. While we still may not agree in the end, at least we have had the chance to consider each other's viewpoint.

**Know your district's student handbook and disciplinary policies.** Your district has a set of policies that clearly outline student behavior expectations and the consequences for breaking these rules. In some areas, there's no wiggle room when it comes to consequences. For example, bringing a weapon to school may lead automatically to suspension or expulsion. In most areas, there is a range of possible consequences laid out for particular behaviors. For example, for "harassment," a student might be given anything from a detention to suspension, depending on the severity of the incident. Bookmark these consequences in the beginning, while you are learning; in time, you'll come to know them by heart.

It's also important to be aware that the law provides discipline restrictions for students with disabilities. When a student with a 504 plan or IEP is sent to my office because of a discipline infraction, I make sure I understand what is and is not considered an acceptable behavior consequence. That way, I am never out of compliance or breaking any provision of IDEA.

**Differentiate your discipline.** Just as we need to differentiate our instruction for various learners, we need to make discipline decisions depending on the student's situation. For example, when a student moves in from a different district and does not yet understand the behavior expectations in your school, you may need to be more lenient in your consequences. I recommend considering the incident's specific circumstances as well as the student's age, home life, and typical behavior patterns before making a disciplinary decision.

**Prioritize student safety.** Look at discipline referrals through the lens of student safety. For small infractions—being chronically late to class, being insubordinate, or failing to complete assignments—I react differently than I do when a student is placing others at risk. I try to change behavior through positive reinforcements and rewards whenever I can; however, if a student is harassing, threatening, or bullying, or has actually made a physical assault on a classmate, I slip into my no-tolerance zone and chose the maximum consequences.

**Investigate fully.** Do not determine a consequence for a student until you are sure that you know the full story. I usually begin my investigation by getting the perspective of each student involved, either verbally or in writing. Then I speak to teachers, staff, and students who witnessed the incident. For significant issues, such as a physical assault or theft, I consult security video footage, if it is available. In short, I seek any and all information that may help me truly understand what happened and why. That way, I'm better equipped to make the best possible decision for all students involved, fully and confidently prepared to talk with parents, and ready for any questions or concerns that may arise.

**Let time be your friend.** Just because a student is sent to your office for disciplinary action does not mean you need to deal with it right away. It is perfectly OK to finish whatever task you were working on and let the discipline situation percolate awhile. Often, if the child has time to sit alone and think, he or she may grow less defensive and emotional, gradually moving toward honesty, resignation, and acceptance. It also buys you time to talk with teachers and gather outside information before working with the student and parent.

**Get a second opinion.** When faced with a tricky discipline issue and unsure about how to proceed, I always call a trusted colleague to get a different perspective. I explain what investigations I've done, outline the discipline history of the students involved, and describe how I intend to proceed. I am always pleased by the rational, matter-of-fact viewpoint that emerges from someone who's been in a similar situation but isn't in it *right now*. Often a colleague will challenge me to consider other options, or give me some new ideas for better solutions. Seeking a second and third opinion generally makes the final decision a better one.

**Avoid group consequences.** It makes me cringe when I hear of a teacher or principal who punishes a whole group because of the actions of a few. I once worked with an aggressive, impulsive veteran teacher who was assigned daily lunch duty. On any given day, something would set her off—a student who didn't properly clean up a mess, a table that got too loud and rambunctious, a group of students who didn't follow the very strict rules she had set in place. When that happened, she would bellow over the typical lunchroom din and announce a "quiet lunch." Students were not permitted to talk—not a whisper, not a giggle, not a *word*. It made me crazy; there were 200 well-behaved students forbidden to talk in what was their only unstructured social time of the day, when only a handful of students had caused the problem. Since then, I have stayed fiercely opposed to group consequences of any type. When there is a discipline problem, I encourage teachers to home in on the students involved and let the other ones go about their day.

**Involve parents whenever possible.** Regardless of whether it is a onetime incident or a repeat offense, involve parents in the conversation as soon as you have a thorough understanding of what actually happened. For the most part, parents will be powerful allies in helping students make positive behavior choices.

I have three pieces of advice here:

1. *Be prepared for pushback, and if it comes, do not engage.* In rare cases, parents will vehemently deny that their child was involved or could possibly engage in the behavior you describe. I recommend restating the facts simply, explaining the consequences, and opting not to engage in an argument. (In a moment, we'll look at steps to take if the situation escalates.)

2. *Student safety comes first.* On the other side of the coin, in very rare instances, a parent will significantly overreact to a discipline situation and issue severe consequences at home. If you believe a parent's overreaction to a student discipline issue may put a student in danger, work closely with your guidance counselor to carefully craft your communication. My guidance counselor and I will call the parent together. I'll talk first, explaining the incident and consequences; afterward, the counselor will reassure the parent with something like "We really believe this was simply a mistake and your child has learned from it. We will handle the consequences here at school and will make sure everything is in place so this doesn't happen again. There is no need for you to do anything further at home."

3. *Always honor privacy.* When communicating with parents, keep the focus on their child, and their child alone. In situations where more than one student has been involved, expect to encounter parents who will want to know what consequences you've set for "the other kid." There is absolutely no reason to share this information. I simply explain, "Just as I would never discuss your child with another parent, I will not discuss this child with you." They may not like this answer, but for the most part, they understand and accept it.

**Do not buckle in response to threats.** You'll hear all sorts of threats from parents who do not like decisions you've made. The most common is the threat to go to your superiors to complain about how you handled a particular discipline situation. I've gotten pretty good at not letting these threats bother me; in fact, I find them to be an odd mixture of pathetic and humorous. When a parent tells me he or she intends to go to the superintendent to outline all the ways I am incompetent, I smile and hand over the superintendent's business card or jot down the e-mail address. My boss knows I am competent, and he knows my track record. If he actually does get a phone call from a disgruntled parent, I know he will understand that the call is coming because the parent wasn't able to push me into changing my decision.

Of course, principals who are new on the job don't have the reassurance of a long-standing record or reputation. Policy and procedures should be your rock. If you do what is right and stick to it, you won't need to worry about getting the support of your supervisor.

In rare cases, a parent may follow the Board of Education's appeal process in an attempt to overturn your disciplinary decision. This can feel deeply personal and thoroughly exasperating, but it almost never has anything to do with you. I have learned to step back and let the appeals process work itself out. Trusting the system allows me to let go and accept the final resolution.

**Treat discipline as a learning opportunity.** Regardless of the discipline infraction, there is always an opportunity for the student to learn from the situation. In fact, learning should be a primary focus of the consequence! When working through a discipline infraction, it helps when both school officials and parents ask themselves questions: *What can we do to help this child make better choices next time? How can we prevent another incident like this? What does this child need from us right now?* Whether it's a fight in the lunchroom or cheating on a midterm, it is important for the adults to work together to ensure the student sees—and eventually takes—the opportunities for change and growth.

## Behavior and Discipline: Conversations to Help Manage Student Conduct

We opened this chapter with three scenarios you may encounter as you manage student discipline. Each involves students who have made unacceptable behavior choices; each also involves communication with parents and making decisions about consequences. As we take a closer look at each scenario, we will discover possible options for handling the situation fairly and appropriately—with a constant eye toward open, honest communication.

### Scenario 1: The Fight

In this scenario, you have investigated a fight during the bus ride to school. Your investigation revealed that both of the students involved had an equal part in the events. You revoke their bus privileges for two weeks and assign them both to an in-school suspension. That evening, you receive an e-mail from the mother of one of the students, Danny. She is refusing to acknowledge her son's part in the fight, choosing to believe it was all the fault of the other student, Colin. She also is accusing you of several things you simply did not do.

Principal Troyer:

I am writing to you regarding the incident that happened today with my son, Danny. Let me start by emphasizing how angry and upset I am with how you handled the incident. I intend to take this to the superintendent unless you are able to make this situation right.

Danny got home today soon after I got off the phone with you. He was crying so hard he could not even breathe. He said you screamed at him and accused him of starting the entire fight. He told me he had nothing to do with the incident, and I believe him. Colin has been bullying him for months, and no one at the school has done a thing about it.

Here are the questions I expect you to answer:

1. What makes you think Danny had anything to do with this fight?
2. What consequence did Colin get for starting this whole thing?
3. What do you intend to do to make sure Colin stops bullying Danny?

I look forward to your response.

Mrs. Baker

After reading the e-mail, you decide to wait until you are calm and collected enough to reply. The next day, you send this response:

Dear Mrs. Baker,

Thank you for your e-mail. I am glad you had a chance to talk to Danny about yesterday's incident. I recognize that you are unhappy about the situation, and I am aware that you feel there is no way to make this a positive experience for you or your son. With that said, I believe there are some parts of his perspective that I need to correct. For one, it is unfortunate that Danny told you I screamed at him and accused him of starting the fight. Let me reassure you that I did neither of these things. I do not ever "scream" at students; it is not, and never has been, the way I interact with children. Further, I never accuse a child of anything unless or until I have completed a thorough investigation.

That investigation revealed clearly that both Danny and Colin played a part in what happened on the school bus. In fact, both boys admitted they had said unkind and inappropriate things to one another as they rode to school yesterday, and they both told me they understood their role and responsibility in the fight. I do not know why Danny changed his story when he got home, but this is something I have known other students to do in order to avoid trouble at home or seek a way out of the consequences. Often, children Danny's age simply do not want to disappoint their parents.

As for your allegations that Colin has bullied Danny, I have not heard any reports of this from you, his teachers, or the boys' peers. In fact, the two of them are largely considered friends. If you do have concerns of bullying, I am eager to hear about specific incidents that have occurred as well as what reporting was done by the boys, the staff here at school, or you from home. This information will give me a place to start investigating your claim immediately, as students' safety is a top priority for us. However, I believe this was an isolated incident in which tempers flared and the boys reacted angrily, which quickly led to a physical altercation. I would encourage you to talk with Danny about how he can avoid this situation in the future; after all, as he grows and matures, he will need strategies to avoid an altercation when he grows angry or upset.

As for Colin, I am not able to discuss the disciplinary consequences set for him. This information is confidential, as I am sure you can understand. Just as I will not discuss Danny's situation with others, I will not discuss Colin's with you.

I hope this addresses your concerns. I am sure the superintendent would answer any questions if necessary; however, as always, feel free to give me a call if you have further questions.

Sincerely,

Principal Troyer

Your response does several things. First, it acknowledges that the parent is unhappy, but it points out the opportunity for the student to grow and mature. It also makes it clear you will not discuss consequences given to another child, that you will not change your mind when threatened, that you have conducted a full investigation, and that your decisions were based on your commitment to student safety. All of these serve to make your final decision one that will stand—no matter how forcefully you are challenged.

## Scenario 2: Sticky Fingers

In this scenario, you are the principal of a middle school and are beginning to wrap up your tasks midway through a Friday afternoon when a student, Ashley, is sent to your office. She is not a frequent discipline problem, and when you ask why she was sent to see you, she simply tells you, "I didn't do anything."

**You:** *So you really have no idea why you were sent to see me?*
**Ashley:** *No.*
**You:** *And what class are you coming from?*
**Ashley:** *Physical education.*
**You:** *Well, the P.E. teacher rarely sends students to the office. I think there's something going on here, Ashley. Tell you what—I'm going to have you go gather your things for the weekend. You'll spend the rest of the school day here, thinking about what may have occurred. While you're here, I'll be gathering statements from other students who may be aware of what happened; I'll also speak with your teacher. In the meantime, if something occurs to you that you'd like to share with me, please do so; maybe some time to think about it will help trigger your memory. And I would like you to have a conversation with your parents about this. That way, when I call them Monday—which I will do—they'll have an idea of what might have happened.*

There's no need to rush to action when it comes to discipline. Take the time to get the whole picture and make a considered decision about consequences.

When students begin arriving on Monday, you pull Ashley into your office immediately.

> **You:** *Good morning. I hope your weekend went well. Have you had time to think about what happened on Friday?*
> **Ashley:** *I guess so.*
> **You:** *I need to know what "I guess so" means, Ashley. Keep in mind that I have several statements from students who were there, and they are very clear about what happened. I also talked with your teacher over the weekend, so I have a good understanding of her perspective. I expect you'll be honest with me when you tell me your side.*

You have done a thorough investigation, so you are well aware of what happened. Now, you're nudging this student toward a learning opportunity.

> **Ashley:** *Well, it's just . . . well, the teacher thinks I broke into someone's locker and took her graphing calculator.*
> **You:** *Did you break into a locker and take a calculator?*
> **Ashley:** *Well . . .*
> **You:** *Make sure you tell me the truth. This whole thing will be so much easier if you are honest with me.*
> **Ashley:** *I just borrowed it. I was going to give it back.*
> **You:** *Where is this calculator now?*
> **Ashley:** *It's in my backpack. I didn't mean to . . . I just borrowed it.*
> **You:** *Do you understand that you can't borrow someone else's property unless you have their permission? Borrowing without asking is just taking—it's stealing. And you know there are consequences for stealing, right?*
> **Ashley:** *Yeah.*

**You:** *I'm guessing that you wanted that calculator and you didn't think about the consequences before taking it.*

**Ashley:** *I guess so.*

**You:** *Did you talk to your parents about this?*

**Ashley:** *Yes.*

**You:** *Do they know you took the calculator?*

**Ashley:** *They know I borrowed it.*

**You:** *Please understand that when I call them, I will have to tell them that you took it. That you stole it. And I'll tell them about consequences. Typically, stealing means an automatic suspension. However, since you have never had a discipline issue before, we may be able to work with you if you are willing to take responsibility and make this right. Perhaps if you return the calculator with a genuine apology, and if I believe you have learned from this incident and will never do it again, I may not need to remove you from school.*

You know the district's discipline policy, and this is an area where principals have leeway. The right decision is to adjust the consequence for this particular child.

**Ashley:** *OK.*

**You:** *So, I'd like you to get the calculator from your backpack. We are going to return it to its owner together. We will talk to the teacher to explain that this will not happen again. She will be keeping an eye on your actions to make sure of that. OK? Finally, we will call your parents and ask them to come in so we can talk about this. Are you ready to take responsibility for what has happened?*

**Ashley:** *Yes.*

**You:** *I'm glad to hear that, Ashley. Finally, let's look at this as an opportunity, OK? If you learn—right now, right here, because of this situation— that borrowing without asking is stealing and stealing is never OK, we will have turned a bad situation into something good.*

Here, you have made the decisions about the disciplinary consequences, and now you're stepping back to allow the teacher to take the lead role in managing the next steps. You're also stressing the "silver lining" of this whole incident and encouraging the student to learn from this experience.

## Scenario 3: The Plan

In this scenario, one of the students in your high school, a boy named Eric, has recently begun making lots of poor behavioral decisions; however, the standard consequences have not made a difference. For help, you turn to your district's behavior specialist, who completes a Functional Behavior Assessment (FBA) of Eric. Using the results, you work with a team of Eric's teachers to create the following Behavior Intervention Plan (BIP), which will help him manage his behaviors at school. *Note that each state, district, and school may have a very different and more specific BIP template than the one presented here.*

---

**Student:** Eric Jones

**Team:** Behavior specialist, principal, student, parents, and teachers: Mr. A, Mrs. B, Mr. C, and Miss D

**Targeted Behaviors:**
Impulsivity
Inappropriate language
Insubordination
Noncompliance with staff requests
Rapid escalation of emotions/outbursts

**Frequency of Behavior:**
3–4 times per day

---

**Predictors:**
Seeking attention of peers/adults
Avoiding tasks that are challenging/difficult

**Team Goals:**
Deliver direct instruction regarding appropriate behavior
Validate Eric's feelings
Offer choices for replacement behaviors
Reduce disruptions for other learners in the class

**Student Goals:**
Reduce incidences to <1 per day
Turn to teacher team for support
Know when to ask for a mental or sensory break
Increase tolerance to change and challenge

**Action Steps:**
- When Eric begins to escalate, teacher will give a discreet nonverbal reminder
- If behaviors continue, teacher will quietly suggest a break
- If break is refused, teacher will escort Eric to the hallway to instruct him on alternative behaviors
- If Eric continues to escalate, another member of the team will be called to escort Eric to the sensory room
- When calm behaviors return, Eric will process the incident with a member of the team, determining how to handle himself differently in future situations
- Eric will return to classroom and resume work, adhering to classroom expectations

**Resources/Materials:**
Frequent breaks to sensory room
Daily check-in with home base teacher
Daily communication log between school/home
Weekly group sessions with guidance counselor and peers

**Rewards for Appropriate Behaviors:**

Verbal praise

Choice of seating

Increase in responsibility

Free time on classroom computer/tablet

**Monitoring Progress:**

Data collection, to be compiled and shared with team weekly

Completion of Eric's self-reflection, to be shared with team weekly

**Date:**

**Date for Team to Reconvene/Evaluate Plan:**

**Signatures:**

Behavior Specialist:

Teachers:

Parents:

Principal:

In the sample shown, we see that a behavior plan differentiates the discipline problem according to the student's needs. It involves the opinions of others, affects only one student and not a whole group, and includes frequent communication with parents. All will serve to help the Eric find success in his personal behavior choices.

These scenarios describe ways in which discipline can challenge you—not only in making decisions but also in defending your right

and role as the school disciplinarian. In time, you will grow to be confident and skilled in handling all sorts of discipline referrals at your school. As a result, most students, teachers, and parents will grow to respect your behavior expectations and will support you in your efforts to uphold them. They will be very appreciative of the work you are doing and will be grateful for the behavior expectations you have in place.

# Managing Adult Conflicts: Parents

### 10

### Scenario 1: The Defensive Parent

*A teacher sends a student from her sophomore English class to your office. Immediately, you know why: the student is wearing a skirt that is extremely short—far shorter than the district policy of "two inches from the knee." You sigh and shake your head; she's been in your office multiple times for dress code infractions. After ascertaining that she does not have alternate clothing in her locker, you ask her to call her parents to bring in something from home. When the student's mother arrives, she hands her daughter a pair of pants and then asks to have a private word with you. Her jaw is tight; you can sense her agitation. You usher her into your office, and when she takes the offered seat across from you, she sits with an audible huff, simultaneously crossing her arms in front of her and one leg over the other.*

### Scenario 2: The Panicked Parent

*It's mid-August, and you are busy preparing for a new school year. Early on a Monday morning, as is typical, your district releases teacher assignments for elementary school classrooms. By 10:15, you've received multiple voice messages from the mother of one of your 3rd grade students. She sounds angry and upset, yet does not explain why. In each message, she insists you call her back immediately. You've just wrapped up a breakfast to welcome newly enrolled students and have a scheduled meeting with a team of teachers in 15 minutes, so the call back will have to wait. Then your secretary appears at your door to tell you that the parent is in the office and is refusing to leave until she speaks to you.*

### Scenario 3: The Litigious Parent

*A middle school basketball player assaults a player from an opposing school during the last few minutes of a highly competitive game. Together with your school's athletic director, you decide to suspend this student from the team for the remaining four games of the season. His mother and father immediately call their attorney, who faxes you a letter informing you that he will pursue legal action in appealing the decision. Pending that appeal, the letter states, the student must be permitted to play with the team.*

These scenarios are examples of how a principal can make a seemingly fair, logical decision and then be caught off guard by the reaction of a parent. No matter how experienced you are, handling a volatile situation with a parent can be challenging. For a first-year principal, though, it can be especially difficult. Why?

For one thing, parents tend to challenge a first-year principal more often and more aggressively than they will challenge an experienced one. There is a perception, I believe, that a new principal can be pushed around, because he or she has not yet developed the strength or courage to stick to contested decisions. Bear in mind that the most aggressive parents will want to establish themselves early as someone to be feared—someone who will refuse to accept the principal's authority.

Second, conflict with parents is especially challenging for beginning principals because rookies often aren't prepared for the lengths that parents will go to make their point or come out on top of a dispute. It can be unnerving, surprising, and even frightening, especially if a parent makes a threat or implies he or she will escalate the situation to the superintendent or school board. It's natural to be anxious about how to handle these complicated situations.

In my first year as an administrator, I was serving as an assistant principal of a very large middle school, learning from a very experienced principal who never seemed ruffled by parents. I, however, still grew very nervous when interacting with parents in contentious situations.

One day late in winter, I handled a simple behavior issue with a student. The boy was a rather impudent 8th grader who had dodged disciplinary action several times throughout the year. This time, though, all evidence pointed straight to him. In this case, he had snuck into the locker room and stolen another student's iPod from a gym bag. When he realized I was looking into the situation, he had thrown the iPod into the dumpster behind the school. I conducted a thorough investigation, and surveillance video confirmed my findings. I determined that restitution and a one-day suspension was a fair and appropriate consequence.

When I shared my plans with my principal, she warned me that the student's father probably would not react well to this consequence. If past interactions were anything to go on, when this parent arrived to pick up his son, he would be aggressive and threatening. Indeed, that's exactly what happened. The student's father stormed into the main office, marched past the secretary, entered my office without knocking, and began to rant. I found myself growing defensive and upset, trying to get a word in somehow. I felt that if I could just get him to *listen*, I could explain why I'd made the decision I had and why it was the right decision. But he was having none of it.

My principal had made it her business to stick close by, and so she came into my office when she heard me floundering. The angry parent whirled toward her. "This has *nothing* to do with you," he snarled. "I'm talking to *her*." He pointed at me.

She smiled at him. "The decision is final," she told him. "We'll have you take your son home now. He's waiting in the lobby."

"This isn't over," the father snapped, rising up taller and throwing his substantial shoulders back. "I'm calling the superintendent the moment I get home."

"Let me save you some time," my principal said sweetly. "I wouldn't want you to have to look up his number." She reached out her hand, and I saw she was offering him the superintendent's business card. He snatched it out of her hand and stormed out.

I turned to my principal, panicked. "Now what? Is he going to call? What is going to happen?"

"Nothing's going to happen," she said gently. "We'll call the superintendent to explain that he might get a phone call, and we'll tell him why. And that will be it. Our superintendent stands by the decisions of the principals," she told me. "The parent can appeal your decision, but you disciplined appropriately, so there's really nothing to appeal. We may never hear another word about it."

She was right.

## Strategies and Solutions for Managing Conflict with Parents

Few interactions with difficult parents will be as contentious as this experience of mine was, but some will—and some will be more complicated. Most times, conflict with parents can be managed peacefully, calmly, and with the utmost professionalism. Here are some tips on how to do that.

**Know your district's discipline policies and procedures.** The policies and procedures adopted by your district's Board of Education are written to help you keep students safe. Make it your business to know these policies so you can confidently stand by them when you are caught off guard—and communicate their rationale clearly. If you follow policy when making decisions, you are never wrong—no matter what a parent says to you.

**Keep your cool.** As the highest authority in your school, you are expected, more than anyone else, to remain calm, rational, and professional at all times. If you get angry or defensive, the situation will deteriorate quickly. Invest some time thinking about your personality and how you de-escalate best in tense situations, and use the strategies that work for you. For example, if you find yourself growing upset, excuse yourself briefly. Walk to get a drink of water; take a few deep breaths. It is important to remain composed and rational; do whatever it takes to do so.

**Meet in person.** When parents call or e-mail and it is evident that they are angry or upset, invite them to come to your office for a discussion. People will say things on the phone or in e-mail that they will not say to you in person. Further, you gain an advantage by being able to read body language and facial expressions.

**Be open to listening, but on your time line.** Make it clear to parents that you are happy to meet with them. Often, parents just want to feel heard; if you give them time and attention, the situation often dissipates. The only times you should refuse to meet with a parent are when you feel physically threatened or if you have previously addressed the issue with the parent and you are confident there will be no further resolution.

However, when a parent is especially furious with a decision you've made, it is wise to wait at least 24 hours before meeting. Given time, many parents will calm down significantly; they will also have a chance to talk to friends or a spouse and may have gathered a calmer perspective. It is as simple as saying, "This sounds like something we should talk through together. I wish I could meet with you today, but unfortunately my calendar is packed. Would you be available to meet with me tomorrow?"

**When meeting in person, be aware of your body language.** Ask yourself, "How do I appear right now?" Think about how you react when you are defensive, and work to ensure you don't fall into those habits. Sit calmly and speak softly. Don't let yourself make defensive movements, such as crossing your arms or standing in a physically aggressive manner.

**Think about your physical environment.** Make sure your office is neat and clean and your desk is as clear as possible. An office that looks organized and professional projects an image of you as a capable, competent leader. Better still, set your office up to be a calm and welcoming place. Think soft lighting, plants, area rugs, and personal photographs. If this is not possible, find an alternative space to meet with parents.

**Don't let your ego get in the way.** Be willing to change your mind if the parent brings a legitimate perspective that sheds a different light on your initial decision. If a meeting with a parent convinces you that it would be best to do something differently, then do so. Don't insist on taking a hard line and sticking to your initial decision if it becomes apparent there is a better one to be made. There is no room for stubbornness or pride when the goal is to do what's best for students.

**Keep the parent's perspective in mind.** Many parents feel it is their responsibility to "defend" their child from the decisions of school administration. As you navigate through tricky parent interactions, it does help to remind yourself that what may seem like a misguided stance to you still comes from a well-intentioned place. Even verbalizing this—"I know how much you love your child, and I understand your impulse to stick up for him no matter what"—can help defuse a tense situation.

**Articulate what you know about the parents' feelings.** Similarly, it often helps to clearly identify your understanding of how the parent is feeling. Simply saying, "I can see how upset you are. If it were my child, I would be angry as well," can help a parent feel heard.

**Be an ally.** Remind parents that you are seeking the same goal. You can say, "Keep in mind that we are actually on the same team. We both want the best for your child, and I truly believe that this decision is the best decision right now." I've found this to be a good way to break down barriers and open parents' minds to my position.

**Keep the conversation focused.** It is common for parents to portray their opinions as representative of a larger consensus or find inconsistencies in the treatment of their child compared to other children in similar situations. Anticipate this and be ready to resist getting off track and tangled in discussions about secondary issues. Don't give them hope of discussing another child's case, and if you feel that there is something to the parent's claim of a larger common concern growing among parents, make plans to do an internal investigation and talk about it in a separate meeting.

**Articulate an end time.** It is wise to begin meetings with parents by setting an end time. You can simply say, "Please understand I have another commitment in an hour, so we'll keep an eye on the time so we make sure we cover everything we need to discuss." If you find yourself going over and over the same issue, you can reference the end time as a way to move forward.

**Know your exit strategy.** At any time, particularly if you feel threatened, you can calmly and professionally end the conversation. Once again, simplicity is best: "Mr. Smith, I feel we have talked this through thoroughly. Thank you for your time and input." I have found it helpful to physically move toward the door, open it gently, and gesture that it is time to leave. Another trick? Plan an exit strategy ahead of time. For example, tell your secretary that if you haven't emerged from your office in 30 minutes (or whatever time frame you feel would be enough), he or she should call in the office and remind you it is time for your next commitment. You can then say to the parent, "Unfortunately, I need to move on to another appointment. I hope we have addressed your concerns. I do appreciate you coming in today."

**End with a personal touch.** As your meeting wraps up, stand and walk the parent to the door. When saying good-bye, you can end on a positive note with a smile, a gentle handshake, or a touch to the parent's shoulder. This will soften your interaction with parents and make it more personal; further, it is a reassurance that you do have compassion and that you understand how they are feeling.

**Have backup, and know when to ask for help.** Never go into a volatile parent meeting without telling someone—a colleague or secretary—about the situation. Ask a staff member to stay close by in case you need someone to intervene. If a parent is truly furious and you feel there is no changing the situation, or if you are genuinely frightened, call for help from a colleague or the police.

**Cultivate support.** There will be situations where a parent will threaten to contact your supervisors to complain about you. Try not to let this bother you. Your supervisors should know your work as a fair, thoughtful, and thorough building leader; for that reason, they should uphold your decisions. However, make sure you save them unpleasant surprises by communicating with them immediately if you think an issue may come across their desks. If they aren't taken aback but, rather, know all the details of the situation beforehand, they will be better able to fully support you. An important caveat: do this sparingly. You don't want to be too high-maintenance or imply that you cannot manage the challenges of your job. For example, in typical discipline situations, parents will be understandably upset—but not angry or placing blame on you. Your supervisors do not need to be informed about these. Only reach out if you genuinely feel a parent will contact them seeking a reversal of your decision, which is usually quite rare.

**Follow up.** Regardless of the outcome, contact parents a few days after your interaction with them to thank them for their time and involvement in their child's education. Doing so will communicate that you truly do care about the child and that you hope to have a positive relationship in the future. Similarly, seek out scenarios in which you could proactively communicate with these parents about something positive—a good choice you observe the student make, academic celebrations, or specific areas of improvement. A simple phone call or e-mail can begin to rebuild a fractured relationship—and serve you well going forward.

**Know when to walk away.** Some parents are *so* passionate about their perspective that they will *not* accept another perspective. They stick resolutely to their convictions, even when it seems to make very little sense, and even at the cost of friendships or professional relationships. In some cases, they may be dealing with mental instability, in which case it's helpful to remember that their real battle is not with you. Try not to take the actions of these parents personally. Get on with the business of serving your school, keeping student welfare as your primary concern and bringing in your superiors and supportive resources as required.

## Turning Conflict into Collaboration: Conversations with Angry Parents

One of the biggest challenges in working with angry parents is mastering diplomacy in even the most heated conversations. Parents have a primal instinct to protect their children, so when they feel something is "threatening" their child—reasonable or not—they will come to you feeling any number of strong emotions. They may be furious because of a negative interaction with a classmate. They may feel upset because of academic struggles. A discipline decision on your part may have them prepared to dispute your every word. Regardless of their emotional position, it's your job to be calm, tactful, open-minded, and fair, as demonstrated in the examples below, where we revisit the scenarios from the beginning of the chapter. In each scenario, the advice from this chapter is put into practice, turning each confrontation into an opportunity to work with the parent in the best interest of the student.

## Scenario 1: The Defensive Parent

A parent arrives in the office because she has been called—again— to bring her daughter appropriate clothing that adheres to your school's dress code. Now the two of you sit across from one another in your office, and it's clear that she is furious.

> **You:** *Mrs. Aseo, I can see that you are upset. Why don't you tell me what you're thinking?*
>
> **Mrs. Aseo:** *I think it's preposterous that you would ask Mia to change clothes. I could walk down the hallway right now and see a hundred other girls with skirts just as short. Shorter, even.*
>
> **You:** *Respectfully, Mrs. Aseo, this is not about other girls. Mia's skirt is simply far shorter than our district dress code allows.*
>
> **Mrs. Aseo:** *But what about all the other girls? Why aren't you punishing them?*
>
> **You:** *I would prefer not to talk about other students. This is about Mia and her outfit today. Also, I encourage you not to consider this a punishment. Mia's not in trouble. I just need her to wear a skirt that adheres to our dress code.*

Mrs. Aseo is using a common tactic of bringing other students into the conversation about disciplinary consequences for her child as a way to make you second-guess your decision. Your response is to calmly explain that you will only discuss the situation as it relates to her particular child.

> **Mrs. Aseo:** *It just seems like you're picking on her. This is the third time you've had Mia change her clothes. Are you just as hard on other girls? Do their parents get called three times in one semester for dress code infractions?*
>
> **You:** *Again, it is inappropriate for us to discuss other students. Let's keep focused on Mia. Can you help me understand why you're so upset?*

Here, you are seeking out the parent's perspective.

> **Mrs. Aseo:** *Well, aside from the unfairness in enforcement, I believe my daughter should be able to dress in a way that she feels comfortable and confident. I trust her completely. If she wants to wear short skirts, I support her. This is ridiculous!*
>
> **You:** *I understand, and I admire your decision to support your daughter. Let me offer you some perspective, though. Our job is to prepare students for what they will encounter after high school. There are certain rules we have that serve as valuable guidelines once students have graduated and moved on. For example, in the workplace, there are certain protocols to follow, and how a person dresses is one of them. A skirt like Mia is wearing today would not be appropriate to most employers. I want Mia to understand that there are certain things you shouldn't wear in certain settings. If she loves ultra-short skirts, that's fine—but there are other places and times to wear that type of clothing. School is not one of them. I just want her to understand that.*

Although you are staying firm, you have articulated what you understand about Mrs. Aseo's feelings so it is clear to her that you are keeping her perspective in mind.

> **Mrs. Aseo:** *But this is high school, not work. She understands the difference.*

**You:** *Does she, though? Based upon her repeated dress code infractions, she doesn't appear to. I think you and I should work together as a team to help Mia understand why we can't accept the decisions she's making. We should have a unified message.*

**Mrs. Aseo:** *What do you mean "work together"?*

**You:** *In the mornings, if you see her wearing something you know is not appropriate for school, you could ask her to think about whether it is an outfit she should be wearing to school. You can ask her to change into something else.*

**Mrs. Aseo:** *The thing is, I think it is appropriate. I think the dress code is too strict. And it's sexist in the way it is slanted against girls.*

**You:** *I am sorry you feel that way. Unfortunately, that's a different issue altogether. The dress code was adopted by the Board of Education, which means it is a policy to which all students must adhere. For now, I would just ask that you try to work together with us here at school, rather than supporting your daughter unequivocally. This is a situation in which it would probably be better for you to challenge her choices and insist she follow the rules that have been set for all students.*

**Mrs. Aseo:** *I see you aren't going to change your mind.*

**You:** *It would not be appropriate for me to do so.*

**Mrs. Aseo:** *Well, OK, then. I wish you would reconsider.*

**You:** *I hope you know that I want to do what is best for Mia. I know that's what you want, too. Again, let's try to work together on this. It would help if you talk to her about why rules are in place and set an expectation that she follow them. In the end, I am sure this will be the best thing for her.*

While staying firm, you are reaching out to the parent to get her support and work as a team to do what is best for the student.

**Mrs. Aseo:** *I'll think about that.*

**You:** *Thank you. Please let me know if you have further concerns. I can't say it enough—we are a team in guiding Mia through school. Let's keep working together, OK?*

**Mrs. Aseo:** *Sure. Whatever.*
**You:** *Thank you for coming in today. I hope you have a nice day and a great weekend!*

Mrs. Aseo's closing comments telegraph that she's not happy—and that this situation may not be over. Frankly, not every conflict is going to be resolved with one conversation, and you won't always make everyone happy, especially when the issues are complicated.

## Scenario 2: The Panicked Parent

A parent is highly upset about her child's placement for the upcoming school year. She has made several attempts to contact you within a short window of time, but you've been busy tending to other priorities. Then she shows up in the office and refuses to leave until she speaks with you. Although you had hoped to put off a conversation until the parent had some time to calm down, it's happening now.

> **You:** *Hello, Mrs. Smith. It's nice to meet you! Let me start by saying I know you have been trying to contact me. I assure you I have not been ignoring you; this is just an extremely busy morning for me. I apologize.*
> **Mrs. Smith:** *I'm sorry, but this is very, very important. It can't wait. I have serious concerns about the teacher Brittany's been assigned to.*
> **You:** *I understand that. How can I help?*
> **Mrs. Smith:** *I have heard terrible things about this teacher. Everyone talks about how she assigns massive amounts of homework and doesn't support the students.*

Mrs. Smith is using a tactic common in parental–principal interactions—implying that "everyone" feels as they do or that they are "not the only one" with this concern. When this happens, it's best to clarify that you make administrative decisions based on policy and formal investigations, never gossip.

> **You:** *Reports like this are something we take seriously and investigate fully. However, my main concern right now is Brittany's success in the upcoming school year. I'd like to keep our conversation focused on your daughter.*
>
> **Mrs. Smith:** *But I need to tell you what I know about this teacher.*
>
> **You:** *Mrs. Smith, I want to hear what you have to say, but I simply cannot do it now. There are three reasons: First, I am meeting with several new teachers this morning, and they are waiting for me. Second, I often find when a parent is upset about something, the conversation goes much better when there has been time to take a step back and reflect a bit. Third, since I'm new to this building, I am still learning about the particular classroom environments of each teacher. I would like to gather more specific information so I'm better prepared for us to have a productive conversation. Does that all make sense?*
>
> **Mrs. Smith:** *I guess. But I feel like this is important. I need you to consider a change immediately.*
>
> **You:** *We have several weeks until school begins, so time is on our side. As I said, I would be more than happy to meet with you. Are you available tomorrow morning? I have some open time between 8:20 and 11.*
>
> **Mrs. Smith:** *I don't want to wait.*
>
> **You:** *I am going to ask you to trust me on this. Please know that I will certainly listen to you, and I hope you will hear me out as well. At this time, though, I must get back to my meeting. Would you be willing to come back tomorrow?*

You are doing two things here: providing time for the parent to calm down and buying time for yourself. You're new on the job, and you don't know much about the teacher in question. Having the parent come back in a day or so gives you the opportunity to review records, ask questions, and determine if Mrs. Smith's concerns might be legitimate.

> **Mrs. Smith:** *Yes, I can come back tomorrow. But I'm not going to let it go.*
> **You:** *Thank you. That will allow me to complete my work for today and be better prepared for our talk tomorrow. Why don't you stop in around 9:00?*
> **Mrs. Smith:** *I'll be here.*
> **You:** *One more thing. Can you try not to worry about it in the meantime? You and I will work together and find a solution. We both want what is best for Brittany. We'll figure it out.*

You are reassuring the parent by explaining your leadership style; you are also acknowledging her worries and moving her away from an adversarial position and toward one of cooperative problem solving.

> **Mrs. Smith:** *I'll try. It won't be easy, but I'll try.*
> **You:** *Thank you.*

At this point, you stand and walk together with Mrs. Smith to the door. Before opening the door for her, you turn and shake her hand.

> **You:** *Thank you again; I'll see you tomorrow. I'm sure we will both feel better after we've talked this through.*

Ending these meetings with some kind of connection—in this case, with a handshake—helps to further personalize the situation and turn it toward the positive.

## Scenario 3: The Litigious Parent

This scenario describes parents who plan to dispute your decision to suspend their son for the remaining four games of a basketball season after he assaulted an opposing player during a game. You have received a letter from their attorney stating that the boy must be permitted to play pending a legal appeal. When you receive the fax, you pick up the phone and call the boy's father; you ask him if he can come into your office after school. He arrives immediately after the last bell.

> **You:** *Let me start by thanking you for coming, Mr. Troutman. I know we all want the best for your son, and I feel it is best to come together in person to discuss this situation we are in.*

Note that you articulate that it was best to meet in person. In this case, communication by phone or e-mail—or by an attorney in a letter—would only widen the disagreement between you and the parent.

> **Mr. Troutman:** *I don't feel you want the best for my son at all. Why would you suspend him from the team if you want what is best for him?*
> **You:** *Let me first say that I understand your perspective. You do not feel that punishing Zack by taking him off the basketball court is appropriate. You want him to play in the final four games of his middle school season. I understand that.*
> **Mr. Troutman:** *That's exactly right.*

Here, you show you have considered the parent's perspective and understand it. The parent doesn't have to make his argument, because you already have done it.

> **You:** *Let me ask you a question. Do you think it was appropriate for him to assault the other player like he did?*
> **Mr. Troutman:** *"Assault" is a harsh way to put it. I didn't feel like it was that bad. The referees were terrible during that game, and the other player had been taunting our team all night. Quite frankly, that kid deserved it.*

**You:** *As you know, we take sportsmanship very seriously here at our school. Your son knows we have no tolerance for actions like that. And while I do feel he acted impulsively and didn't intend for things to get out of hand so quickly, I do know he has a clear understanding of the consequences of such an action.*

**Mr. Troutman:** *Well, as you know, I've called my attorney, so none of this even matters. We're going to appeal.*

**You:** *Unfortunately, a decision from school administration cannot be appealed legally. You can appeal it through our deputy superintendent, but the appeals process takes time. I would rather not discuss any legal action at this point, because I think we can work toward a mutual under-standing. Can I give you some additional things to think about?*

**Mr. Troutman:** *If you must.*

**You:** *Mr. Troutman, there were almost 800 fans in the stands that day, and there were at least 20 student-athletes participating. They all saw what happened; they all saw a situation where an athlete was in an unsafe situation. It is my responsibility to ensure it does not happen again, and to do so, I need to show those fans and those kids that we do not tolerate those kinds of behaviors.*

In this case, you are letting the parent know that your first priority is student safety.

**You:** *I'd also like you to think about the position Zack would be in if I allowed him to play the remaining games. When something like this happens, people feel there should be a consequence, and they would wonder why he was exempt. It would put him in a very uncomfortable position.*

**Mr. Troutman:** *So you're punishing him because of what other people will think?*

**You:** *Not at all. I just want you to know I have a responsibility to all the people who were in the gym that day, not just your son. And there are a lot of people who would lose respect for both you and me if he were to play out the rest of the season.*

This is a key point, because it allies you with the parent. It makes the two of you seem as if you're together in this situation.

**Mr. Troutman:** *I can see that, I guess. But this could damage his playing career.*

**You:** *You know, I believe the opposite is true. If Zack learns from this mistake now, while he is in middle school, he will do all he can to make sure it never happens again. This would be much worse if it were to happen a few years down the road when the stakes are higher—when a championship is on the line, when a team is counting on him, when there might even be college scouts in the stands. Middle school is a great time to have these conversations with our athletes and help them understand the implications of their actions.*

**Mr. Troutman:** *I can understand that. But you won't consider changing your mind at all?*

**You:** *No, sir. I truly believe this is what is best for him.*

**Mr. Troutman:** *I will call my attorney and discuss this with him. I will let you know if I have further questions.*

**You:** *Please do. I am here to support you as well as your son. I know it's not easy to be a parent sometimes—that's why we must make sure we work together.*

Here, you have articulated again that you understand the parent's feelings and you are his ally in the situation. The objective is to diffuse a potential litigious situation and make it one in which the two of you are on the same team.

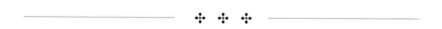

Though the goal of these conversations is to get to a place where parents and the school enthusiastically agree, that does not always reflect reality, so even a situation in which a parent begrudgingly acknowledges an understanding of the school's position can be considered a success. After you and the parent have had some time to reflect on the conversation, a quick follow-up phone call to show your concern for the situation and the student might be more welcome than you anticipate.

# Managing Adult Conflicts: Parents and Staff

### 11

### Scenario 1: Neighborhood Discord

One morning near the end of your first year as a middle school principal, a parent tells you that her son has been accused of bullying the girl who lives next door. The accuser is the girl's mother, their neighbor. This parent tells you that the neighbor has accused her son of terrible things—both directly, and by talking about it to others in the neighborhood. She explains that she has spoken with her son's teachers and they dismissed her concerns, telling her there is no evidence of a problem at school and urging her to ignore the accusations. She can't, though. She feels the whole neighborhood is involved in some sort of plot against her son. She is distraught and has no idea what to do.

### Scenario 2: Teacher-to-Teacher Discord

In your first few weeks in your elementary school, you learn that two of your 1st grade teachers cannot seem to get along. They refuse to communicate with one another about the most basic things, they gossip about one another to colleagues, and they even argue openly. You make a plan to discuss it with both teachers, separately.

### Scenario 3: PTO-to-Teacher Discord

Within a few months of taking the position as a high school principal, it's clear that there is little to no relationship between members of your PTO's Executive Board and the teachers in the school building. In fact, you have heard several snarky comments made from PTO members regarding the staff. You set up a meeting with the PTO president to gain her perspective.

These scenarios are just a few examples of how a principal can be caught in the cross fire of conflicts between adults who aren't getting along. Sometimes, collegial relationships between staff members falter and fail. Sometimes, there is a problem between teachers and parents. And sometimes, principals might find themselves caught up in conflicts among parents. A neighborhood argument may seep into a disruption at school, members of the PTO may be fighting with one another, or a discipline issue involving several students may turn into all-out war among the adults involved. As the principal, any adult conflict that affects your school and the learning climate within becomes your responsibility.

Not long ago, I arrived at work early on a Friday morning, eager to finish several tasks before the real hustle of the day began. As usual, it was just Susie, the school secretary, with me in the office. The phone had begun to ring with regularity, as it does in the mornings; I tuned it out, focused on whittling down my in-box while I had the chance.

Suddenly, Susie appeared at the door of my office. "That was Mrs. Evans on the phone," she said. "She wants to talk to you. Now."

I looked up. "Sure. Put her through."

"No, she wants to talk to you in person. Right now. She's on her way." Susie lifted her hands helplessly. "I have no idea what she's so upset about. I'm sorry. I tried!"

Within minutes, a furious Mrs. Evans walked into the office. I invited her to take a seat, reassured her that I was there to listen and help, and asked her to tell me why she was so upset. She launched into an emotional 10-minute diatribe about her son's teacher. I pieced together the story slowly. It seemed that the day before, Ben had come home miserable and teary-eyed, saying that his teacher had refused to allow him to go to the restroom all day long. Mrs. Evans wanted the teacher to be reprimanded. She wanted the teacher suspended. She wanted a written summary of the teacher's action put into a personnel file. And if I didn't do it, she would call the local newspaper and report that students at our school were forbidden to use the restroom throughout the day. *It was unacceptable . . . downright criminal . . . what kind of organization is this, anyway?*

As she spoke, my first reaction was dismay. *How could something like this happen?* Then I caught myself. I knew Ben's teacher very well, and this didn't sound like Ms. Myers at all. There had to be some explanation.

"Let me start by apologizing," I said. "I am sorry Ben came home upset, and I'm sorry you are upset now. And I completely understand your concern and frustration. If it were my son, I'd be very upset, too."

Mrs. Evans nodded triumphantly.

"However. . . ." I paused before going on. I wanted to choose my words carefully. "I just have to be honest with you, Mrs. Evans. This just doesn't sound like something that would go on in Ms. Myers's classroom. She is a kind, compassionate, and understanding teacher. I can't imagine her refusing to allow Ben to use the restroom."

"*I* thought she was great, too," Mrs. Evans said, crossing her arms. "It appears we both were wrong."

"Tell you what," I said. "Let me look into this. I'll investigate, and call you back today with an explanation. If this truly did happen, I assure you I will handle it appropriately. But I'd like to get the full story first."

Mrs. Evans left—still rather grumpy but a little calmer than when she'd first arrived. I immediately scooted upstairs to talk to Ms. Myers.

After I summarized the story, she sighed. "It would have been better if I had warned you about this," she said. "I should have known Ben would bring home *that* story instead of the real story."

It turned out that Ben had been pushing his teacher's buttons over the past several days. He'd been breaking basic classroom rules, he'd been talkative and disruptive, and he'd begun mocking behavior expectations. In fact, the day before, he'd bragged to his classmates that he'd gone to the restroom, yanked piles of paper towels out of the dispenser, and tried to clog up the restroom toilets. Hearing this, Ms. Myers had determined it was time to tighten her supervision. Part of her plan was to allow Ben to use the restroom only when accompanied by a responsible classmate or during whole-class restroom breaks.

"We took four class restroom breaks yesterday," Ms. Myers told me. "Each time, I invited Ben to come along, and he said no. He chose to stay in the classroom with several peers, insisting he didn't need to go. Then, two or three minutes after we had all returned to the class and were settling back into work, he would ask to go."

"And you refused," I finished.

"Yes!" she said. "He didn't like the structure I set up, so he was trying to set *me* up. And it worked!"

I smiled at her. She had, indeed, been outmaneuvered by a 10-year-old—but only briefly. I reassured her that she had my full support. I would just explain the real story to Ben's mom.

It wasn't easy for Mrs. Evans to hear the full story—after all, it meant she had to flip her frustration away from the teacher and onto her child—but eventually she accepted that her clever son had twisted the situation around to get the adults pointing fingers at one another rather than at him. Together, we worked out a reasonable restroom schedule, put in a behavior plan with consequences for poor behavior, and met with Ben to show him our plan as a united group. Fortunately, everything ended well.

## Strategies and Solutions for Mediating Conflict Among Parents and Staff

Adults can be drawn into petty conflict almost as easily as children can. Add *actual* children to the mix, and even simple misunderstandings and minor incidents can get so blown out of proportion that they damage professional and personal relationships. These are the times when it's your responsibility as the principal to step in as a mediator, find a solution, restore the peace, and preserve a positive and effective learning environment. Remaining calm, impartial, and compassionate will serve you extremely well, but it isn't always easy. Here are ideas for successfully navigating this tricky territory.

**Recognize that in most cases, conflict exists because all parties really, really care.** Adult conflicts will drive you batty. You'll wonder why everyone can't just get along. You'll think, "Really? Why am I spending my time on this?" Reminding yourself that conflict comes when people feel strongly about something can help you see these situations in a more positive light. We feel passionately about children, about learning, and about schools. It is a very emotional business; parents, teachers, and even community members are very invested in their work with kids, and when they feel their intention is challenged in some way by another adult, they may behave in ways that are not helpful to the situation. And even though their behavior sometimes leads to problems, there is no arguing that a group of people working hard toward the goal of helping children—even if it gets messy at times—is a very, very good thing. I try to take a moment to acknowledge this emotion. When I do, I find that the adults often admit they aren't thinking clearly because they care so much, and it can help dissipate the situation.

**Ask questions and listen, but remember the difference between listening and agreeing.** It is essential to establish an understanding of why the conflict exists in the first place. Take time to ask questions of everyone involved. *When did the conflict begin? Why did it start? Who are the people directly responsible for the situation? What previous mediations have been tried, and why did they fail? What role might the child play in the situation?* When gathering this information, I work hard to just *listen*. This is a challenge for me; I am the type of person who talks more than my share. But I have learned that when there are adults in conflict, they all deserve a chance to share openly. This may happen in the same room with all parties present, or it may happen individually. I'll hear one side, then I'll hear the other side, then I'll reconnect with both parties with a summary of events and a solution that works for all. Either way, I make sure I have heard from everyone involved.

When I listen to an upset adult, I do all the reassuring, calming things I know to do: I nod, I murmur, I "tsk," and I raise and lower my eyebrows to express empathy. This is genuine. I do empathize with parents who are upset about an experience their child had, and I very much empathize with teachers who feel they must defend themselves as educators. When I speak, I try to convey that I understand even when I do not agree. I'll say, "While I have a different take on the situation, I can certainly understand how you are feeling, and I have a lot of compassion for you in this situation." Use simple statements like this to clarify that you are listening carefully and taking the conflict seriously.

**Filter out the gossip.** People are people, and they talk to one another, especially about conflict. Easy access to texts, e-mails, and posts in online community groups only adds to the buzz, and if you're not careful, it can skew your perspective. When mediating a conflict among staff and parents, stick to the facts and perspectives of the staff and parents involved. Politely shut down any arguments that start with, "Everyone I have talked to agrees that . . ." or "I heard some people talking, and they said. . . .".

**Work to see both sides.** This isn't always easy, but understanding why parties in conflict feel as they feel and act as they act is a big step toward effective mediation. Once you have a sense of both sides, you can help the opponents see the other perspective. Try opening that conversation by saying, "Let's consider why they are feeling this way." Even if adults can't *agree* with the other side's perspective, it certainly helps if they *understand* it.

**Take responsibility when there is responsibility to be taken.** I've often found myself in a situation of conflict in which nothing appears to be of my doing, but if I look deeper, I can find something I could have done differently to solve the problem. I could have intervened earlier. I could have been more forceful. I could have predicted things would spiral out of control and reacted accordingly. Instead, I missed all the warning signs. In these situations, I will be the first to take responsibility. I'll say something like "I feel like I could have done more to avoid this problem. I wish I had called you earlier to talk it through before things escalated. I take responsibility for not intervening earlier."

I do this a *lot*. As an example, not long ago, I took over as principal for a different school in my district. The majority of the work to begin the school year had already been completed, and I didn't worry much about checking it. In the first couple weeks of school, though, a group of teachers came to me in frustration because of some significant inequities in assigned duty responsibilities among staff members. Although I hadn't written the duty schedule, I said to them, "I am sure we can find solutions to this. But first, I want to say that I should have taken the time to review the schedule before we started our year. I want to take responsibility for this situation." My willingness to do so immediately alleviated some of the frustration the teachers were feeling. Ironically, taking responsibility for problems does not diminish your credibility at all. In fact, it shows you are willing to admit your role in the conflict, however small it might be. Doing so automatically makes you part of the team working toward a solution, rather than a far-removed third party.

**Apologize.** If you're a principal, saying "I'm sorry" often helps, even if the situation is not your fault. An apology doesn't have to mean you're sorry for something you have done. It can be, "I'm sorry you're so upset," "I'm sorry you are feeling frustrated and angry," or "I'm sorry it has come to this. I wish we had found a resolution earlier." Sometimes, people in conflict just need *someone* to apologize before they can move on. It might as well be you.

**Remember how much pressure is placed on teachers, and give them a break.** Often conflicts that involve teachers arise because they are feeling enormous pressure—from parents, whose expectations are extremely (and understandably) high; from other teachers; from state and federal mandates; from the community, who expects them to work more and get paid less; and even from you, who need them to be highly effective teachers for your own accountability. The stress of this can be brutal. When teachers feel stretched to their limit, conflicts can arise and feel more personal than they really are. Keeping this pressure in mind will help you understand the teachers' perspective as you determine the path to resolution.

**Know your biases.** In conflicts among staff, be careful to avoid favoritism. We all have teachers we gel with quickly and easily, or we may have a personal understanding of their perspective, but that should not sway us when mediating, and it certainly should not lead to us taking sides. I fight against this when working with conflicting staff members when one may be a very active teacher—volunteering time, coaching extracurricular activities, serving on a leadership team—and one may give very little "extra" to the school. I can easily make the mistake of siding with the active teacher, simply because I know how hard he or she works and I am so grateful for the extra investment in our school. That's a mistake, though. I've learned that being active doesn't mean being right. I have to actively remind myself to leave my biases at the door when mediating conflict.

Another bias to watch for is personal affection. In many ways, school becomes a second home, and the people who work there become like family. It's important not to let your affection for staff members cloud your judgment. I once worked with a teacher I very much enjoyed; she was funny, smart, and an excellent teacher. When I heard rumblings that she was difficult to work with, I could hardly believe it; I'd seen none of those problems in my dealings with her. Over time, though, I realized she could be very disagreeable and problematic. I had to push myself to see the perspective of other teachers because I badly wanted her to not be the problem—because I *liked* her!—but it turned out that she frequently was.

**Identify tactics.** When investigating a conflict, you may find that people resort to tactics to bolster their "case." It helps to watch out for these tactics so you know how to respond. For example, some people resort to passive-aggressiveness (pouting or ignoring others), dismissal (responding with comments such as "Whatever. I've been through this before"), gossip (trying to gather colleagues on their "side" by talking in negative terms about others), or acting innocent (as if they have no idea that there is a conflict, much less acknowledging a role in it). When I see these things happening, I remind myself that it's just a defense mechanism that is being used to sway me from the real conflict at hand.

**Get creative!** Being in a position of authority, you have the somewhat limited luxury of trying unorthodox solutions to help everyone move on. For example, I have moved teachers to different grade levels or content areas, or switched how teachers are teamed. I have strategically placed students with—or away from—a particular teacher or peer because of damage resulting from disagreements between adults. Your options aren't limited to the workplace, though. I have also gathered conflicting adults together in social situations to get to know one another without the stressors of the classroom. I make these types of "creative" decisions when I know there will be a positive outcome—for the adults, sure, but mostly for the students caught in the cross fire of adult conflict.

**Be frank and honest when you encounter stubborn or unrelenting adults.** If you find that one of the adults in the conflict simply will not accept compromise, point it out: "I feel you are not willing to work with me to improve this situation. What can we do to make you part of the solution rather than the problem?" Pointing out stubbornness may alleviate it somewhat; after all, it can be embarrassing and humbling for someone to hear he or she is being difficult. If that still doesn't work, or if your directness only serves to elicit more negative emotion, it may be time to accept that your mediations are not working. Depending on the situation, you may need to put your foot down and make a unilateral decision that will, if nothing else, resolve the situation once and for all. For example, if you are working through a teacher–parent conflict and see no resolution in sight, you may need to say, "We seem unable to reach a compromise here, so I see no reason to continue the conversation. Moving forward, I simply ask that we treat one another with respect and keep our focus on the child. All further communication should be funneled through me." In another example, if you have a significant conflict between unrelenting staff members, you may need to say, "Look, this is unacceptable. Your behavior is unprofessional and must change immediately. If it does not, you will be subject to disciplinary action." Follow through with whatever steps or reprimands may be required. It will be difficult, but sometimes that's the only way to get improvement—to clearly and forcefully insist upon it.

**Know when to give up.** Unfortunately, there are times a conflict simply can't be resolved—an adult will not be persuaded to accept a scenario that would resolve the situation; irreparable damage has been done; or there is too much anger, resentment, or hurt feeling involved to continue hoping for a compromise. At times, it may even seem that dissenting adults enjoy the conflict and like simmering in misery. In those cases, it's best to move on. After all, adults are adults, and you are not a magician. Don't pour all your energy into something that will never change. Unless students are being adversely affected—in which case you must be direct, as explained above—walk away and let it go.

## Easing the Effects of Conflict: Conversations with Feuding Parents and Staff

Here again we revisit the scenarios outlined in the beginning of the chapter. In each case, the suggestions from this chapter will be applied, and the effects of a disagreement between parents and teachers will be diminished or eliminated.

## Scenario 1: Neighborhood Discord

You are speaking with a parent, Mrs. Pouran, who is quite distraught because her son, Amir, has been accused of bullying the neighbor's daughter. The neighbor has been vocal about it, both directly to Mrs. Pouran and to other families in the neighborhood. Mrs. Pouran has come to you for help.

**Mrs. Pouran:** *I just don't know what to do. I feel like an outcast in my own neighborhood.*

**You:** *Why don't you summarize for me what has happened?*

**Mrs. Pouran:** *Well, on Friday, the neighbor rang my doorbell just a few minutes after the kids got off the bus. She was livid. She literally screamed at me for five minutes, standing on my front step, and wouldn't let me get a word in.*

**You:** *What was she saying?*

**Mrs. Pouran:** *Terrible things. She said Amir has been hitting her daughter, kicking her, calling her awful names. She said this has been going on all year, and she accused me of doing nothing about it.*

**You:** *Was this the first time you'd heard about Amir bullying this girl?*

**Mrs. Pouran:** *Yes! I was completely shocked and taken aback.*

**You:** *What did Amir say when you asked him about it?*

**Mrs. Pouran:** *He said there had been an incident on the bus that day, but it was because the girl had been bothering him for several weeks and he was sick of it. He said he told her to stop it. I'm sure he said, "Shut up," which obviously isn't kind, and I have had to talk to him about that in the past. And the girl got really mad and started yelling at him. He said he pushed her a little just to get away from her. But he swears he hasn't been bullying her, and I tend to believe him.*

**You:** *Did you talk to your neighbor about Amir's side of the story?*

**Mrs. Pouran:** *I went over to her place the next day to tell her what Amir said, but she insisted he was lying and that she was going to come meet with you about disciplinary action.*

**You:** *What is your previous experience with this neighbor?*

Here, you are asking focused questions that will help you understand the history behind the situation.

**Mrs. Pouran:** *Well, she's always been a hothead. She gets really angry about the silliest things—the mailman is late, the trash guys make a mess. It's always something. But I've been able to get along with her until now. I'm just so upset now because she's talking all throughout the neighborhood about how awful Amir is, and he's not! He's a great kid. And he pushed the girl because she got in his face—just like her mother is wont to do.*

**You:** *If this neighbor has a temper, then certainly your other neighbors know that, and they can keep perspective with whatever they are hearing.*

**Mrs. Pouran:** *Probably. I hope so. But I still feel sick inside, because it's so personal. They're talking about my son.*

**You:** *We always feel things so deeply when there is an issue associated with our child. You want to defend him and protect him, but sometimes that seems impossible to do.*

Here, you are expressing empathy and inserting a reminder of how the emotion that comes along with parenting or teaching children can sometimes take the upper hand.

**Mrs. Pouran:** *Yes, absolutely.*

**You:** *And I wonder if that isn't how your neighbor is feeling, too. Her daughter probably came home upset about being pushed, and she reacted in a very emotional, impulsive way because she loves her daughter and wants to protect her.*

Notice how you are gently introducing the other perspective into the conversation.

**Mrs. Pouran:** *I understand that. I really do. But she is so irrational about this—she was in a rage! She doesn't seem interested in talking about it or thinking about Amir's perspective. She just wants him to get in a pile of trouble here at school.*

**You:** *Amir is a very nice boy. I, too, have a hard time believing that things are as bad as she is saying. Has anyone spoken with your neighbor's daughter?*

**Mrs. Pouran:** *I wanted to, but she wouldn't let me.*

**You:** *Well, trust me when I say I will not take any disciplinary action without talking to both kids. I'll call them in today and get both sides of the story. If it is as Amir says it is, it just seems like the two will need to talk it out and maybe meet with the guidance counselor about their conflict. I am confident I can work it out with the students.*

**Mrs. Pouran:** *And what about me, with my neighbor? How should I handle this?*

**You:** *I think your best course of action is just to lie low. I'll handle the students, and I'll do everything I can to have a fair, appropriate outcome for the kids. As for the adults, you will have to work it out on your own— but now may not be the right time, because you are both so emotional about it. With some cooling-off time, it might just pass.*

**Mrs. Pouran:** *Sure, that makes sense, but she may hold a grudge for years. I'm telling you, she was as mad as I've ever seen anyone be.*

**You:** *In that case, you'll need to work on letting go. There are times that there simply isn't a resolution to a conflict; you'll have to do your best to coexist in the neighborhood and just hope the kids can move on. We don't want to turn an adult problem into a kid problem.*

**Mrs. Pouran:** *Thank you. That's what I'll try. Thank you for listening. And I'll look forward to hearing if there's anything you need me to do based on your conversation with the kids.*

## Scenario 2: Teacher-to-Teacher Discord

In this scenario, you have begun your work as an elementary principal and discover there are two 1st grade teachers who do not get along. Molly and Delia refuse to communicate with each other, they disparage each other to colleagues, and they even argue openly. Finding this unacceptable, you make a plan and discuss it with both teachers. Here is how the conversation goes with Molly.

**You:** *OK, Molly. What's going on with you and Delia?*

**Molly:** *We have never really gotten along.*

**You:** *Why? What's the history here?*

**Molly:** *I was hired here three years ago and replaced someone Delia was apparently very close to. So she resented me from the beginning. She didn't want anything to do with me and made that very clear. She was on the committee that interviewed me, and she was very verbal in not wanting me to be hired.*

**You:** *Well, that's something you could only have heard from others.*

**Molly:** *Yes, she obviously told all the other teachers. It's not like it's a secret.*

**You:** *But let's keep this conversation focused on the facts. Anything you've been told by others may not be accurate, you know.*

**Molly:** *But they did tell me.*

**You:** *Again, let's keep it focused on the two of you and the facts between you two. I'm not interested in what anyone else may have said that would stir the pot and make the situation worse.*

In these kinds of conversations, it's always a good move to filter out the gossip.

**You:** *Now, what has happened to get you to this place?*

**Molly:** *From the first day, she has never offered a single helping hand or suggestion. She undermines me when we have grade-level meetings* *by talking over me or interrupting me. She's constantly comparing our students' achievement data and tries to make herself look good. It makes me furious.*

**You:** *When I spoke with Delia, she said she feels like you are competing with her, and that it's been like that since you first joined the staff.*

**Molly:** *Competing? I just want to do a good job! And I have tons of great ideas that she just shuts down.*

**You:** *Could it be that she felt threatened when you joined the staff? There you were, fresh out of college, full of great ideas, with lots of time and energy to devote to teaching. . . .*

Here, you are sharing the other side's perspective.

**Molly:** *Well, I guess I can see that. I worked a ton of hours those first couple years, and Delia had little children, so she couldn't devote that much time. But that wasn't my fault!*

**You:** *Of course it wasn't your fault. But it just helps to understand how she may have felt—and how she still might be feeling.*

**Molly:** *Yes, but how she treated me, and how she treats me, is not cool. It's like she tries to sabotage me.*

**You:** *So this conflict has been going on for three years now. What has been done to try to help the situation?*

Here, you are asking questions to develop a history of why the conflict exists and what has been done to alleviate it.

**Molly:** *Nothing. The previous principal basically ignored it.*

**You:** *Nothing?*

**Molly:** *Well, he got us together to talk about it, which didn't work at all. We basically just sat there and stared out the window. I mean, we don't like each other. We won't like each other. That's the way things are.*

**You:** *I'm going to be honest, Molly. Based on what I'm hearing, I don't feel like you're interested in solving this conflict. There's a lot of anger here, and it just doesn't sound like you're willing to let go of it.*

You are giving frank feedback to challenge the stubbornness of the adult.

> **Molly:** *I'm sorry to be this way. But what can I do? I'm done with her.*
> **You:** *Have you ever considered a new role? Perhaps teaching at another grade level, where you and Delia would not need to work together? Or maybe a transfer to a different school in the district?*

Sometimes, introducing a creative solution is the way to move past the problem.

> **Molly:** *I actually have. It probably would be good for one of us to consider a move. But I love this school, and I love teaching 1st grade. I've heard she feels the same.*
> **You:** *Well, I'll continue to consider that as an option, but in the meantime I have to tell you this: the way things are now simply cannot continue. For one thing, the way you and Delia have been behaving toward one another is unprofessional. Adults simply should not act like this. But in addition to that, your conflict isn't helping students. I'm not asking you two to be best friends. I'm asking you to find a way to coexist and communicate with one another about important school information.*
> **Molly:** *What about her?*
> **You:** *I'm telling her the same thing. And I'm telling you both that if I don't see an improvement, we will have to sit down and formally write a plan, which would probably include getting the two of you together with an impartial staff member in attendance to mediate. And if we can't improve it from there, there will be disciplinary action. I don't want to do that, but it is a solution of last resort.*

Here, you are being directive, insisting upon a change.

> **Molly:** *Well, I understand. I will do what I can to foster a basic working relationship.*
> **You:** *I appreciate that. I'll keep monitoring the situation, and I'll do whatever I can to help.*

## Scenario 3: PTO-to-Teacher Discord

This scenario describes a situation in which you realize the PTO Executive Board of your high school seems to have a strained relationship with the teachers. You aren't sure why, so you invite the PTO president, Karen, to meet and talk it through.

> **You:** *Thank you for coming in to talk today. I was hoping we could review how things are going so far and get your perspective on a few things.*
>
> **Karen:** *Sure. I'm happy to help. I've really enjoyed working on this board so far!*
>
> **You:** *I'm glad about that. You've been doing great work. I would like to talk to you about the PTO's relationship with the teachers. It is, after all, supposed to be a parent and teacher organization. Do you feel like it is a reciprocal relationship between parents and teachers?*
>
> **Karen:** *Well, if I'm honest . . .*
>
> **You:** *Yes, please. I really would like your honest opinion.*
>
> **Karen:** *Well, OK, then. I don't want to cause problems, but sometimes it feels like there's no relationship at all.*
>
> **You:** *Tell me more.*

Here, you are showing that you are actively listening—not necessarily agreeing, but certainly listening.

> **Karen:** *In talking with the other PTO Executive Board members, we all feel the same—underappreciated. We are working really hard to support the school, to raise money, to volunteer at events, to take care of landscaping projects outside the school—and it's like the teachers don't even notice. It's like they take it for granted. I can't remember the last time I had a teacher actually take the time to say thank you—not in person, not in a phone call, not in an e-mail, not even in passing at a school event. It's frustrating. Quite frankly, it makes me angry and resentful.*

**You:** *I can imagine. If I were in your shoes, I would probably feel that way too.*

## You are acknowledging the emotions that are involved in this conflict.

**Karen:** *I don't think they have any idea how hard we work. Sometimes it feels like a full-time job to manage all the various PTO events and activities. We love the work, because we love helping the students—but a little appreciation would be nice.*

**You:** *Has it always been this way?*

**Karen:** *It's definitely become worse over the years. The previous principal left us alone to do our work a lot. In fact, there were times he didn't even attend our meetings. I think that set a precedent that our meetings aren't important.*

## Delving into the history often sheds light on a conflict.

**You:** *Wow. That must have been difficult, to see things get worse over time, and to do all this wonderful work without support. I know you are volunteering all this time because you really care about the children in this school. And I appreciate it.*

**Karen:** *I know you do. I just wish the teachers did.*

**You:** *I am in no way defending them, but I do think I can offer their perspective.*

**Karen:** *I'd love to hear it.*

**You:** *Well, first of all, there is enormous pressure on teachers these days. They are under scrutiny from the community and from the district. Sometimes I think they get so focused on their curriculum and instruction, they lose sight of some of the other things going on. Not that this is an excuse; it's merely an explanation. It's how they are feeling.*

**Karen:** *Yeah, I guess I can understand that.*

You are sharing the perspective of "the other side."

> **You:** *But that still doesn't make it right. Quite frankly, I think it's unacceptable that the PTO members feel so unsupported and unacknowledged by the teachers. I'd like to think of some creative solutions to solve this problem.*
>
> **Karen:** *Like what?*
>
> **You:** *Well, for one thing, I want to attend every meeting and be very active in your work. That will help set the expectations for teachers. Further, I can appoint two or three teachers to be regular PTO representatives. These teachers will attend all meetings and send out news and updates to staff—just weekly reminders of all the things you are doing to support their work. I can also encourage all teachers to attend at least one meeting a semester. That will help.*
>
> **Karen:** *That would be great. Teachers never attend our meetings. I'd love to see some regulars there.*
>
> **You:** *You know what else we could do? We could have a social hour—on an upcoming weekend evening, someone could host a PTO/Teacher Open House. We could provide food and drinks, and everyone could just relax, hang out, and get to know each other. I'd be glad to host it at my home.*
>
> **Karen:** *I think that's a fantastic idea. One of the biggest problems we have is that the PTO and teachers don't seem to know each other. We're working toward the same goal—student success—but we're doing it completely independently of one another. Getting together in a social setting may help bridge the gap between us. I'm sure I could get the PTO board to provide the food and drinks for the gathering.*
>
> **You:** *Let's do it! Let's start planning now, and we'll put it together for a month or two from now. I think that will really help.*

This is an illustration of how to find creative solutions to help resolve a conflict.

**You:** *With your permission, I will talk to the teachers openly and honestly about how the PTO board is feeling. I truly think they would be sorry to hear this. They are not a group of people who would be deliberately hurtful. If they know your perspective, I really think they'll do all they can to change.*

Again, sharing the perspectives of others can pave the way to resolution.

**Karen:** *I'm fine with that. It may help us communicate more openly if we know one another's perspective.*
**You:** *Great. I think we have a good starting point here. Let's touch base in a few weeks to discuss our progress. Thank you for being willing to come in and talk it through.*

As a principal, you will find yourself in situations in which you are mediating between dissenting staff and parents. There are many reasons for conflict—things that have happened in the past, differing perspectives, highly emotional situations—but it will often be the principal's job to investigate the situation and mediate each side toward a solution. By proceeding carefully, with an open mind and an open ear, you will gain valuable perspective for both sides of the conflict. Ideally, you'll get to a place where the adults are all getting along, which, of course, will only serve to benefit the students in your school.

# Leading Effective Meetings  ⑫

### Scenario 1: The Staff Meeting

*You are the principal of a middle school, and class is back in session after winter break. It's Tuesday, and you're holding a regularly scheduled staff meeting in the school library. There is a lot to cover on this month's agenda, and you will have several people presenting information. Each staff member has received an electronic copy of the agenda, and your secretary has made additional hard copies that people can pick up as they walk in. You start the meeting on time.*

### Scenario 2: The IEP Meeting

*The law dictates that you must attend every meeting for a student individualized education program. With a high special education population in your school, it seems you have an IEP meeting every morning before school, so you are getting a lot of practice leading the meetings. It's not long before you have an efficient outline of how each meeting will go. Your special education teacher does the majority of the talking, but you open each meeting, keep it moving along, and bring it to a conclusion.*

### Scenario 3: The PTO Board Meeting

*At the beginning of each PTO Executive Board meeting, held in a conference room in your high school, you share a Principal's Report to give the board members a summary of the latest goings-on. The board is a fun-loving, talkative group of women who are all friends, and they love to be social. You know you will have to stay focused on your report in order to get out of the meeting in a reasonable amount of time, leaving them to finish their agenda without you. You know you will be most successful if you can capitalize on the strong relationships you have with them and use a light-hearted approach.*

I can't help but open this chapter with a quote, often posted or shared on social media from worn-out professionals all over: *When I die, I hope I'm in a meeting, because the transition from life to death would be so subtle.*

Yes, this quote is dramatic, but there have been times I've remarked on its truth. After all, in the life of a principal, there are a *lot* of meetings. There have been times when I've muttered (and only to my dear administrative assistant, to whom I can say anything and not be judged), "Susie, I'm not a principal. I'm a 'meet-er.' That's what I do. I *meet*."

In education, the word *meeting* is overused, of course—applied to everything from conferences to professional development sessions to information exchanges to even casual, unscheduled conversation. I remember a day not too long ago in which I looked at my calendar and saw that I had an IEP meeting first thing in the morning, then bus duty (where I "met" with a parent who was dropping off her child), then a post-observation meeting with a teacher, then a PTO meeting, and then a meeting with a group of students to plan an all-school activity.

I try to stay positive about the number of meetings I have. Most times, this is not difficult to do. I actually look forward to meeting with people, because I enjoy working together to talk through different scenarios. And I naturally let myself emerge as the leader whenever appropriate, articulating the intent of the meeting and moving it forward toward a satisfactory finish.

I learned the importance of leadership in meetings by working for two principals with very different styles. One led meandering meetings with no focus. We rarely got through everything on the agenda—when there even *was* an agenda. There was a lot of cross-talk, meaning it was difficult to hear whomever was supposed to be talking. A few years later, I served under a principal who approached meetings with laser focus. She created clear, specific agendas that outlined each topic, indicated the person who would be speaking about it, *and* provided the estimated time that each agenda item would take. Teachers were expected to listen carefully, pay attention, and speak only if it contributed to the topic at hand. Meetings were thorough, helpful, and efficient; we often ended early and had time to complete any to-do tasks that had emerged in the meeting.

## Strategies and Solutions for Leading Efficient and Effective Meetings

The second principal I mentioned approached *all* meetings in the same way, whether it was a small gathering or a large group. There was always an agenda, always an opening statement that presented the intended outcome, and always a suitable conclusion at the end. Almost everything I know about leading school meetings came from watching her work, and these strategies have served me well.

**Create an agenda, and use it to guide your meetings.** How many times have you been in meetings that seemed straightforward but derailed due to a lack of planning? Following an explicit agenda is helpful in any meeting, but it is especially important if your meeting involves a lot of participants, where there is a greater risk of losing focus. For these larger meetings, the agenda created should outline each topic, the topic's presenter, and the amount of time the topic will require. I try to e-mail agendas to participants beforehand so everyone knows what to expect, particularly if they will need to prepare in some way. I also bring hard copies, because I find having the agenda in front of everyone helps everyone stay focused and stick to the expected pace; it also allows me to gently nudge those who stray back onto the established path. For smaller or more casual meetings, if you don't prepare a written agenda, make sure that you have a firm idea of how you want the meeting to progress and state that intention outright at the beginning. I have found that regardless of what my "agenda" looks like, it helps to open by explaining the intended outcome to all participants.

**Be strict about starting on time.** I am rabid about starting meetings on time; I find there is rarely a legitimate reason to begin late. Beginning on time does several things. First, it sets the expectation that everyone needs to be there and ready to go. Second, it ensures you will be able to cover all topics without running out of time. Third, it is respectful to honor the time given by meeting participants. Fourth, it helps you avoid appearing scattered and unprepared. There will be occasions that a staff member may be late, sometimes with very good reason, but if the expectation is set that the meeting will start on time, I find everyone works hard to comply.

**Make sure everyone is introduced.** In small meetings, personal introductions should happen immediately, so everyone knows the name of others at the table and is aware of the role that each person will play in the meeting. In larger meetings, such as with a large staff that knows one another well, it's good to just make sure there aren't any new faces that need an introduction—a student teacher, a long-term substitute, or someone who is attending the meeting for a one-time presentation (e.g., a district nurse or a technology specialist). The tone of the meeting will be more relaxed if each attendee has heard the name and role of all other people in the room.

**Lead with positives.** If it is a large group, such as a whole-staff meeting, I follow my opening statement and introductions by thanking individual people for something they have done that was particularly helpful or remarkable. It is also nice to allow some time for people to share some good news that may be happening in their lives. This sets a positive tone while allowing attendees to feel connected to one another. Smaller meetings should also start with positives, even if it is a simple compliment. I often begin meetings with a parent and teacher with something like "I'm so glad we were able to get together to talk about Eashana's progress. She is such a delightful girl; she truly makes our school a better place. I know her teachers all agree!"

**Tailor the tone to the meeting's topic and its attendees.** There are times that a meeting can be a lighthearted, fun affair. In these situations, participants can be relaxed, there can be humor, and the pace of the meeting will occur in a natural, comfortable way. There are others where the mood may be sober, systematic, and businesslike. Depending on the participants in each meeting and the topic on the agenda, set the appropriate tone and lead it accordingly.

**Learn to interrupt politely, professionally, and respectfully.** At times you will need to stop the direction of the conversation and help return the participants to the intended topic. This can be done with an apology and by articulating why you are interrupting. "I apologize for jumping in, but I would like to remind us all what we are here to talk about. Let's swing back to the main topic, OK?" I have to do this a great deal in IEP meetings, where our intent is to go over a student's present levels and discuss goals and objectives. Often, however, the conversation will veer off to sharing chatty, amusing anecdotes about the child; suddenly, everyone is chiming in, and I can see the meeting stretching out to twice as long as it should be. That's when I will kindly interrupt to say, "It is so fun to hear such sweet stories about Andrew at school. We're lucky to have so many successes to share. In order to complete all the things we need to cover today, though, let's bring it back to our goals and objectives." Sometimes, especially if I know we have a particularly chatty group, I'll begin the meeting by telling them with a smile, "I am appointing myself today's meeting taskmaster. If we get off track, I hope you'll forgive me if I interrupt and bring us back to the focus of our meeting." As with anything else, the tone and delivery of these words matters just as much as the words themselves; saying them with a kind, cheerful, and understanding tone will soften the words and lead toward your desired outcome.

Here are some polite, professional, and respectful phrases you may use to interrupt a wayward conversation and keep your group focused:

- "I am so sorry to interrupt, but I am hoping we can refocus our conversation back to our main topic. We were discussing ways to . . ."

- "Excuse me for stopping the conversation. I'd like to revisit our main goal of this meeting. Remember, our hope is to come up with . . ."

- "Here I go, interrupting again! I am keeping an eye on the clock, and I see our time is limited. Let's quickly review what we have discussed and revisit the conclusions we've reached."

- "There are excellent questions being asked, and I appreciate the thinking I hear happening in this meeting. Can I ask that you jot down any questions you have? That way, we can stay on track with our meeting agenda, and we can address all questions at the end."

**Move the conversation along.** Much like learning to interrupt appropriately, it is beneficial to learn how to move a meeting along, wrapping up each topic when it has been thoroughly discussed. It's best to openly and clearly articulate what you are doing so no one assumes you are being rude. You want to communicate that you appreciate everyone's contributions and honor everyone's time. Here are some phrases that get the job done:

- "I think we have come to a good conclusion here. In order to move along, let's quickly review each person's responsibilities and next steps, and then we'll move on to the next topic on the agenda."

- "I am so pleased with this conversation; in just a short amount of time, we have come up with several possible solutions to our problem. Does anyone have a strong feeling about the direction we should take from here?"

- "Thank you for all the contributions. I'm keeping an eye on the clock, and I see we are running out of time. Do we all feel we have come to a reasonable conclusion?"

**Read body language and react appropriately.** In large meetings, make sure you are constantly scanning the room, both when you are leading the discussion and when you are not. Read expressions and body language. Are people engaged and interested? Are they taking in the information, or do they seem to have shut down? Is anyone angry? Frustrated? Overwhelmed? If so, does the emotion seem to be present in everyone, or just one or two people? Sometimes it's best to step in and intervene—"I realize this topic is a frustrating one, and I can see some of you are overwhelmed. Let's talk about some possible solutions"—but there are other times it's best to carry on and address concerns individually after the meeting. Additionally, in long meetings, watch body language to determine when focus is waning; that's a great prompt to call for a break. This gives your participants time to clear their heads so they come back with renewed energy and enthusiasm.

**Don't speak if you don't have to.** Before adding to the conversation in a meeting, ask yourself if what you are going to say will genuinely contribute to the discussion. If it won't, don't say it— doing so will just draw out the time everyone will be there. Often I'll catch myself repeating something that was just said, changing the words around a bit, because I agree with the point and I want to reinforce it. Bad idea. It wastes everyone's time, and, besides, it's annoying ("Didn't so-and-so just say that?"). Repeating the ideas presented by others doesn't contribute to the conversation—it just delays a conclusion.

**Don't drone, and stop anyone else who does.** What's worse than someone who speaks needlessly? Someone who drones on and on, dragging the group along, by studying a problem from all angles and circling around solutions. If you are leading a meeting and someone begins to drone, stop it with a simple and respectful phrase. Try these:

- "I understand and appreciate what you're saying. Let's move on so we are sure we cover everything we need to cover today."

- "Thank you for the thorough and thoughtful input; we will certainly keep all of that in mind as we work toward solutions."

- "I am eager to hear the input from others. Any reaction to what we've heard so far?"

It's important to keep a keen eye on *yourself* to make sure *you* don't drone on and on. This may happen if you feel strongly about a situation or if you are a bona fide expert on a topic. However, ask yourself if you're dominating the conversation and, if so, force yourself to back off. I have a couple tricks to avoid this situation—small ones, but they work well for me:

- Keep a pack of gum in your bag and slip a piece in your mouth if you sense yourself talking too much. The chewing will remind you to stay silent unless necessary. Hard candy also works well.

- Bring a large bottle of water and take a long sip whenever you're tempted to begin pontificating.

- Find something to fiddle with. A pen works well, but I've snatched any number of things to keep my hands busy and to serve as a reminder to stay silent: a bottle lid, paper clips, a small wrapper, or a ring or bracelet.

- Take notes. I have been known to fill pages of notes just to keep my hand busy and my mind focused on the topic. The physical act of writing notes serves as a reminder to speak only when there is something short, concise, and helpful to say.

**Listen.** As leaders, we often want things to go just the way we think they should, so we struggle to really listen to the perspective of others. I'll never forget the day I was in a meeting about technology and I was advocating for a bulk purchase I thought we should make. I made my argument, and when our district's director of technology started to respond, I interrupted him. "Look, I get your point," I said, "but I really think we should—." Justifiably, he interrupted me right back. He looked at me straight in the eye and said, "I haven't *made* my point yet." Duly chastised, I quieted down, let him speak, and listened to his perspective. In the end, he was right—of course he was!—and I learned to listen carefully to voices other than my own.

**Leave room for questions, but make sure they affect the whole group.** Moving toward the conclusion of a meeting, you can ask, "Now it is time for us to take questions and offer any clarifications. If your question is specific only to you, I can address it after the meeting or sometime later today. For now, I'd like to take questions that affect all or most of the group." You can also ask if there is anything else—"For the Good of the Order," as many people call it—to gather any final thoughts or input from others. If there is nothing further, your meeting is almost complete.

**Know when to bring things to an end.** When a solution has been reached, all points have been covered, or time has run out, it's time to end the meeting. You can summarize major points that were made, review next steps, and remind the group if and when they will convene again. End with a message of appreciation for the time and input given to move the meeting successfully along.

# Being Efficient and Effective: Conversations to Guide Meetings

Although meetings may dominate your schedule, they do not have to weigh you down. With the right approach, meetings can be productive, be helpful, and improve the operations of your school.

Now, we'll revisit the scenarios outlined in the beginning of the chapter. In these conversations, you will find suggestions for how to guide your way through three different types of meetings that are likely to be a regular part of your work.

### Scenario 1: The Staff Meeting

In this scenario,* the middle school where you are principal is back in session after winter break. You always have a staff meeting on

---

*We will skip the details of the meeting and cover just what you say to manage its pace and efficiency.

the second Tuesday of the month. You have many things to cover, and you have several people planning to present information to the staff. You have prepared by sending an agenda to each staff member electronically, and your secretary has made hard copies, which people can pick up as they enter the room. You start the meeting exactly on time.

> **You:** *Welcome, everyone. Thank you for being on time and ready to go. You all received the agenda via e-mail, and I see you all have a copy in front of you. As you see, today's meeting will begin with a presentation from our test coordinator talking about upcoming assessments. Next, I'll share information about upcoming computer upgrades, the guidance counselor will talk about our Student Leadership Team, and the athletic director will review some upcoming events. We'll finish by watching a webinar that will show you some of the new things our online grading system can do. Over break, they really upgraded the system, and I think you'll like some of the new bells and whistles! We'll work through our agenda quickly; hopefully, I'll get you out of here early!*

Your opening remarks succinctly outline the events and goals for the meeting.

> **You:** *As always, let's start with just a few minutes for positives. First, I want to say a special thank-you to everyone in the guidance depart- ment. We had to make some changes to some student schedules over break, and the counselors all got together on their own time to make sure they'd communicated with everyone and that we were ready to go the first day back. Thank you so much. I also want to thank the office staff—as always, they are all so quick and efficient in getting things done. I am so lucky to work with such a supportive group. Does anyone else have celebrations or appreciations to share?*

Starting the meeting on a positive note sets the tone for the rest of your time together.

**You:** *Thank you to everyone who shared. Now, let's move right into our agenda. Let's have the testing coordinator review our spring assessment calendar and important training dates for everyone who is proctoring tests.*

### The test coordinator speaks.

**You:** *Thank you. That is a lot of information; does anyone have general questions or need clarification?*

### Questions are posed and answered.

**You:** *Those are excellent questions. Thank you. Remember, you can also ask further questions at any time. For now, though, let's move on. I want to tell you about upgrades to our computers. I recently met with our technology coordinator, and we talked about how best to schedule these to minimize disruption in your work. I'm going to project the schedule onto the SMART Board and talk you through our thinking.*

### You share your information and respond to questions.

**You:** *I'll keep you posted if anything changes on this schedule. For now, let's move on to our discussion about the Student Leadership Team.*

You continue moving through the agenda, introducing each person who is sharing information and leading follow-up questions and discussion.

**You:** *That covers all the items on the agenda. We still have a bit of time. Is there anything else we should discuss? Does anyone have anything to share with the whole group?*

Here, you are asking for questions and allowing participants to add anything else they think is important. When all voices have been heard, your meeting is complete.

## Scenario 2: The IEP Meeting

Although the teachers and parents do the bulk of the talking in IEP meetings, your role is to kick the meeting off, keep it moving, and end it in a timely manner. In this meeting, you are going over the IEP of a 5th grader named Jack. Attendees include Jack's father, Mr. Li; the special education teacher, Ms. Hicks; and several other related service personnel.

> **You:** *Thank you everyone for coming. Let me start with introductions. I'll introduce myself, and then we'll work our way around the table. For now, let's just state our name and role in Jack's education.*

Everyone introduces themselves with their title and their role at the meeting.

> **You:** *Great—let's get started. We are here to conduct our annual review of Jack's IEP. Mr. Li, I know I speak for the entire group when I say how much we enjoy working with Jack. He's a great kid—energetic, enthusiastic, and a very hard worker. And he's made terrific progress over the past year.*
>
> **Mr. Li:** *Thank you. He loves going to school. I'm grateful for everything you do for him.*
>
> **You:** *I'm so glad to hear that. To make sure we cover everything today, we'll get started right away. I'll be turning it over to Ms. Hicks, and she will cover Jack's present levels of performance, go over specific goals we have written for him, review accommodations and modifications that will help him succeed, and gather input from you regarding your goals for him in the future.*
>
> **Mr. Li:** *Sounds good.*
>
> **You:** *Great! Ms. Hicks—take it away.*

Here, you begin with a positive by praising the student, and then review the goals of the meeting in a verbal agenda. And since you have nothing to say that will contribute to the conversation, you let others take over the conversation.

> **You:** *Ms. Hicks, thank you for everything you shared. You were thorough and clear, and the goals make perfect sense for Jack. Now, let's shift to related services; we'll have the speech-language pathologist share her goals, and then we'll conclude this portion of the meeting with the occupational therapist.*

You are moving the meeting along by articulating next steps.

> **You:** *Thank you to all of you for putting so much time and effort into making Jack successful at school. Before we conclude the meeting, I'd like to ask everyone—especially you, Mr. Li—if we feel we have considered all the factors necessary in this IEP—Jack's present levels, his assessment data, the most appropriate accommodations and modifications. Have we successfully covered all of those? And does anyone have additional questions or concerns?*

Note how you are offering a time for questions, and you are asking if anyone has final thoughts to share.

> **You:** *Since we all seem to be in agreement, let's go ahead and sign the necessary paperwork. Mr. Li, we will implement the new goals in the IEP immediately. We will meet again in a year's time, although, as you know, we actually can meet anytime. If there is a need to update this plan sooner, we certainly will.*
> **Mr. Li:** *Sounds great. Thank you again!*
> **You:** *Thank you to everyone on the team! I know that together we're doing great things for Jack.*

Because there are no further questions or concerns, the meeting can come to a close.

## Scenario 3: The PTO Board Meeting

In the final scenario, you are joining the PTO Executive Board at the beginning of their monthly meeting. The board is made up of a group of four women who are all close friends. You really enjoy working with them—they are fun and spunky, and they do a tremendous amount of good for your school—but they are a talkative and social bunch, and their meetings last a long time. Most of the agenda doesn't involve you, but you do need to share a summary of things going on at school. You hope to stay focused on your report and dismiss yourself from the meeting quickly, letting them go on with the rest of their agenda. Fortunately, you have built a relationship with them in which you can address their tendency to get off topic by using a lighthearted approach. After the meeting has been called to order, you begin.

> **You:** *Hello, ladies. Ready to get started?*
> **PTO President:** *Yes. Of course! We're always ready, aren't we, gang?*
> **PTO Treasurer:** *Always. That's why we drive everyone crazy.* (Laughter)
> **President:** *And never get anything done.*
> **Secretary:** *And drive everyone crazy.*
> **Treasurer:** *Like I said. Crazy.*
> **You:** *There you go, ladies. Up and running already.* (Deep, dramatic sigh)
> **President:** *See? We drive you crazy. Sorry, sorry, sorry. Let's focus. Let's start, as always, with the Principal's Report. We promise not to interrupt.*
> **Treasurer:** *We do?*
> **You:** (Laughing) *Yes, you do! OK, let me summarize my Report to the President. First one to interrupt has to buy lunch.*

Here, you have set the tone of the meeting based on the personalities of the attendees.

> **You:** *I'm going to start by sharing some great news. We recently got results from the spring administration of the ACT, and our scores were*

*higher than they've ever been. The group of students that took it did an excellent job; I'm so proud of them. It shows that our teachers' instruction is really effective.*

**Vice-President:** *True. And that our students also have really great moms. Like us!* (Laughter)

**You:** (Laughing) *OK, I'm going to keep moving because I know there's a lot to get to. Another bit of positive news is that spring athletic season is under way, and it looks like we're going to have a great season. I'm especially excited about our baseball and track teams. I could see us really competing on the state level this year.*

The sharing of celebrations starts the meeting on a positive note. You have also interrupted in a respectful and professional manner to keep the meeting moving.

**You:** *Since I've shared our good news, I'll just quickly go through the rest of my report. I just have three more items to cover. I'll talk about how we are using the literacy resources the PTO purchased last fall, plans for graduation day, and our summer school program. After that, I'll open it up for questions.*

After verbally outlining your agenda, you've offered a chance for questions at the end of the meeting. In this case, you would continue to offer specifics about each of the items.

**You:** *Now that I have covered everything, do you have any questions?*

**Treasurer:** *I have one. My daughter said she had the chance to take a look at the new reading material in the library. Is that something all students get to do?*

**You:** *Not necessarily. If you recall, those resources were for our higher-level English classes; they wouldn't be appropriate for all readers.*

**Treasurer:** *I don't recall anything anymore.*

**Secretary:** *You recall when it's happy hour.*

**Treasurer:** (Laughing) *So true. I never forget that!*

**President:** *The best hour of the day!* (Laughter)

**Vice-President:** *Here we go again, making our principal crazy!*

**You:** *I always look forward to these meetings. I love how you love to laugh! Thank you. That was a great question. Are there any others I could address?*

Here, you tactfully keep the meeting moving forward.

**Vice-President:** *I don't have anything else.*

**Secretary:** *Me neither. So we're done?* (Laughter)

**Treasurer:** *Time for happy hour?* (More laughter)

**You:** *OK, then, let me just summarize some of our main topics, and then I'll slip out and let you work through the rest of the items on your agenda. I've shared some celebrations with you, explained how we are using some of the PTO purchases, and covered graduation and summer plans. And that covers all of my topics! Give me a call if you have any questions; I'll be out and about and can come back anytime if you have questions for me. As always, I thank you for your time and all you do for us here at school. We couldn't do it without you!*

Notice how you are ending your portion of the meeting by summarizing main points and expressing appreciation.

The conversations in this chapter all emerge from positive meetings that move along smoothly, but not all of your meetings will be this easy. Some will be contentious, some will be long and arduous, and some will conclude without the solutions you sought. The strategies in this chapter don't guarantee great meetings, but they will go a long way toward ensuring more productive ones that make the best use of your time—and the time of those around you.

# Keeping Up with District, State, and Federal Mandates

## Scenario 1: New Laws

*About a month into your tenure as an elementary school principal, your district's literacy director calls you in for a meeting to discuss new legislation relating to assessing elementary reading proficiency. As you enter the room and sit down across from her desk, you can tell she is a bit rattled.*

## Scenario 2: New Processes

*Your superintendent calls a meeting with all district principals to explain a change in the process for hiring new staff members. As he talks, you are overwhelmed by the implications of the changes he is making. Afterward, you call a colleague to process the new requirements that have been laid out for you.*

## Scenario 3: New Requirements

*After a regular meeting with all administrators in the district, you ask your district's food service director if he has a few moments to talk. You have read a little about recent changes to the National School Lunch Program, and you're curious about the new requirements' effect on your school, staff, and students.*

As a principal, there are many times you will be at the mercy of district, state, and federal mandates. Because district mandates tend to come from a leadership team that makes decisions to best serve *all* enrolled students, they may not make sense to you in relation to your own building and your students. Similarly, state and federal mandates can give district and building leaders pause, not least because they tend to be broad and aggressive, the result of complicated political maneuverings by people who may not know much about the realities of public education. That can mean decisions have been made that do not factor in what it takes to operate a school and do not consider the best interests of children.

An obvious example is the battle in some school districts related to required assessments. In an effort to bring students in the United States up to the achievement levels of students in other countries, legislators have passed laws that require students to be tested to determine progress—and tested again, and again, and again. Most teachers and principals find it baffling; after all, for every moment we are *testing* a child, we are not *instructing* a child. And if we can't instruct, how can they learn? And if they aren't learning, how can they show their learning on a test? The cycle is maddening. Yet, even as many teachers and principals lament the loss of instructional time and the number of tests students are required to take, the law is clear: testing must be done. So we do it. But we also do what we can to minimize the damage it causes and advocate for a different and better way.

One thing I try to remind myself is that many mandates truly come from a place of good intentions. As an example, several years ago, districts in our state were required to implement an online system that allowed students (or their parents and peers) to electronically report incidents of bullying directly to the principal. When the program rolled out, my in-box was flooded daily with reports that turned out to be unfounded. Students created false reports as a joke on their friends, reports were filed to get back at a peer for something inconsequential, and parents spontaneously filed reports based on little or no evidence. I silently cursed the amount of time I was spending implementing this new mandate, weeding through the reports each day, conducting investigations, and trying to tell truth from fiction. Yet, once things calmed down a bit, I realized that for every few bogus reports, there was one that was legitimate—a student who was truly suffering due to unkind or cruel treatment at our school, or a parent who was watching her child grow depressed and reclusive as a result of bullying. I came to realize that even if this direct reporting system helped just one child, then the time it required from me was well worth it. In the end, I straightened out my perspective, found ways to share the burden of the work, and applauded the intent behind the mandate.

## Strategies and Solutions for Keeping Up with Mandates

What can a building leader do to stay on top of district, state, and federal mandates? Here are several strategies to try.

**Rely on a network of experts.** Depending on the size of your district, you may have a support system already in place to help you keep abreast of changes and new mandates. Large districts tend to have people at the central office level who keep up with legislative changes and communicate them to their principals. If this is not available to you, it's wise to build a network of colleagues with whom you can communicate when there are new mandates to implement in your building.

**Ask questions about mandates, even those that don't seem directly related to your work.** Even if you don't think some mandates will affect you, it's smart to be inquisitive and ask questions of others around you. Over time, you'll develop a better understanding of all the different behind-the-scenes issues that affect how your school really runs. I love to ask questions of people in my district whose job descriptions are very different from mine, because I always discover that what they do really does have an impact on the daily operations of my school. Facilities, maintenance, transportation, food service, instructional technology, operations—all these departments adhere to countless district, state, and federal mandates that filter down and affect the work at the building level. Learning about them will help you understand why some things are the way they are.

**Find solid sources of news on the mandates that affect your school and read them regularly.** In my state, our Department of Education sends out a weekly e-mail newsletter to anyone who is interested in reading about new requirements for principals and teachers. Subscribing to receive these updates helps me understand what is happening at the state level. Similarly, professional organizations offer frequent e-mail updates, providing succinct, helpful reviews with suggestions to implement new mandates in practical and efficient ways.

**Attend state and national professional conferences.** There are many reasons to attend professional conferences—not the least of which is learning about new mandates you will need to implement. It's wise to attend sessions related to legislative changes so you know the very latest information that relates to your work. These events also provide an opportunity to network and build relationships with peers who can be ongoing sources of information and ideas.

**Don't jump the gun.** Newly announced mandates that seem overly aggressive, sweeping, and broad can easily lead you to believe you'll have to make huge changes at your school. In actuality, they may turn out to have very little impact on your day-to-day operations. For that reason, I have learned not to react too quickly when I'm told about new mandates. Especially in the case of state or federal legislative requirements, there are often follow-up political checks and balances that may change things several more times before official policy is set. It's always best to wait and see how things really play out before you make big changes that affect everyone involved in your school.

**Look for justification and understanding, and communicate this to others.** In the example I shared earlier of my school's mandated system for reporting bullying, even though the mandate created a lot of unfounded investigative work for me, there is no doubt that the system was put into place to protect children who were suffering. Keeping this in mind, I was able to use the system to help students, all the while getting to know them better; I was also better able to communicate the program to others. So when I talked with teachers or parents when their child was involved in a bullying report, I was able to start by saying, "Remember, this system is put into place to give a voice to students who may not otherwise have one. If we all remember our goal—protecting kids—we can work through this problem in a positive way." And as you look for and communicate the intent behind a particular law or mandate you're faced with, you may naturally find support in implementing it.

**Share the burden.** It's impossible for a principal to manage every single federal, state, and local mandate without help—which is why you should appoint a designee to manage some of them. As an example, my administrative secretary logs all of our safety drills and submits the information to the county and state as required by law; my assistant principal manages all of our required standardized assessments; my guidance counselor filters through the majority of our bullying reports. All three of these people only come to me when they encounter something they don't feel equipped to manage. By divvying up responsibilities, we are able to successfully implement requirements without any one of us being stretched too thin.

**If you have an opinion, share it.** Although seeking understanding about mandates can usually make them easier to swallow and sharing the burden they impose will often make implementation easier, this isn't always the case. And no one has a better idea of how mandates will affect your school than you and the staff you lead. So when you hear about discussions or legislation that may result in invasive new requirements for your school, get involved in the conversation. Call your legislator, offer to be on committees or study groups, be part of pilot programs, and so on. If you do not support the proposed changes, you can bring a perspective to the conversation that may alter elements that are impractical or detrimental. If you support proposed changes, your voice will help to make the mandates more sound and implementable.

**Join your professional organization.** Becoming a member of professional organizations on both the state and national level is an excellent way to keep up with the most recent changes in mandates that affect education. These organizations can shed light on the thinking that leads to changes, summarize how it affects you, and offer suggestions for implementation. Moreover, professional organizations usually have an excellent, informed staff that are just a phone call or e-mail away.

## Staying in Compliance: Conversations That Will Help You Keep Up with Mandates

Many of our leaders, both within the field of education and in the political world, want to have a lasting impact on schools. This is one reason education is constantly shifting and changing. For those of us in the trenches, it means making frequent adjustments to how we operate.

Here, we will revisit the scenarios outlined in the beginning of the chapter. These conversations will help guide your thinking as you navigate your way through the job of keeping up with mandates.

## Scenario 1: New Laws

In this scenario, the director of literacy, Stacey, calls a meeting to fill you in on some recent legislative mandates related to students learning to read at the elementary school level. As you enter the room and sit down with her, you sense immediately that she is rattled and anxious.

> **You:** *OK, tell me more about this new law.*
>
> **Stacey:** *Well, here it is in a nutshell. All students have to pass a state-approved standardized reading assessment at some point in 3rd grade. If they don't, we will be required to retain them in 3rd grade. As you know, retention is an incredibly dated practice. It is rarely used anymore because it's been shown that it doesn't really help kids learn more successfully over time. And it can damage a kid both socially and emotionally. But retention is what we are going to have to do if students don't pass this test. I mean, there are still some things to be hammered out, but it sounds like the law is going to be implemented in some shape or form. The state legislature seems quite committed to it.*
>
> **You:** *I've read a little bit about it in the weekly updates from the state Department of Education, but I didn't realize it was so far along in the process.*

By subscribing to a state education resource and reading its updates, you're staying abreast of the big developments.

**Stacey:** *It's moving rather quickly now; it passed the House, and it's working its way through the Senate. I wouldn't be surprised to see it implemented for this upcoming school year.*

**You:** *I do have some questions, then, because there are parts of the law that don't make sense to me. For one, what if we're talking about a student receiving special education services who has a specific disability in reading? I'm talking about a case where we have evaluated the child, have acknowledged that he is not reading on grade level, and have written goals to help him.*

**Stacey:** *Luckily, students receiving special education are exempt from retention. We just have to amend all the IEPs to indicate that exemption.*

**You:** *Well, that's a relief. Are there any other exemptions?*

## You have an expert in the room, and you're looking to her for more information.

**Stacey:** *Fortunately, yes. Students are exempt from retention if they are in the ELL program and have lived in this country for less than three years or if they have been previously retained.*

**You:** *Again, what a relief. It would be so unfair to retain students who aren't reading on grade level because they are learning the language. And if a child was retained before 3rd grade, another retention could be devastating. We're talking about kids being at least two years older than their peers.*

**Stacey:** *Exactly.*

**You:** *So, how do you feel about all this?*

**Stacey:** *Well, you know my philosophy. I believe students learn at their own specific pace, and it pains me to think about punitive consequences for not passing a certain benchmark on a test at an arbitrary point in their education.*

**You:** *I agree with your philosophy, but since it's looking like some form of this law will soon be a reality, we should try to see the good in it. Districts all over the state are going to have to do everything they can to get kids reading on grade level. There will have to be intense, focused,* *appropriately planned interventions in place. So we're going to do what we've been asked to do, and in the end, if more students become proficient readers, that's a positive outcome. We'll work closely with you in the district office to make all of this work.*

Here, you're striving for balance—seeking the silver lining in a mandate that you're not particularly enthusiastic about, and sketching out a very preliminary plan for compliance.

**Stacey:** *That's reassuring to know. I have my own ideas on how to get started, but it will be great to have some help putting all of this in place.*
**You:** *Great! I want to hear your ideas. Until all parts of the new law are put into place, though, let's proceed with caution. I don't want to make decisions too early.*

No need to jump into any big decisions before the mandate is official.

**Stacey:** *That's great. And until then, we'll just stay focused on teaching kids, right? That's what we're here to do.*
**You:** *Teach kids. Yep. That's what we'll do.*

Mandates will come and go, but both you and your district leadership have the same primary, underlying mission—to ensure students receive the best education you can provide.

## Scenario 2: New Processes

In this scenario, your superintendent calls a meeting with all district principals to explain a change in procedures for hiring new staff members. The process seems long and difficult; you can't help feeling a little overwhelmed as he explains the new expectations. After the meeting, you call a colleague, Lee, to process the new requirements that have been laid out for you.

**You:** *Are you as concerned as I am about this new hiring process?*
**Lee:** *Yes. It seems like it will take twice as long to hire someone. With all the new steps to the process, I worry we'll lose our top candidates to neighboring districts. I mean, a screening interview, a committee interview, watching the teacher lead a lesson, an individual interview, and then all those reference checks we're supposed to complete? That's going to take a lot of time.*
**You:** *That's exactly what worries me. Of course, I get what the superintendent is trying to do. He wants to be sure we hire only the very, very best.*
**Lee:** *Of course. He absolutely means well.*

Here, both you and your colleague have identified the justification for and have some understanding of the new mandate.

**You:** *If we could just eliminate one or two of the steps, I'd feel much better about it.*
**Lee:** *I hate to be blunt, but it doesn't matter how concerned we are; it seems like a done deal. Now it's about finding a way to get it done.*
**You:** *Well, let's not get ahead of ourselves, though. Before we start brainstorming an action plan, maybe we could call the superintendent and talk him through some of the things that have us a little nervous.*
**Lee:** *You think he would rethink it?*
**You:** *You know him better than I do. What do you think? If a group of principals got together and came up with a solid alternate plan that would streamline the process but still provide the kind of quality check everybody wants, perhaps he'd reconsider.*

Here, you are advocating taking a step back before springing into action, as well as considering sharing your opinion.

**Lee:** *Maybe he would. I agree that it would be important to meet with him as a group, so he knows it's not just one person complaining about what feels like "more work."*

**You:** *After all, we agree with what he's trying to do. He knows the best candidates teaching in the classroom will lead to better instruction— which is what's best for kids. And that's all any of us want.*
**Lee:** *Right.*

Again, your guiding focus is what's best for students.

**You:** *Let me reach out to a few other principals and see if we're all feeling similarly about this. Then I'll figure out if anyone is interested in meeting with him to suggest options. I'll get back to you, OK?*
**Lee:** *Great. I'm happy to help in any way.*

## Scenario 3: New Requirements

After a regular meeting with all administrators in the district, you ask Dan, your district's food service director, if he has a few minutes to talk. You are seeking to understand some federally mandated changes to the school breakfast and lunch program.

**You:** *Thank you for taking a few moments to talk with me. I'm interested in knowing more about recent changes in the school lunch program. I've been reading a bit about it in some of the updates I get from my professional association, but I'm unclear on all the specifics of the changes.*

Here, you're making use of information you receive from your professional organization, and you're reaching out to someone whose work is not obviously connected to your own.

**Dan:** *Oh, the changes have completely altered how we do business. When I think back two decades to the school lunches I ate as a student—wow. Whole different world.*
**You:** *Tell me more.*

**Dan:** *Well, the National School Lunch Program was established in the 1940s, so it's not a new thing. There have been overhauls throughout the years, but there haven't been big changes in at least 15 years—not until these recent updates. This all came from a presidential initiative to expand and improve the quality of school breakfast and lunches.*

**You:** *How is it playing out?*

**Dan:** *Well, the new regulations from the U.S. Department of Agriculture require that we offer fruits and vegetables as separate meal components, where previously we just offered one—a fruit or a vegetable. Now, there has to be fruit served at both breakfast and lunch and vegetables at lunch, with significant limits on starchy vegetables. We need to offer whole-grain products, offer a protein at breakfast, and have low-fat or fat-free beverages. And that's just the beginning.*

**You:** *Wow. What else?*

**Dan:** *There are regulations on the number of calories in each meal. There cannot be any trans fats, and our food offerings have to be low in sodium. It's important to stay in compliance with all of these mandates to get reimbursed for our food costs—especially the full reimbursement we get for students who receive free or reduced-cost meals.*

You are tapping into your network of experts to learn specifics about the mandates in place.

**You:** *It sounds like a daunting task.*

**Dan:** *It is, but as with anything else, we're just figuring out how to get it done. We've had to retrain all of our staff members and adjust how we order and distribute food. And we launched a significant education campaign for our parents and students. But it was part of what we had to do, so we did it.*

**You:** *That's why I wanted to touch base with you. I get a lot of questions from parents who want their child to purchase a school lunch, but they are concerned about the quality of the food and the nutritional value.*

**Dan:** *And I appreciate you helping me at the building level by educating families about our school lunch program. It can be confusing for a*

One of the first things you should do as a beginning principal is take a long walk through every part of your building. Open every door. Walk through each classroom, each workroom, and all locker rooms and offices. Explore the boiler room and heating areas. Get to know the kitchen and cafeteria. Memorize the fire exits and shelter-in-place areas. Outside, walk around playground areas and athletic fields. If your school has a field house, a weight room, or a stadium, inspect those carefully. Finally, find the roof access door and climb onto the roof—you'll undoubtedly find several baseballs or basketballs that have been hurled up there!—and inspect it for standing water or loose roofing tiles. Look out and scan the expanse of your campus from this bird's-eye view.

Ideally, this inspection should take place in the company of your school's head custodian, who should know the physical space better than anyone. Ask a lot of questions, even if you think those questions are silly. Gather a sense of the history of repairs and future planned projects or improvements.

When I was hired as a principal, the superintendent sat me down with a list of things for me to prioritize. Close to the top of the list were the words "Building Upkeep and Updates." He explained, "You are taking over the dirtiest building in the district."

"Dirty?" I sputtered. I wondered what he could possibly mean.

"Dirty," he said. "As in, not clean."

He went on to explain that the current custodian had just completed a probation for failing to meet expectations for cleanliness and maintenance. He had simply seemed unable to work through his daily tasks—emptying trash, preparing the lunchroom in time for the students to eat, cleaning up afterwards—much less completing more challenging jobs such as replacing ballasts and bulbs, repairing broken equipment, and cleaning high-traffic areas thoroughly. The assistant custodians were doing their best to keep up, but things had fallen into disrepair.

"Take a walk around the school," my superintendent told me. "You'll see."

The walk was illuminating. As I toured the building, I realized that up to this point in my career, I'd taken for granted how much the physical environment factors into overall school climate. It struck me that a messy, disorganized, and indifferently maintained building cannot support the environment of high expectations, focus, and professionalism that is crucial to a school's success; nor does it communicate to parents that their children will be working in a safe and nurturing space.

As I walked, I kept a mental list of the problems I saw. Outside, the hedges were overgrown, and weeds had popped up willy-nilly throughout the playground. The school sign was badly in need of paint, the concrete on sidewalks leading to the front door was crumbling in spots, and some of the playground equipment was blocked off with caution tape. Inside, I found several areas with dull, chipped paint. Drywall tape was peeling. In classrooms, desks didn't match, and areas near the baseboards weren't swept. Corners of classrooms and workrooms were stacked with piles of stuff.

I decided we needed a plan. I grabbed a composition book, summoned the (reluctant) custodian, and began all over again. Together, we walked through every inch of the school campus, studying it with a critical eye. I wrote down everything that needed to be cleaned, updated, or organized. I also took note of everything I should be aware of—where fire extinguishers were located, where dry goods were stored, where to find the elevator inspection information, and so on.

We finished our inspection back in my office. Together, the custodian and I worked through my list. We prioritized each task by importance and ease of completion. We noted which tasks would need to be outsourced and which our existing custodial staff could accomplish.

"There is a lot to do here," the custodian told me, shaking his head. "We'll never get it all done."

"Actually, we *will* get it done," I told him cheerfully. "We'll start right now."

He looked at me in dismay. I realized he was hurt—after all, I was criticizing how he had cared for the building in the past. More than that, though, he was clearly overwhelmed. It occurred to me that he probably had no idea how to begin to tackle the jobs I'd listed for him to complete.

In fact, it did prove to be too much for the custodian to manage. Soon after our meeting, he requested a transfer to another building, and I replaced him with one of the second-shift custodians who had a whole arsenal of skills. Not only did he value organization and cleanliness, but he was also an expert with a toolbox. He worked his way through our list of repairs—fixing, replacing, painting, and removing materials that were not being used. Within one year, the building was gleaming, and there was very little clutter. Everyone noticed the difference. Time and again, parents and visitors—and my superintendent—commented on the transformation.

Why is it so important that a school building be at its best? It's simple: it *must* be a space that promotes learning. It needs to be inviting, warm, and free from distractions. It can't look like a haphazard conglomeration of supplies, materials, and resources; it can't show a laundry list of necessary repairs. If the building is a mess, it undercuts everything the teachers and students are trying to do.

## Strategies and Solutions for Maintaining Your Facility

Getting to know the building and establishing a good working relationship with the custodial staff is a priority for a new building principal. It's the first step in ensuring a healthy, safe, and positive learning environment. It conveys your commitment to top-to-bottom excellence. Here are some additional strategies to try.

**Keep records that support problem solving.** When working with the maintenance team to solve problems that arise in your building, it will help to be knowledgeable and prepared. For example, if a teacher calls you the morning after a severe rainstorm to say he has discovered a puddle of water on the floor, you will need to determine the history and severity of the problem—what repairs have been made, and if there have been previous roof or structural issues. I find it helpful to work with my custodian to maintain a binder where we store reports for fire, water, and health department inspections; water, gas, electric, and HVAC manuals and updates; window replacement and repair records; elevator inspections; and so on. This system allows us to have productive conversations with teams called in to diagnose and fix damage, and it supports faster and better decision making when there are maintenance emergencies.

**Plan to be creative with how space is used.** Being a principal requires managing constant change, and the use of your facility is no exception. Shifts in enrollment, severity of special education caseloads, and staffing adjustments are just a few reasons you may need to change how you make use of the square footage of your building. For example, if you have a large influx of students move in at semester break, you may need to create a new classroom. You may need to convert a workroom into an office, a lounge into a commons area, or a stage into a classroom. I find that I am often considering alternate ways rooms and spaces could be used—sometimes without even being aware that I am doing it. When an idea hits me that may lead to using space in a more effective way, I jot it down and then reference it later, if and when the need arises. I find it helpful to frequently revisit the question, "Are we using space in the most effective way?"

**Inventory your resources and storage space.** It is important that you know what resources are available and where things are stored. Extra desks, cleaning equipment, academic supplies, old equipment, and various materials are all stashed somewhere in the building. Knowing where they are will help you run your building efficiently. I was reminded of this recently when our school's testing coordinator asked me to purchase over 100 headphone sets for an upcoming online state assessment. I recalled seeing a large box of headphones stashed in the back storage room of the library. In retrieving them, we saved quite a bit of money. Seeking to get a better handle on our resources, I created a Google Doc outlining the contents of all of our main storage areas. Everyone on staff is able to refer to—and edit—this list, so it is always up to date and truly reflects what resources are available.

**Plan for updates and upkeep.** As mentioned before, be aware of areas of concern in the building, and use this awareness to develop a list of things you'd like to improve or update. Be thoughtful in how you prioritize tasks that are necessary to keep your building a fresh, clean, and organized space—one that promotes instruction and learning most effectively. Keep the list as a working document. Refer to it often as a way to keep track of improvements and updates.

**Set an expectation for excellence.** When you know your facilities well, you can more effectively lead your staff to meet your expectations for safety and cleanliness. When staff, students, and parents see how committed you are to taking care of the building, they will follow your lead. You can set the expectation by pointing out areas of improvement.

In my first year, as we worked to improve our facilities, I found myself gently pointing out areas in which teachers could help us achieve our goals. Years of inattentiveness had left our teacher workrooms cluttered with old materials, textbooks, and supplemental resources. I encouraged teachers to work through the space and discard items no longer used. I explained that organized, updated work areas would give them more efficient and easy access to their resources. They were happy to comply, because they had had enough of the clutter and disrepair; they just needed the expectation to be set, and they were happy to meet it.

**Be generous, flexible, and cautious (all at once).** School districts are often asked to share their facilities with community groups. It is wise for districts to be generous with their facilities, as it helps build a positive working relationship with community leaders. Further, opening your facility whenever possible allows members of your community—who may otherwise not see your school—to experience some positive things happening in your building.

With that said, it requires flexibility on the part of you and your staff; at times, you may need to adjust athletic practice times, performances, or even teacher use of the building. Quick note here: It's important to think cautiously and carefully about community use of your building, because there are some groups or organizations that may make you uncomfortable, such as aggressive religious, political, or social gatherings; political organizations; or groups that may discriminate against particular members of your community. I called a friend of mine for some insight on this. He works in a neighboring district and is charged with filtering through requests to use school facilities. He gave me several examples of requests that he denied for this reason, including political organizations that wished to host a rally for their party, requests to host protests for and against family planning clinics, and even, once, a request for a wedding reception—open bar and all.

**Create an emergency protocol, and commit it to memory.** In an emergency, response time is critical. The location of your school's power and heat switches, water sources, fire alarms, fire extinguishers, automated external defibrillators (AEDs), medical supplies, and even telephones should be documented in a formal emergency protocol that you (and your team, as backup) can access electronically and remotely and as an old-fashioned paper document. Then you should memorize this information. It is impossible to predict when you will need to activate these safety resources, and it's your responsibility to know how to do so. I can't help but think of a colleague whose quick action and awareness of where to find the AED stored in his school's cafeteria helped to save the life of a teacher experiencing cardiac arrest.

## Knowing Your Building: Conversations to Help You Manage Your Facility

School districts face constant and inevitable change. Shifts in enrollment brought on by aging communities or new growth projections may create the need to renovate deteriorating buildings or, conversely, oversee new construction. These changes can be exciting, but they open districts up to some crucial decision-making challenges with financial and political implications. As a building principal who knows the facility better than anyone, you should make sure you are an active, knowledgeable voice in conversations about your building.

We will now revisit the scenarios that opened this chapter by making our way through possible conversations you may have.

## Scenario 1: The Tour

In this scenario, you have officially received your keys, and you want to get to know your facility. You ask your custodian, Sam, to take you on a full tour, and he is happy to comply.

> **Sam:** *Where would you like to start?*
> **You:** *Let's just work our way down each hallway. You can tell me which grade levels and departments are in each classroom. When we pass any storage areas, maintenance rooms, or custodial closets, let me take a look at them so I know what is inside.*

Here, you begin your tour with your custodian, taking special care to learn what resources you have stored in which areas. As you begin walking, you tell Sam what else you'd like to see.

> **You:** *As we walk, can you make sure to point out any safety equipment, such as fire alarms, fire extinguishers, AEDs, handicapped entrances, and so on?*
> **Sam:** *I'd be more than happy to do that for you.*
> **You:** *The other thing I would like is for you to show me the automatic shutoffs for gas, water, and electric. I hope we never have an emergency that would require that, but I'd like to be prepared.*
> **Sam:** *Absolutely. There are also manuals describing the location of the shutoffs and how to operate them; I'll show you where we keep those, too.*
> **You:** *I've brought along a map of the tornado drill locations and fire exits; as we get to each area, let's pause so I can gain an understanding of how those types of drills will work.*

Here, you are learning about the location of safety areas, materials, and equipment.

> **Sam:** *I see you also have a notebook.*

**You:** *Yes, I'm going to take some notes as we walk along. First, I want to note what we have in our main storage areas so I know what resources we have and where they are stored. I hope to create a database or a fluid document that will serve as an inventory list for the staff. And second, I want to note specific areas that we agree need some upkeep— paint, updates, or repairs, and so on. Afterward, we'll make a plan for maintenance requests and updates.*

Written records support effective planning for updates and upkeep.

**Sam:** *That's great. I'm glad that the facility is a high priority for you.*
**You:** *I really believe that in order for students to learn their best, the building needs to be in great shape. As much as our budget allows, we should keep things looking as updated, neat, and clean as possible. So you're right, I do prioritize the building. I want it to look great.*

Note how you are setting the expectation for excellence.

**Sam:** *You and I are going to get along just fine. I take a lot of pride in this place. It's kind of my home away from home. So it's obviously my first priority, and I'm glad to hear it's high on your list, too.*

## Scenario 2: The Construction Project

This conversation illustrates how your input can influence district decision making that affects your facility. In this conversation, you tour the building with district leaders and an architectural team, who are considering an addition of several classrooms.

**You:** *How many new classrooms do we anticipate an addition would provide?*
**Superintendent:** *We would need to add at least eight classrooms to accommodate projected enrollment. We need to plan space for about 200 additional students in the next five years.*

> **You:** *Wow. That's a lot of additional students. Have we considered if the existing heating and cooling system can handle that much extra space?*
> **Architect:** *Yes, that will be part of the plans. We anticipate we will need to increase the capabilities of your current system.*
> **You:** *What about our core space—the cafeteria, the commons area, our central office, and the gym? We are using those spaces to capacity now; how will they be able to grow to accommodate the extra students?*
> **Architect:** *We can consider some alternate space in the addition to ensure all students have access to those types of areas.*
> **You:** *What about restrooms and drinking fountains?*
> **Architect:** *Our plans include one full restroom facility and two additional drinking fountains. Will that work for you?*
> **You:** *That sounds good. It would be best if they were centrally located within the addition so they are not too far from any particular classroom.*
> **Architect:** *We'll make sure we consider that when we finalize our plans.*

Notice how you are pointing out the best use of space. You know from experience that a long distance from classroom to restroom can cause learning distractions, so you know you must advocate for thoughtful placement of these areas.

> **You:** *Thank you! Now, let's talk about safety. Will there be external doors for a fast exit during a fire drill? And will there be windowless areas to be used during a tornado drill?*
> **Architect:** *There will be an external set of doors, but unfortunately there are no enclosed tornado shelter areas. Can we think of a solution to that?*
> **You:** *Absolutely. When the addition is built and in use, I can revise my tornado safety plan to have students spread out in the main building in safe areas.*

The questions you are asking are helping to identify future needs. You are also keeping the location of safety resources in the forefront of your mind.

**You:** *Let me ask another question. I'm wondering about work areas. Currently, each department and team is composed of four teachers. Each team has a workroom that stores their shared resources; the teachers also use it as a work space during their planning time, as their classrooms are often used during those periods by a traveling teacher. Do the plans include two additional workrooms for this purpose?*

**Architect:** *We had planned on only one workroom.*

**Treasurer:** *We can look at the final cost estimate and see if we can add an additional workroom. Are there other spaces you may need that we should consider?*

**You:** *With our current enrollment ratios, we have four special education students and 15 English language learners per 100 students. If those ratios remain unchanged, we would need space for an additional special education classroom and ELL classroom. We will also need additional storage space. There's never enough of that!*

**Architect:** *We had planned on two small rooms for those special services classrooms.*

**You:** *That's great. I will take a look at our final enrollment numbers and make a plan for using that space. Again, though, let's make sure we consider additional storage space if possible.*

Here, you are firm in advocating for storage space as a way to maintain your high standards of upkeep. Organized space and quick access to resources is important for every school staff.

**You:** *Can I ask if we have considered how we can fill these classrooms? Have we budgeted for technology, desks, tables, chairs, textbooks, and related materials? Should we consider an additional copy machine? How about an increase in my supply budget?*

**Treasurer:** *We will have a startup budget for you to purchase materials you need for the first day, and we are planning to increase your supplies budget according to the per-pupil ratio we currently use. Therefore, none of that should be a concern.*

**You:** *Great. Just one more question. What about custodial staff? Currently, our custodial staff is responsible for 25,000 square feet for each 8-hour shift. We will need to increase our custodial staff, correct?*
**Treasurer:** *Absolutely. When we know a final square footage total for the addition, we will increase the staff or move one of your part-time custodians to full time.*

You are consistently advocating for the resources you need to maintain a clean, neat, and functional building.

**You:** *It seems you've considered most of the things I am concerned about. I am excited about the potential for an addition to ease the overcrowding we are experiencing—and also about welcoming new students to our school. Thank you so much for involving me in the decision making. I am glad we are working together as a team on this!*

## Scenario 3: The Event

This conversation captures a common occurrence in many schools: an invitation to allow the community to use the facility for a big event. In this case, you tell the city you will honor their request to host a large community concert in your gymnasium. You meet with your head custodian to brainstorm important considerations.

**You:** *Thank you for meeting with me on such short notice. I wanted to discuss an upcoming event that will be held at our school. The city council has asked us to host a large holiday musical performance. They have agreed to cover all costs and anticipate more than 2,000 people will attend. As you know, our gym has a capacity of 2,500, so we're looking at a crowd that will be packed in pretty tightly! Let's talk through this and make a plan. Where should we start?*
**Custodian:** *The first thing that comes to my mind is staffing. We'll need several extra custodial staff to keep up with things like trash, troubleshooting technology, and keeping up with restroom facilities.*

*In addition, given the time of year, we must also plan for weather; we may need some of our extra staff to be on hand for snow removal, for example. I think we'll need to schedule five extra custodians to manage the event.*

**You:** *That sounds great. Let's schedule them as soon as possible. One of my considerations was traffic management and parking. I was thinking I should contact City Hall to see if the council's funding will include a police officer to manage traffic flow. For parking, let's use the plan we have in place for football and basketball games. We'll ask one of our school's clubs to volunteer to park cars that evening. What else?*

**Custodian:** *We'll need to make sure the heat is right. We will need the heat on, obviously, but with that many people here, we'll need to make sure the sensors are on so the chiller works correctly and adjusts itself as the gym's temperature rises. I'll make sure I monitor the temperature throughout the night in case I have to make manual adjustments.*

**You:** *Thank you. What about a performance area?*

**Custodian:** *Perhaps we should ask the council if they would like to rent a stage area complete with the lighting required by the musical group. We could use our mobile stage, but lighting and sound would be a challenge.*

**You:** *I will check in with them. I agree that renting a stage would be more appropriate in this case. Another thing I think about—with this many people who are unfamiliar with the facility—is safety.*

**Custodian:** *I agree. It'd be a good idea to open the night with a short announcement about the location of emergency exits. The fire extinguishers are all very visible, so I am not concerned about that. And I'd want everyone who is working that night—custodians and support staff— to review the location of all AEDs, just in case there is a medical issue.*

Awareness of safety—and safety equipment—is definitely a priority.

**You:** *Great. Another good idea might be to have a security officer here, just in case.*

**Custodian:** *That's all I can think of at this point. Are we forgetting anything?*

**You:** *I think I'll call a colleague of mine and see if there's anything else we should think about. And I'll stay in contact with the city's event coordinator; we can solve problems as they arise. The event ought to be a lot of fun! Thank you for your help in managing it!*

Even in the first year, a building principal needs extensive knowledge and understanding about the school building and the space surrounding it. There is a direct correlation between how the school is cared for and the effectiveness of the learning environment, and, thus, the resulting pride that students and staff have about their building community. For that reason, the principal must make it a priority to know and understand the facility, and then oversee the appropriate use, updates, and upkeep on an ongoing basis.

# Managing Your Budget

### 15

### Scenario 1: The Plan

*You sit down with your administrative secretary, whose job description includes managing your school's financial transactions, to strategize how to allocate money for the year. You will be relying on her extensive experience, as well as her understanding of how the previous principal allocated funds.*

### Scenario 2: The Problem

*In your first meeting with the principals of other schools in your district, the district's treasurer gives everyone a spreadsheet summarizing general supply money that rolled over in the budget from the previous year. The treasurer explains that this is the amount of money you have to start the school year. You stare at the sheet in dismay. It appears you will begin your year with only a couple hundred dollars, but you see from the spreadsheet that your colleagues all have many thousands of dollars. You realize you've taken over from a principal who clearly wanted to go out with a bang; he spent the budget down to the very limit. After the meeting, you ask the treasurer for a few minutes of his time.*

### Scenario 3: The Windfall

*In the spring of your first year as principal, your district went on the ballot with a bond issue. After a long and difficult campaign, the issue narrowly passed. The superintendent calls to tell you that in January of this—your second year—there will be $20,000 added to your bond account. You blanch. What does that mean?*

These scenarios describe situations you may find yourself in as the person ultimately in charge of your school's budget. In many cases, you will have an administrative assistant or treasurer who will help you manage the money coming in and the money going out, but you are the one responsible for decisions about spending.

Managing a budget is something I felt very wary about when I first started as a principal. I took the responsibility very seriously; I knew I was dealing with taxpayer dollars, and I wanted to make sure I spent it responsibly. And secretly, I was afraid of making a mistake. I knew of administrators who had gotten into trouble for managing money poorly, making decisions that were too self-serving, or being careless about financial budgeting and record keeping.

The fact is, a school budget is quite complicated, and it is made up of many subsets. Depending on the size of your school, there are budgets for almost everything—the music program, the theater program, athletics, academic departments, student services, special education services, and on and on. In many cases, the principal is charged with overseeing all of these budgets—or at least overseeing the person who oversees these budgets. It is an enormous responsibility and one that cannot be taken lightly.

When I was a new assistant principal in a middle school, I had very little to do with the budget, and I was happy to keep it that way. The principal made all the financial decisions, from creating the budget in the spring to making financial choices throughout the year. She worked with the district's finance department to reconcile the school's checking account, develop purchase orders, manage fund-raising efforts, spend funds from local bond revenue, and so on.

That year, though, a neighboring school district was shaken by a financial scandal. The president of an athletic booster club was convicted of embezzling thousands of dollars over the course of a few years. He'd adjusted numbers in the organization's financial records, skimmed cash from ticket and concession sales at sporting events, and reported bogus expenses and taken the money as his own. It was a big story in our city; headlines and reports were splashed all over local media outlets, and many people took to comment boards to weigh in on the situation.

The topic came up in a casual conversation with my principal soon afterward. I expressed that I *never* wanted to be responsible for public funds or be charged with managing a budget. It was too scary to think about what could happen if I made a mistake. In her trademark fashion, my principal briskly informed me, "Well, it sounds like it's time to teach you how it's done."

"Um, I'm not sure I want to learn. Because then I may have to do it."

"You need to learn to do it so you can do it right," she replied. "There is absolutely nothing to be frightened of. As long as you follow protocol, have some checks and balances in place, and keep a close eye on money coming in and money going out, you won't have to worry a single second about managing a budget."

## Strategies and Solutions for Managing Your Budget

Being in charge of a budget of many thousands of dollars can be a scary thing. Even scarier is that everyone in your school community will look at you as the expert. In your first few years as a principal, you'll probably feel like you ought to know much more about managing a school budget than you actually do.

I'm happy to pass on the wisdom passed down to me by my mentor, and I'll present it to you as she presented it to me: broken into steps.

## Step 1: Meet with Your District's Treasurer

I'm convinced that most school district treasurers have brilliant minds; every one I've worked with has a deep, clear understanding of school finance and can answer questions beyond my scope of understanding. They know all about state law in regards to school funding, and they seem to effortlessly and simultaneously manage huge amounts of money, be the financial expert for a whole school community, and help countless people avoid financial missteps. I admire them a great deal, because the legal ramifications of a single mistake could be both personally and professionally catastrophic for them. But they seem to do it all without breaking a sweat. For those reasons, it's a good idea to make the treasurer an ally and a resource.

**Ask a lot of questions.** When you are hired, it makes sense to call your district's treasurer (or the designee that works with budgets) to ask some basic questions. *What is my role in managing my budget? How much money am I allocated each year?* As you receive answers, your questions will grow more complicated. *How do we reconcile our accounts? When do we open and close purchase orders? When are accounts replenished? Do unspent funds roll over to a general fund?* Depending on your district, you may have anywhere from exclusive control of your building's funds to very little control. Only by asking specific questions will you determine how it will work in your case.

**Request specific training.** Even after asking questions, you may need some time to sit down with a treasurer or business manager to discuss specific systems that your district utilizes to manage building-level finances. Again, if you are in a large school, you may have someone in your building to manage all of this; if not, it will be important for you to learn. The training may cover the intricacies of the district's financial reporting system, which can generate

budget summaries, manage purchase orders, produce fiscal out-
lines, handle bond funds, and so on. The more you know, the better!

## Step 2: Make a Plan

Assuming you will have a large amount of control over your building's budget, and assuming you have a good understanding of how
much money you have to work with, it's time to make a plan for
how you will allocate it.

**Determine your priorities.** What do you, as a leader, value
the most? What would you like to address immediately, what do
you *need* to address immediately, and what are the financial implications of those decisions? You may wish to increase the number
of books in the library, update aging custodial equipment, replace
classroom furniture, or improve science labs and literacy rooms.
Take some time to think carefully about your priorities for the
year, what existing programs need support, what materials and
resources are needed to support instruction, and any upcoming
maintenance or repairs that will be required. I always make a "wish
list" of everything I'd like to purchase, from new crayons to a new
snowblower, and I number them in order of priority. My spending
plan emerges from this list.

**Take a look at the bigger picture.** If you are part of a large
district, there may be plans for spending district money that
change how you will allocate money in your budget. Your central
office may have specific plans for capital improvements, equipment replacement, furniture or technology updates, maintenance
issues, and so on. Make sure you know what will be taken care of by
district funds as opposed to building funds.

**Set up an emergency fund.** Just as with your home budget,
you won't want to count on everything going exactly as you'd
planned. There will be unexpected equipment failure you will need

to get repaired, teachers will come to you with requests for financial support for new initiatives or ideas that you want to support, or something that you've budgeted for may turn out to cost more than you'd anticipated. I keep a cushion of several thousand dollars in my general account to help manage these unforeseen situations.

**Audit yourself by having someone else be part of your financial decisions.** I rarely—if ever!—make financial decisions alone; rather, I ask my secretary or a colleague if my thinking is sound. I speak to *someone* about every single purchase I make. That way, there's someone else who knows about it and could speak to why a purchase was made and from what account it was paid.

**Work closely with your district's finance department.** I never guess when I'm unsure about something related to my budget. I call someone in the district's financial department whenever I have questions. They are never bothered; they'd rather I ask for permission or clarification than have to help me clean up a mess later.

**Gain an understanding of general costs.** School equipment, repairs, and supplies are notoriously expensive. The first time I heard about the price of certain items—bookshelves, copy machines, cafeteria tables—I thought there had to be an error. Even simple classroom chairs seem shockingly, outrageously expensive. But that is simply how it is—with the myriad safety regulations in place for schools and the legal ramifications that may arise from poor-quality furniture and equipment, we must purchase a particular grade of items for our school. And that costs a lot of money.

**Learn where you have control and where you don't.** There are some budgeting items you will not have control of—their use will be determined by district, state, or federal mandates. For example, in some states, special education spending is determined on a per-student basis. The amount of money you receive, allocate, and spend will depend on the number of students with an IEP. This is true of several other programs, too. So it's important to know what you will manage in your budget and what has been predetermined for you.

**Find out what works best for your school.** As you decide how to allocate resources, think about what your school needs. For example, I have worked in buildings where the principal took the amount set aside for general supplies, divided it by the number of teachers, and told them they had that amount of money to spend. Period. I have also worked in a building where the principal "gave" no money to staff but, rather, made decisions individually and on an "only-when-you-need-it" basis. In both cases, the system in place worked very well for each respective school, but had the systems been switched, it would not have worked as well.

**Find out how things have been done in the past, and decide if that system still makes sense.** If you find that the previous principal's system was not successful, or there were financial decisions made that you cannot support, you may need to immediately begin asking questions and making decisions for change. However, if things worked well and budgeting allocations seemed fair and equitable and made financial sense, it's wise to keep things as they are, at least until you're experienced enough to change things for the better.

## Step 3: Implement Your Plan

After you have made a solid plan for how you will manage your budget, move to put it into place.

**Get approval.** Send a copy of the plan to the district treasurer for approval. I do this every year, accompanying the plan with a note asking him to look it over to see if there are any mistakes, oversights, or areas of concern. I encourage him to call me to talk it through, particularly if he has any suggestions for improvement.

**Get your team on board.** After you have your treasurer's approval, sit down with your administrative secretary and your administrative staff to share your financial vision for the year. Explain the plan and seek input or ideas from them. Once everyone understands and endorses the plan, contact anyone who will be affected by your decisions and communicate the plan as it pertains to them. As an example, I recently took over a building in which we decided to purchase general supplies for the whole staff and store them in a central area; each teacher then received an allocation to buy classroom-specific items. Because this was a change from their previous practice, I sent out an explanatory e-mail and encouraged anyone with questions to contact a member of the office staff. In my communication, I was open and honest about my reasoning, showing them the cost savings that would come with ordering general supplies in bulk. It helped everyone understand the thinking behind the change.

**Set a schedule for monitoring and management.** Throughout the year, check in at regular, established intervals to see if the plan is unfolding as you had anticipated. I ask my secretary to run a budget summary monthly so I know how we are proceeding with purchases and balances. If needed, I make adjustments. If things are looking tight, I suspend purchases for a while. If we have more money than I'd thought—much more fun than the alternative—I look back to my "wish list" and determine if I can make a purchase I may not have thought we could manage yet.

## Managing Your Money: Conversations to Support Responsible Budget Decisions

The scenarios at the beginning of the chapter all refer to situations you may experience in your first few years as a principal. The following conversations may lend some insight into how to manage each scenario.

## Scenario 1: The Plan

In this scenario, you are meeting with your administrative secretary, Susie, to talk about how to allocate funds for the upcoming school year. A large part of Susie's job is to handle financial matters at your school, and she brings a lot of experience and history to the position. You begin by asking her how things were done in the past.

> **You:** *OK, I'm taking a deep breath! I have a lot to learn about budgets, and I'm so glad you are here to help me. Let's start by talking about allocating general supply money to teachers. How did the previous principal manage this?*
>
> **Susie:** *He allocated $100 to every teacher, and they could spend it on whatever they needed in the classroom. They turned in their receipts to me, and I had him approve them before I reimbursed the teacher. The rest of the general supply money was left to me to order whatever was needed—copy paper, construction paper, staples, pencils, markers, and whatnot. We store them in the teacher workroom.*
>
> **You:** *Does that system seem to work well for everybody?*
>
> **Susie:** *It really does. The teachers tell me when we're running low on something, and I just reorder it online using our purchase order. It arrives in a day or two.*

You are learning what has worked best for the school in the past. The experience and expertise of your administrative staff is an invaluable resource.

> **You:** *What about other accounts? Related arts, gifted, special education?*
>
> **Susie:** *Yep. They all have their own accounts. Related arts first: The previous principal allocated quite a bit of money to physical education,*

*art, and music because a lot of the things those teachers need to pur-*
*chase are specific to their work—sports equipment, art supplies, sheet*
*music, and instruments. He would also allocate a significant portion of*
*the budget to the library because he felt like the library was a place all*
*students would utilize, so it was important to keep it updated with the*
*newest books and technology. That gets expensive, but he was very*
*committed to it.*

**You:** *I agree with his thinking, though. The library can be the center of*
*the school, but only if students want to go there—which they will, if they*
*like what they find when they go. I'd like to continue with that this year.*

## Here, you are establishing one of your main priorities.

**Susie:** *Now, in terms of gifted and special education, those allocations*
*are actually not in your control. The amount of money for both of those*
*is determined on a per-student basis. So we'll pull up the information*
*on how many students are involved in both those areas and multiply by*
*the amount determined by the state, and that's how much money goes*
*to those accounts.*

## Here, you are learning about programs for which you do not control funding allocations.

**You:** *That makes sense. Now, let's talk about equipment. I have worked*
*with the custodian to create a list of things I'd like to consider replacing*
*or repairing in the next few years, but I don't know how to prioritize it*
*without considering what funds are available to us.*

**Susie:** *There is the general equipment repair account. The previous*
*principal allocated $2,000 to handle small repairs. I see in this report*
*that last year we used it to repair several broken doors, for carpet clean-*
*ing, for the tractor we use for snow removal, and to resolve a couple*
*problems we had with clogged sinks that needed new pipes. Then*
*there is the equipment replacement account. Last year the principal*
*put quite a lot in that account because he suspected one of our copiers*

*would probably not last the year, and he was right—it didn't. We had to buy a new one in mid-January.*

**You:** *Is there anything you think may need to be replaced this year?*

**Susie:** *Nothing as expensive as a copier. There's been talk of a new laminator, and the garbage disposal in the kitchen has been acting up, but other than that we should be OK. The two of them together should cost about $2,000, whereas we spent $10,000 on the copier.*

## You are gaining an understanding of the cost of certain items.

**You:** *Great. So that's it for equipment and repair?*

**Susie:** *There's also the account for small equipment purchases—light bulbs, batteries, trash cans, and so on. Previously we just put about $500 in that account, and it always was just enough.*

**You:** *Maybe I should just mimic the previous principal's budget! It seems like everything worked very well. And while I learn about this whole budgeting thing, it seems silly to change anything.*

**Susie:** *I actually think that's smart. "If it ain't broke, don't fix it." With that said, though, there is one more thing to consider. The previous principal allocated some money for his technology budget because he planned to replace a set of computers in the science lab. Before we went ahead with that, though, the district office decided to use grant money to replace science computers throughout the district. That means the money the principal allocated was never actually spent.*

**You:** *And that means . . . ?*

**Susie:** *That means it rolls over into the general fund. So you have an unexpected additional $10,000 in that account.*

**You:** *Wow! That's great. But I think I'll wait until I know what our priorities should be before deciding how to budget that money. We may want to reserve it for unexpected expenses or emergencies. In the meantime, let's stay with the system that has worked in the past. Until I get settled in and learn more, I wouldn't feel comfortable doing things differently. So let's just pull up the budget from last year, make any updates we*

*need to, based on our carryover balance and accounts that operate on*
*a per-pupil equation, and we'll be set!*
**Susie:** *Sounds great. I'll do that now.*

By working together with your secretary, you have learned how things were done previously and decided the system still works; further, in learning about an unexpected fund rollover, you have decided to reserve the money for emergencies until your priorities are firmly set.

## Scenario 2: The Problem

In this scenario, you are in a principals' meeting with your colleagues, and the district treasurer has given everyone a spreadsheet that shows how much money is in each building's budget for the beginning of the year. Apparently the principal you replaced spent your building's budget down to almost nothing, while your colleagues all have a lot of money to use for the beginning of the year. After the meeting, you flag down the treasurer to ask him a few questions.

**Treasurer:** *Well, I can guess what you want to talk about—that terribly low number on the spreadsheet next to the name of your school?*
**You:** *Yes! My goodness, what happened?*
**Treasurer:** *Unfortunately, you are the victim of circumstances. Your school had a bad year in terms of things needing to be replaced and updated, so your budget was low anyway. But the retiring principal made the decision to give all of his teachers several hundred dollars to spend however they wanted to improve their classrooms. So most of the remaining money in his already strained budget was spent.*

You are gathering an expert's perspective on how things were done in the past.

**You:** *That's something a principal can do? Spend down everything?*

**Treasurer:** *Absolutely. It's not generally done—most principals want a carryover of several thousand dollars—but it is within a principal's rights to do so.*

**You:** *So what can I do about this? I have no money to buy supplies or resources—or anything.*

**Treasurer:** *Well, the good news is that many repairs and replacements have occurred, and the teachers are now well supplied. My advice is just to tell the staff that until the budget is replenished with operating and bond funds, there will be no purchases.*

**You:** *Yes, that's what I'll have to do. It also sounds like I need to figure out what has been recently replaced or purchased, and make a plan for managing the budget.*

Notice how you will be making changes to previous financial decisions, and you are going to make a plan for future purchases.

**Treasurer:** *Yes, that's a smart approach. If you'd like, I can go through all of the receipts and purchase orders so you know where money was spent.*

**You:** *I would love that. Thank you!*

**Treasurer:** *I would also be happy to go over your budget with you once you've got it almost finalized. I might be able to give some insight on how to carefully save money.*

Here, you're making a plan to tap district expertise to guide responsible financial decisions.

**You:** *Hopefully, by stopping all purchases for a time, and by being extremely careful about how money is spent, I can build up funds and have some wiggle room with the budget.*

**Treasurer:** *I always advise principals to have a cushion of money in their general fund account. Unexpected repairs or needs come up, and you'll want some money to be able to support those things. An emergency fund, so to speak.*

**You:** *I agree. It makes me nervous not having that cushion. That will be my goal for this year.*

It is essential to keep some money aside in the case of unexpected funding needs.

**You:** *I really appreciate your perspective on this. I'll give you a call to set up a time to go over past purchases and the year's budget. I also hope I can call you throughout the year to check in. I'm new to all of this and hope I can tap into your knowledge throughout the year.*
**Treasurer:** *I'm more than happy to help. We can check in often. Don't worry—we will get it straightened out. I promise!*

You are auditing yourself by discussing financial decisions with someone else, and you plan to keep a close eye on your financial plan throughout the year.

## Scenario 3: The Windfall

Your district narrowly passed a bond issue on the spring ballot, and the superintendent calls to let you know there will be an additional $20,000 for you to spend on improvements for your building. You don't even know how to begin.

**You:** *How much again?*
**Superintendent:** *Yes, $20,000. Don't get too excited, though—that actually isn't much money, given the cost of many items you'll want to consider.*
**You:** *What do you mean?*
**Superintendent:** *Well, as you know, the bond issue was for $10 million—most of which will be spent on exterior improvements on all buildings in the district. We are going to replace several HVAC systems, fix some structural problems that have crept up due to the age of some of our*

*schools, and replace almost all of our roofs. Bond funds need to be spent on something that will last more than five years.*

## Gaining a whole-district perspective can support better decision making at the school level.

**Superintendent:** *So we allocated $20,000 for each school to spend on things you need to replace at your school. Frankly, you could easily spend that amount by simply replacing student desks or updating your digital learning lab.*

**You:** *I'm learning that things cost a lot more than I had thought.*

**Superintendent:** *Absolutely. Because we need to buy from vendors that sell commercial-grade equipment and supplies. The upside is that commercial-grade materials last a long time, even given the wear that occurs from longtime student use.*

## Gaining an understanding of general costs is an eye-opening experience.

**You:** *Do you have an idea of how I should allocate the $20,000?*

**Superintendent:** *Well, you've had some time to take a look at your school. What are some things you think need to be updated or improved?*

**You:** *Well, of course we could use updates in technology. The teachers have mentioned that we need new laptops and tablets. I agree with them to an extent, but I feel like there are other things we need to focus on for now. Funny you mentioned student desks. In many of our classrooms, we have desks that are old and damaged. They don't match, and they are all different styles and sizes. As a result, many of the rooms look messy and disorganized, and I worry about the effect that has on general climate and morale.*

**Superintendent:** *That would definitely be a good way to spend the money—updating classroom furniture. What else have you noticed?*

**Note the need to prioritize spending decisions.**

> **You:** *The sound system in the gym is terrible. Using the public-address system is painful. It is full of static, and the volume is difficult to manage. Sometimes it cuts out altogether. That PA system has marred many athletic events, music performances, and student assemblies.*
>
> **Superintendent:** *Again, a great idea. Unfortunately, those two items alone could add up to more than $20,000.*
>
> **You:** *And I could think of several other things I could replace or improve.*
>
> **Superintendent:** *Why don't you discuss your list of priorities with the treasurer? He will go through each item and can put you in touch with the best vendors to maximize the impact of your dollars.*

Input from the district's financial department can provide valuable clarification and guidance for new principals facing budget decisions.

> **You:** *Sounds good. I appreciate your insight. I'll keep you updated with how things progress.*
>
> **Superintendent:** *Great. Have fun with it. Even though the money won't go very far, it will be nice to think of ways to make your school look more updated or work more smoothly.*

As you grow more comfortable with the policies and regulations to which you must adhere, you'll find that managing your school's budget can be an enjoyable challenge. Once you know the rules, you can make a list of priorities to best allocate your money, keeping an eye on your ultimate goals for your school and your students.

# Planning for Growth and Change

**16**

## Scenario 1: Setting Goals

*You have been a principal for a full year, and you feel like you have a handle on the basic day-to-day operations at your school. You are having your evaluation conference with your superintendent, and one of the first things he asks you relates to your goals for the upcoming year. You are glad you have considered this beforehand, and you pull out a short list of goals you have set.*

## Scenario 2: Making Plans

*After sharing your goals for the upcoming school year with your superintendent, it's time to think about action steps you will need to take to actually meet these goals. You brainstorm with your assistant principal and make a plan.*

## Scenario 3: Communicating Change

*You have worked with several stakeholders to develop a plan for your school's future growth. One of your action steps involves making a significant change in the school's master schedule. This will have big implications for the teachers and the students. Before you roll out your plans to your staff, you meet with the president of your district's teachers union to get her input.*

In your first few years as a principal, you may not be thinking much about setting goals for the future given that you're focusing so much attention on managing your school's day-to-day operations. But the future is coming, and you'll want to be ready for it. If you're like me, one of the things that drew you to administration was the chance to become a transformational leader—to make real, lasting improvements in the lives of both the teachers and the students you serve.

The typical advice given to new principals is that there should be "no changes in the first year." I agree with this advice, provided, of course, that there isn't anything unreasonable, unfair, or unsafe going on that you need to change. On the whole, it's best to be reserved about making changes until you have a very strong understanding of why things are as they are. You'll damage both your credibility and a big chance to build trust if you go in and start changing things too soon and without reason.

I was reminded of this truth recently when, as I mentioned in the Preface, I was reassigned to a different building in my school district. The principal leaving *that* building was taking over my school; basically, it was a principal swap. Although I was still working in my "old" school, wrapping up the last several weeks of the year, I immediately began receiving e-mails and calls from staff at my "new" school. I was invited to attend meetings to plan the next year's schedule. I was asked questions about the service delivery model. I was asked to make decisions on budgeting, facility use, summer school programming, and even the colors for the summer painting project. I decided to place a phone call to my fellow principal, the one whose place I would be taking and who would be taking mine. Thankfully, she is a friend, and this made the conversation easier.

"Are people from my building contacting you and asking for your input on a whole pile of things?" I asked.

"Yes!" she wailed. "Things are so busy this time of year. I feel like I can't wrap things up here successfully because I'm so busy making decisions about another school."

"I get why they are reaching out to us," I acknowledged. "They want us to have a voice in how things will be next year. But I don't know the history of your building at all, so I don't know why decisions were made in the past. And I don't know anything about the actual facility. Heck, I don't even know where the school clinic *is*, much less what *color* it should be!"

"I also have a hunch that the people reaching out to us are the most aggressive and opinionated in the school," she answered. "They may also be the most dissatisfied with current leadership. So people are calling you because they're unhappy with things I've done here. They want to make sure you hear their voices immediately so you'll change things to the way they want them to be. And vice versa." It was an excellent point.

We commiserated awhile, and then we turned toward solutions. Ultimately, we agreed each of us would ask our staff not to contact the other; we would point out that, for the remaining several weeks of school, all decisions would be made by the current principal, the one who actually knew the workings of that building, that budget, and that staff. We agreed to support one another's decisions out of professional respect and good faith. If I didn't like how she set up the building schedule, how she allocated money, or what colors she picked for the paint crew, well, I'd just have to deal with it. And she'd have to deal with my decisions, regardless of whether she would have made the same choices or not. It turned out to be an excellent decision. When we started the new school year, we spent time observing, asking questions, and figuring out the reasons behind decisions that had been made in the past. Only then were we ready to think about things we wanted to adjust, improve, or overhaul completely.

## Strategies and Solutions for Planning for Growth and Change

A new principal will always gain a better understanding of the school's needs when there is time to watch, listen, and learn. Once you've equipped yourself with that understanding, though, you're ready to solidify a vision for the school's future. Whether it's an academic program, operations, or use of staff and facility, there will be things you want to change to make your own, and there will be things you wish to improve upon. Here are some strategies for going about it.

**Ask yourself pointed questions.** Before making a plan for your school's future, run through the questions that will point you in the right direction:

- What issues do I need to address?
- Are teachers as effective as they should be?
- What can we improve upon?
- Are there staffing changes I need to make? Are there any teachers who may be more effective in a different teaching role, or teachers who would do well with a different challenge?
- Are we effectively using research-based instructional methods in all classrooms?
- Am I comfortable with grading and homework practices?
- Am I comfortable with the level of understanding our parents have about what is happening at school?

- Are teachers and support staff speaking in the same terms? For example, does "differentiation" and "formative assessment" mean the same thing to everyone?
- What do our data say about the needs of our students?

**Develop and write goals.** After determining the answers to these questions, it's best to pick two or three areas of particular focus and turn them into specific, measurable goals for the next few years. The goals should be set for three to five years to make sure the staff has time to really get to know your goals and commit to them. Write them down in a simple, clear format you can use to share with others.

**Limit and prioritize your initiatives.** It's wise to keep your list of goals small. You want to avoid spreading yourself—your focus, your energy, your to-do list—too thin, so focus on just two or three things you'd like to change. Make sure you prioritize based upon the most pressing issues and those that have the most effect on student learning. Simply asking yourself, "What will have the biggest impact on student growth?" will lead you to good decision making about priorities.

**Identify key stakeholders and seek their buy-in.** When you have ideas for growth and change, you will want support when you roll them out to the staff and community. Without some initial behind-the-scenes "legwork," you risk finding yourself standing all alone to face any resistance. So, early in the process, present your plans to some important stakeholders—people you know will understand your purpose and help you promote it.

Recently, I presented an entirely new process for our end-of-day dismissal that would get our students on the buses in a safer and more efficient manner. The previous process had been cumbersome and fragmented, leading to significant frustration from parents, students, and teachers, so I knew a change was in order. But I also knew my new plan had to be carefully researched and strategically designed for it to succeed. So I reached out to everyone I needed in my corner. I met with personnel from the district transportation department and our bus drivers. I pitched the plan to my assistant principal, office staff, and school leadership team. I even shared it with a group of highly involved parents. In each case, I asked, "Do you think this will work? Can you think of anything I've not considered? On the first few days of our new plan, could you join me outside to make sure everything works as we hope it will?" By the time I presented the plan to the entire staff, I had a whole group of people who'd given my plan a stamp of approval and were willing to help me put it into action.

You can identify key stakeholders by asking yourself questions like these: *Who cares deeply about the daily operations of the school? Who volunteers a lot of their time to help out? Who are the obvious leaders? Who can help me communicate new initiatives and help me put them into action?* Here's a starter list of stakeholders and when their assistance tends to be most valuable.

- *Principal colleagues*—when a change may affect other schools; for anything drastic that may leave your community comparing initiatives between schools
- *Assistant principals*—when you will need a lot of help and support explaining, supporting, and implementing changes
- *Teacher leaders*—when you will need teachers to be the communicators and catalysts for change; when you need a historical perspective on what has worked and what has not; when you're looking to generate ideas and anticipate barriers
- *Student leaders*—when you're looking for perspective on the day-to-day effect of changes; when you need to ensure buy-in from the larger school community

- *Support staff*—when you want *all* staff members to feel heard and be willing to be part of the change
- *Representatives from the bargaining union*—when a change might lead to contractual problems; when change is likely to be uncomfortable for teachers
- *Your supervisors*—when you need assistance clarifying your vision for change; when you anticipate bumps in the process
- *Community partners*—when the change will benefit from community support or communication assistance; when a change involves mentoring or volunteering
- *PTO members*—when you need parents' perspective on change; when you need assistance clarifying and communicating a change to the larger school community
- *Aggressive, opinionated, "bulldog" parents*—when you need someone to serve as the ultimate barometer for a change's potential success or failure; when you need bold and loud support for new initiatives among community members

Although you will be held responsible for the success or failure of your school's growth and change, you should continue to involve these stakeholders, as well as those who are likely to be most directly affected by your proposed changes, as you develop your future plans. Their input and perspective will be invaluable when making decisions about the future.

**Be specific about roles and deadlines to push your initiatives forward.** When talking about plans for the future, it's easy to be vague about who is actually supposed to *do* something. It is a lovely experience to gather as a group and chitchat about goals—especially lofty ones—but all too often, the conversation is the end of things because no one actually takes action. As a leader, it is your job to point out exactly who is supposed to do what—and when.

**Decide how you will check in and monitor progress.** After you have identified your stakeholders, you will need to determine a process of regular communication to coordinate efforts and make sure everyone meets their individual goals on schedule. Will you bring them together in a more official capacity, establishing a school committee or group ("Leadership Team" and "Principal's Advisory Council" are popular names) with regularly scheduled work sessions? Or will you interact with them more informally, only seeking input when needed? Either way can be successful—what works for you will come down to your personality and leadership style.

**Be open and honest, and own your flaws.** When you talk about schoolwide goals, it's always wise to admit it when there are areas where your knowledge is lacking and issues you're not sure how to solve. This honesty is an essential building block for trust and effective collaboration.

When I assumed the principalship at my new school building, I had been told that the master schedule needed a major overhaul. Because of inconsistent "sections" of classes at each grade level, teachers did not have a common planning time, which presented a domino effect of challenges. Although I knew I should avoid making big changes in my first year, I looked over the master schedule and decided this problem was important enough to address immediately. I grew determined to "fix" it right away. To that end, I completely rebuilt the schedule: I arranged all the classes in a different order, I adjusted class lengths, and I reassigned staff to various duties. I was convinced this brilliant idea was the solution to all our problems, but when I shared it with my leadership committee, they did not agree. They gently pointed out things I hadn't considered. For one thing, there was not enough classroom space to accommodate my suggested changes. Contractual language limited when and how I could use certain staff members. And I had forgotten to figure in the irregular schedule of traveling teachers. Rather than be embarrassed at what I'd missed (something that would have happened early in my career), I took responsibility for my naïve mistakes. I told them, "Well, I had good intentions, but clearly I acted too impulsively. I didn't gather enough knowledge about staffing and space before presenting this schedule to you." I tabled my proposal until such time that I felt confident I understood all the components involved in the building schedule. I have learned that when I stumble in this way, it's best to own it. I'll say, "Oops! I sure didn't think about that one!" I find that people trust me more when I can admit my flaws, smile about it, and move on.

**Be proactive in anticipating barriers that may come up, and prepare to think of creative ways around them.** Do your best to think ahead about things that may thwart your intentions. Will there be staff pushback? Does the negotiated contract prohibit some of the things you would like to do? Is there stipend money available to pay for time teachers put in outside of their regular workday? Are there resources you will need—and, if so, how will you finance them? There are a number of things that can block a plan for improvement, but if you think creatively about how to overcome such obstacles, you'll be prepared to deal with them when they emerge. For example, if you have a goal of providing professional development in a particular instructional area but do not have the funds to hire an expert or send a team to a conference, seek experts within your district or building who can lead PD for the rest of your teachers. Or if you want to put together a task force to study grading practices in your building but cannot have after-school meetings due to contractual limits, allocate some substitute teacher funds to get teachers release time to complete the work together. There are many ways to solve problems if you make it a point to think ahead and look beyond typical solutions.

**Get approval early, before taking even small first steps.** It's nice to get approval from your superiors—your immediate supervisor, the superintendent, and maybe even the Board of Education (if you work in a small district)—before implementing your plans for growth and change. When your leaders know what you want to do, they will be better able to offer support from the very beginning and when challenges arise. They will also appreciate being in the loop from the start, because if they are asked about some of your initiatives by staff or community members, they will be able to talk knowledgeably and positively about the ways you plan to improve your school.

**Be prepared to talk about your goals (again and again and again).** Earlier I mentioned that buy-in is important when you roll out your goals. Beyond the first introduction of the goals, though, you will need to talk frequently about them. Keep circling back around to what you're trying to do—and why it's important—by addressing the goals as often as possible. Since you will be working on your goals for several years, you will need to keep them at the forefront of the minds of students, parents, staff, and community members. As a result, everyone will be aware of what you're trying to do and might be more inclined to join you in your efforts.

## What's Next: Conversations to Support Your Plans for Growth and Change

When you start your work as a principal, and after you've taken some time to understand how and why your building runs as it does, it will be time for you to look forward to the future. In what areas can you seek improvement? What needs to change? How can you plan for your school's future?

Let's revisit the scenarios from the beginning of this chapter. Each conversation is an example of ways you can address your goals by planning for growth and change.

## Scenario 1: Setting Goals

You have completed your first year as a principal, and now it's time for your evaluation conference with your superintendent. Early in the conversation, he asks you to talk about your goals for the upcoming school year. You have already given it some thought, so you pull out your short list of goals to share with him.

> **You:** *I'm glad you asked about goals. I had thought about this, and I've written down what I am going to focus on next year.*
> **Superintendent:** *How did you come up with your goals?*
> **You:** *I took a look at all of our programs and asked myself a lot of questions. I studied how successful I felt we were in delivering excellent instruction, how we had structured our schedule and our programs, and if I was making the best use of the staff.*

You have begun your planning by asking some pointed questions.

> **Superintendent:** *That's a great starting point. How many goals do you have?*
> **You:** *Just two. I want to make sure I keep my goals manageable. And I've thought about them in terms of what I think we really need to address at school—the most important issues.*

Note how you are limiting and prioritizing your goals.

> **Superintendent:** *I think that's solid thinking. So let's talk about these goals.*

**You:** *The first thing I am going to focus on is our use of differentiation in the classroom. From my observations, teachers are doing their best to differentiate for the different levels of learning and kinds of learners in their classroom, but it continues to grow more and more difficult as the needs of students get more complicated. I would like to offer some specific, targeted professional development on differentiation.*

**Superintendent:** *How will you structure the PD?*

**You:** *I have several teachers in the building who I think really have mastered differentiation. I will be offering them some release time to meet with other teacher teams and discuss some of the things they know about differentiation.*

## Notice how you are thinking creatively to find ways to meet your goals.

**Superintendent:** *That sounds like it will work. What is next?*

**You:** *My second goal relates to special education. I have watched throughout the year, and I don't feel we're using inclusionary practices as much as we should be. I feel we have too many students pulled out of the regular classroom for instruction. In most cases, I think these students would be just fine in the general classroom, provided we were able to give them the proper support.*

**Superintendent:** *Tell me more.*

**You:** *I think we've been relying so much on a pullout model because that's just the way it's always been done, and no one has really thought to change it. I want to shift how we think. I'd like all teachers to think of themselves as teachers of all kids. We're a team in this together; after all, we all want every one of our students to have a positive, successful experience at school.*

**Superintendent:** *What is your plan for change?*

**You:** *I'm thinking we'll put some new expectations in place, such as having general education teachers and special education teachers meet to talk about students on a regular basis. They can discuss student* *needs and do some planning together. In each meeting, I would ask them to discuss each child's IEP, check on progress, and determine if each child is receiving the appropriate services. If not, the two of them could brainstorm other options and, together with the parent and the rest of the IEP team, amend the IEP. I think regular conversations will help the teachers build stronger relationships with one another so they will be able to come up with ways to provide instruction in what is truly the least restrictive environment for the students.*

**Superintendent:** *That sounds great. How will you implement these goals?*

**You:** *I have identified some leaders within the school. I worked with them a lot last year, and I know they will agree that we could improve in these areas. With their buy-in, I will roll these goals out to the staff in the beginning of the year, and we will continue to revisit them each month.*

Here, you have identified major stakeholders and have thought about how to ensure their buy-in and how to keep the plan for change on target.

**Superintendent:** *Well, I'm pleased with your plan. Keep me posted on how it goes, OK?*

**You:** *Thank you for your support!*

## Scenario 2: Making Plans

After sharing your goals for the upcoming school year with your superintendent, it's time to think about action steps you will need to take to actually meet these goals. You meet with your assistant principal, Carol, to brainstorm and make a plan.

**You:** *OK, it's time to get to work. The superintendent approved my goals for the next few years. As you know, the first goal centers on differentiation, and the second goal relates to our special education delivery model.*

**Carol:** *It occurred to me that the goals really are interrelated. If we can improve differentiation practices, general education teachers will be better able to provide instruction on the level needed for all learners—special education students included.*

**You:** *Exactly. They are interrelated. And that means we can gather a team of people whose work relates to both goals. We'll use their input to put specific action steps in place. Who comes to mind for you?*

**Carol:** *I'd like to hear from the special education teachers, our Response to Intervention committee, and perhaps the team leaders at each grade level.*

**You:** *I like that. Let's make a task force made up of any of those people who would be willing to guide our work.*

## You have identified your stakeholders, and you are planning to seek their input.

**You:** *How do you think we should communicate with them?*

**Carol:** *I'll e-mail them and ask if they are willing to help us out. Then, I'll create a shared document where they can record their responses to the goals. We'll plan a time to get together as a task force to talk about their responses.*

**You:** *Excellent. We can keep updating that shared document so we have a record of our thinking over time. It will help us reflect on our progress as we go.*

## You are starting to develop a plan for effective collaboration and communication.

**You:** *Now, let's be proactive and think of potential barriers to success. I think we'll need to have some professional development, which can get expensive. We'll have to think about how we can move things around in our budget so we can fund what we need.*

**Carol:** *I can think of another one. The people we ask to be on our task force may wonder when they will fit it in. They already feel overwhelmed*

*and stretched for time. And we may get pushback from the teachers'*
*bargaining unit if we ask for too much time.*
**You:** *I was thinking about that problem, and I think we can get the task*
*force together if we clear one morning a week of all meetings. We*
*could make it a sacred day where no one schedules planning meetings,*
*parent meetings, or IEP meetings. Instead, it can be our task force meet-*
*ing once a month, and then, the rest of the month, members of the task*
*force can share what we've been doing with their teams.*
**Carol:** *I like that! And I think the staff would like it, too.*

You are thinking creatively about how to overcome the barriers
you may face.

**You:** *So let's summarize. You will begin the communication to staff*
*members we'd like to work with on these goals, and you'll set up a*
*shared document to capture the thinking behind the work. Mean-*
*while, I'll start to think about professional development opportuni-*
*ties for staff, and I'll look for resources and possible experts. Let's*
*do this by the end of next week. Then we'll meet again on Friday to*
*finalize who is actually on the task force and determine a time to get*
*everyone together.*
**Carol:** *Sounds great! I can't wait to get started!*

Here, you have outlined specific responsibilities and set a time line.

## Scenario 3: Communicating Change

After working with multiple stakeholders to develop a full plan
for your school's future, one of your action steps involves making
a significant change in the master schedule at your school. This
will have big implications for the teachers' and students' typical
day. Before you roll your plans out to your staff, you meet with the
president of your district's teachers union, Dawn, to get her input.

**Dawn:** *Thank you for inviting me in to talk about the schedule. You indicated there are big changes coming?*

**You:** *Yes. As you know, I worked with several stakeholders this year, and we developed some ideas for changes to meet our goals. One of those changes involves revamping our master schedule. I wanted to get your perspective to make sure there isn't anything I've proposed that we can't do. I need to make sure my ideas still honor the teachers' contract.*

**Dawn:** *Thank you for thinking of that. It's definitely better to talk it through now. If you implemented your plan and it went against the contract, there would be problems there.*

## You are considering barriers that may get in the way of your plans for change.

**You:** *So what I am proposing is to shift to a block schedule format. That means science and social studies teachers would team together for a 90-minute block each day, math teachers would have a 90-minute block, and English teachers would have a 90-minute block.*

**Dawn:** *Can you tell me more about why you want to do this?*

## You must be prepared to talk about your goals and clarify your intentions in ways that stakeholders will understand.

**You:** *Absolutely. Our goals are simple. We are trying to develop our differentiation practices, and we are trying to improve our special education service delivery model. We think giving teachers more time with fewer students will help them have a better understanding of each student's needs, so they will be able to teach them at the most appropriate instructional level. And it will allow our intervention specialists to "push in" to the regular classroom more and get away from the pullout model we have been relying upon.*

**Dawn:** *So teachers will have each class of students for a longer period of time, but they will have fewer students, right?*

**You:** *Yes. With this format, there are fewer students on each teacher's roster, but they have them for a longer period of time. It does mean there are some staffing changes, though. I'd like your input on that issue, too.*

**Dawn:** *Like what?*

**You:** *Well, it seemed like a no-brainer to move to a block schedule, but then I realized it won't be that simple. To make it work, it's going to mean some teachers moving to different content areas. I'm struggling with how to get teachers' buy-in for a change this big.*

Here, you are owning your challenges as a leader.

**Dawn:** *Have you announced these plans yet? What kind of communication have you done so far?*

**You:** *I told the staff there are changes coming. The task force has been charged with getting input from staff members about who might be willing to change content areas and who are passionate about staying where they are. We plan to convene in one week's time to make a final plan.*

Note that you are getting input from stakeholders. It is clear what responsibilities have been assigned and when they need to be completed.

**Dawn:** *The staffing moves will be voluntary?*

**You:** *I hope so. If I don't get enough staff willing to move, though, I may have to reassign teachers to a different role. If that happens, I will certainly give you a heads-up in case anyone is upset and needs to talk it through with you.*

**Dawn:** *Staffing moves are within your rights. And I appreciate the advance notice. It will help me support the teachers while also supporting your building's goals.*

**You:** *Thank you. That will be a great help.*

**Dawn:** *In terms of the schedule changes, are you still in compliance with the negotiated contract in terms of planning time for teachers?*
**You:** *Absolutely. Teachers will still have their 200 minutes of planning time each week. In fact, in many cases, teachers will have more than the required planning minutes.*
**Dawn:** *Well, it seems you've thought of most of the important issues for teachers. I am hopeful you will have a successful implementation of your new schedule!*

By meeting with the president of the teachers union, you are both considering possible barriers and involving a very important stakeholder.

As you settle into your role as a principal, you will begin to have the time and insight needed to plan for your school's future. This is one of the most enjoyable parts of being a principal, because the energy and ideas that come when planning for future change are exciting.

# Hiring Quality Teachers and Supporting New Ones

### 17

### Scenario 1: The Hiring Process

*In the spring of your first year as a principal, the director of human resources calls you to confirm what you had already known—one of your teachers is retiring, and you will need to hire a new teacher for the position. You keep him on the phone so you can run through your ideas for hiring and get his approval for your process.*

### Scenario 2: The Candidate

*You are calling references for a candidate you are considering for a teaching position. You had a committee conduct interviews, and you also interviewed the candidate individually. Everything seemed to work well—the committee was accepting of the candidate, and all his answers seemed fine—but there's something nagging at you about proceeding with the hire. You study his résumé and realize he has not listed his previous principal as a reference. Intrigued, you do a quick online search, find out the name of the principal, and give him a call.*

### Scenario 3: The Brand-New Teacher

*After hiring a new teacher to fill a social studies position, you get him set up in his classroom and tell him about resources he can consult to begin planning his instruction. You also introduce him to the head of the department. You assume all is well. However, you are surprised when you stop in to visit the teacher after school a few weeks into the semester; he seems anxious and rattled. You ask him to have a seat to talk it through.*

Many books have been written on the best approach to hiring quality teachers and supporting new ones. It's an important task. It's often said that teachers are the single most influential factor in a child's educational experience. They can inspire, motivate, and push students to achieve beyond expectation, or they can be the reason a child dreads going to school. Teachers have an enormous responsibility each and every day, and that means the principal has an enormous responsibility, too—to find and hire the best possible teachers and support them in their work.

This chapter is divided into two parts. The first part will offer suggestions for conducting the hiring process in a way that will help you find the most qualified teachers. The second part will discuss how to support new teachers as they begin their career in the classroom.

## Strategies and Solutions for Making Hiring Decisions

In your first few years as a principal, you will notice that spring is an exciting, energy-filled time. Many end-of-year activities are taking place, the promise of summer is in the air, and students and teachers are enjoying the fruits of a year's worth of growth and leadership.

Although the current school year has not yet wrapped, you'll find yourself looking ahead to the one that will follow, because springtime is when the need for shifts in your staffing plan appears on the horizon. Whether it's teachers announcing their plans to retire, stay home with a newborn, or move to a new school or district or it's the district informing you that your school will be adding additional staff to meet rising enrollment, it's time to think about hiring.

When I first began my work as an assistant principal, I had no idea of the time, effort, and energy I would need to devote to hiring a strong teacher. I thought we'd call some candidates, run through some questions, and offer someone the job. It couldn't take all that long, right? Wrong.

Watching my mentor principal that first spring as an administrator, I noticed that she took hiring more seriously than almost anything else she did—as well she should have. She started with an exhaustive look at all the résumés that were sent to her before selecting about six strong candidates to interview. Next, she created an interview committee made up of various staff members, including a custodian, a guidance counselor, a secretary, and several teachers who would be working closely with the new teacher. She always made it clear that *she* would make the ultimate decision, but she wanted their perspectives in terms of personality fit and commitment to helping students learn and grow. She worked hard to prepare the committee for the interviews, effectively training them on how to listen carefully to a candidate's answers. Then, after the exhaustive interview process, there were extensive committee conversations, reference checks, and talks with the human resources department before any job offer was made.

As I first watched my principal work through her process, I remarked to her, "I had no idea hiring was such a big deal."

She looked at me as a wise mother looks at a naïve child. "The chance to hire a teacher is a huge opportunity, because it's a rare chance to find a new person who will bring new energy and ideas—someone who is eager to contribute and make our school a better place," she said.

I nodded. That seemed obvious.

"But it's also a huge responsibility. There is extreme pressure on me and the interview committee to 'get it right.' After all, hiring decisions have a long-lasting effect. Hiring the wrong candidate can affect instruction, student achievement, school climate, and staff morale for decades."

"I guess that's true. I hadn't thought about it like that."

"It's easy to underestimate the effect of a hiring decision—not only for me but for whoever follows me," she went on. "Long after I'm gone, the teacher we hire will be here, still having an impact, positive or negative, for 30-plus years. So it's important to hire well."

Every year, I have silently thanked her over and over again as she has been proved correct. Sorting through applicants, conducting successful interviews, and ultimately finding the best person for the job takes a great deal of time, thoughtful planning, and attention to small details. Here are some important steps you can follow to ensure you are successful in hiring quality teachers.

## Step 1: Develop a Committee

Having a committee of people conduct interviews for a teaching job is important because it ensures buy-in from staff who will be working directly with the new teacher. You need them to feel good about the person you hire.

**Get diverse representation.** You may wish to follow the example of my first principal and assemble an interview committee that will bring a wide range of perspectives. I always include a group of teachers who will be working directly with the candidate, but I also include a custodian, a guidance counselor, a secretary, and several parents. I find that large interview committees can be cumbersome, though, so if I have eight or more people involved, I break them into two groups. The candidate has interviews with both groups, answering different questions for each.

**Clarify roles—and that the final decision is yours.** Explain to the members of your interview committee what will be expected of them, outlining the complete process (see Steps 2–8). Although all the members of the committee will provide valuable input in the decision, ultimately it's you who will decide whom to hire. Be clear about this, even if being "directorial" is not part of your typical leadership style. It's certainly not how I generally operate, but I make a strategic exception here in order to protect my staff members. If the person hired turns out to be a disappointment, they can blame me rather than one another. Taking blame is something I'm perfectly willing to do if it preserves our school's sense of community.

## Step 2: Set Goals

When seeking to hire teachers, the committee should get together before the interviews and spend some time thinking and talking about what kind of teacher to hire in light of what the school needs.

**Provide guidance on hiring goals so that everyone is on the same page.** The following are typical considerations. When you meet with the interview committee, you might distribute a similar list and go through each of the points:

- *Education:* What license or qualifications are needed for the open position?
- *Experience:* Do we want a person who is brand-new, or should we seek someone who has worked in this capacity before?
- *Personality:* What traits and characteristics will fit well with our team?
- *Work history:* What skills and knowledge will help a person succeed in this job?
- *Priorities:* What do we want this person to value (e.g., student growth, subject-area expertise, collaboration)?

- *Leadership skills:* Is it a priority to find someone who has the potential to grow into a buildingwide leader?

## Step 3: Create a Time Line

There is often a sense of urgency linked to hiring decisions; it is easy to feel a need to fill an open spot as soon as possible lest another school hire the best candidate first. Yet scheduling the interview, finding references, and completing requirements from the district's human resources department can slow the process. Principals must find the balance between moving quickly and being careful, thoughtful, and thorough.

**Break the process into stages, and set dates for each.** Identify the number of days (or weeks) you will spend identifying candidates, conducting interviews, checking references, and ultimately offering a candidate the position. Specific dates that members of the interview committee can enter in their calendars will help them stay focused on this task and will set boundaries that respect their time and other responsibilities.

## Step 4: Narrow the Candidate Field

When a job opening is posted and the résumés begin to flow in, the interview committee should carefully study these résumés to build an interview list.

**Remember, résumés are only the first step.** Remind yourself and your committee members that résumés do not and cannot offer a full picture of a candidate. After all, many job seekers get help from a professional to create a flawless résumé. Résumés are a tool that offers initial factual information—college attended, degree earned, grade point average, breadth of experience. All of these should be evaluated with an eye to your list of hiring goals.

**Take communication skills seriously.** Having just warned about not taking résumés as the end-all, be-all, I will provide this caveat: if a submitted résumé describes a candidate who has the credentials and experience perfect for your needs, but you find spelling errors or grammatical missteps, consider that an enormous red flag. This may seem overly picky, but communication skills are an essential attribute for a teacher. Perfection is a reasonable expectation for a teaching candidate's first written correspondence with you.

## Step 5: Draft Original, Nonstandard Interview Questions

A quick online search will turn up many examples of standard interview questions, but the interview committee should invest some time to create more specific, pointed questions. Many colleges and universities aggressively train their graduates to have a successful interview, so applicants are often coached on how to answer standard questions very impressively. The challenge comes in creating questions that will reveal a detailed, authentic picture of each candidate's skill, knowledge, values, and focus in regard to the specific job you have available.

**Try "Why?"** Asking unique, unexpected questions that pertain to the specific job opening challenges candidates to communicate exactly what they will bring to your team. It is certainly within the power of a good and experienced group of professionals to write these kinds of questions from scratch, but there is a shortcut.

Not long ago, I worked with a team to fill an opening for a guidance counselor—a position that can have a significant effect on students, staff, and the entire school community. As we interviewed using a standard set of questions, we found we could dig deeper and even find the type of specific, insightful responses we were seeking simply by following a candidate's answer with, "Tell us why that is important."

For example, if we asked, "What will you prioritize as a guidance counselor?" we invariably got an answer like "Helping students will be my top priority." *Of course,* we thought. *We would certainly hope so.* So, seeking a deeper answer, we would say, *Tell us why that is important.* A weak candidate would stumble and struggle to find an answer; a strong candidate would refer to students needing a network of people to support their needs—teachers, parents, and a guidance counselor—and advocate a "team" approach to determining how to help students grow and succeed. *Helping students grow and succeed:* another phrase that tripped our stock-reply sensors. Again, we would ask, *Why is that important?* A weak candidate didn't know why it was important. A strong candidate spoke of a child's future—as an eventual contributing member of society; as someone who could and would be a part of the workforce; and as someone who would make a good partner, spouse, friend, and parent someday. Just for fun, we would often ask again, *Why is that important?* Our strongest candidates had a broad view of a child's future and his or her place in the world, and they knew their role was to help a child scaffold to that place. By using one simple word—*Why?*—we were able to dig deeper into a candidate's answers as a way to understand the candidate's core beliefs about working with children.

### Step 6: Conduct a Deep Analysis of the Interviews

When all interviews are complete, the interview committee should convene to discuss each candidate.

**Focus the interview debrief on question responses, not feelings.** Comments such as, "I really liked her!" or "He seemed like he'd fit in really well," are inevitable, but guide the conversation so that you delve into what the candidate's responses revealed about strengths he or she could bring and weaknesses that cannot be overcome. Here are some factors to consider:

- Did the candidate reveal a student-focused mindset?
- What responses gave insight into the candidate's potential for leadership?
- What responses gave insight into the candidate's pedagogical and subject-area knowledge?
- Did any responses suggest a need for additional professional development or training?
- What responses gave insight into the candidate's approach to teamwork and collaboration?
- Did any responses trigger concerns about the candidate's commitment to your school's educational goals and philosophy?

**Remember the difference between talent and skill.** Talent is harder to teach than skill. For that reason, even if a candidate doesn't have all the knowledge you'd like but has the passion and energy to learn, it's worth considering him or her for the position. It's a balance: What might the candidate bring to the position *naturally*, and what are you willing to provide in the way of support? This conversation should be part of every interview debrief.

## Step 7: Conduct Follow-Up Interviews

Unless there is a clear front-runner for the position, I conduct follow-up interviews individually with the strongest two or three candidates who emerged from the committee interviews.

**Present specific scenarios, and include some curveballs.** Ask your second-round candidates specific questions about their experiences, and ask them to respond to challenging scenarios.

Examples might include a difficult parent, a struggling learner, or a behavior or classroom management problem—use the list of strengths and weaknesses that the interview team identified to guide your choice here. You can learn a great deal about a candidate's poise, reaction to pressure, and willingness to seek help and support from a scenario response.

I should say here that many principals flip these two steps of the interviewing process; many will conduct individual interviews first, determining two or three candidates they would be comfortable hiring, and then leave the final decision to the committee. This system works very well for some principals, and I have also used this reversed version with great success. Ultimately, the process you use should be one that makes you feel the most comfortable. As long as you feel you are finding the best possible candidates, it doesn't matter which step comes first.

## Step 8: Perform Reference Checks

Reference checks are the single most powerful tool in the interview process. This step should *never* be skipped. Even if the résumé is perfect, the interview was seamless, and both you and the interview committee feel strongly about the candidate's selection, you *must* check references. Asking for honest feedback about qualifications, experience, and commitment to students will complete the picture you have about a candidate. Reference checks will reveal information about a candidate's character, work ethic and attendance and other hugely important details that will affect the work of the school.

**Take note of who is *not* on the reference list.** It is important to study the list of references provided by the candidate to note who is *not* on the list. If a candidate leaves out a student teaching supervisor or a principal, for example, it's wise to wonder—and find out why.

**Check references through personal phone calls.** When making reference checks, instead of relying on standardized checklists or e-mail, I always pick up the phone and make a call. Beyond just the answer to my questions, I can pick up additional information based on the tone the reference uses in our conversation (eager and proud? wary and hesitant?). I also listen for nonverbal cues (sighs, long hesitations) and subtle signs that give me pause (overly canned answers, avoidance of certain topics, overzealousness). Phone conversations also allow me to ask follow-up questions and have a dialogue. When I ask, "Can you tell me more about that?" or "Why do you think that is?" I am able to develop a deeper understanding of the candidate.

**Be wary of overly vague or overly positive reference calls.** If what a reference tells you about a candidate seems deliberately vague, or, conversely, overly positive but only in very general ways, take that as a red flag. References should speak specifically about the candidate's teaching skill or employability. If they don't, there may be something they are keeping from you. Sadly, some principals will give positive reference checks for teachers they want to leave their building. If something doesn't feel right, it probably isn't.

**Don't limit your calls to the reference list.** Typically, teaching candidates will include a principal and several colleagues or student-teaching advisors on their reference list, but those people may have a skewed positive view of a candidate. Understandably, in the short amount of time spent student teaching, the candidate has most likely put his or her very best self forward during that time. Also, not every reference gives the level of detailed information you are seeking, or, as I mentioned above, some may even purposely misrepresent the candidate. For these reasons, I try to reach beyond the provided list to call anyone else I can think of who could speak to the candidate's work ethic, attendance, and commitment to doing good work. For example, if a candidate previously held a job as a nanny or a waitress, I'll call his or her supervisors to ask nonteaching questions.

When an opening occurs in a school, it is usually a valuable opportunity for positive change. By following a careful, thoughtful process, and avoiding some simple missteps along the way, you increase your odds of hiring a truly excellent teacher who has the potential to enrich many aspects of your school's work.

## Strategies and Solutions for Supporting and Retaining New Teachers

Once a teacher is hired, it's tempting to relax and admire your neat conclusion to the hiring process. But the work has just begun. Now it's time to make sure the new teacher is welcomed, supported, and successful.

If you have hired an experienced teacher, there won't be as much to think about compared to the hiring of a new college graduate. An experienced pro will know his or her way around the classroom, and is likely to arrive confident and ready to get to work. Conversely, brand-new teachers tend to be very nervous and eager to please, endearing in their earnest desire to get *everything* right. They will need a different level of support, and they will be our focus in this second part of the chapter.

I always see myself in new teachers—or rather, I see the reflection of me almost 20 years ago. My first teaching job was in my hometown, where I was hired to teach 7th grade English. My principal handed me a curriculum guide and my classroom key, and left me to my own devices.

I was almost sick with anxiety in the days leading up to the first day of school and, in truth, for much of the year. I desperately wanted to succeed in the eyes of students, parents, colleagues, and my principal. But my task was monumental. There were 173 7th graders on my roster, divided into 6 periods of 28 students each. Again, these were 7th graders—hormonal, energetic, hilarious, challenging, jittery adolescents . . . 173 of them, *every day*. And because of space issues, I was teaching on a cart and scurrying all over the building to take over classrooms of intimidating colleagues. As if that weren't enough, I also coached basketball and cross-country. I was barely hanging on, and I felt very, very alone.

I was consumed by the job—by planning and teaching and grading countless papers, projects, and journals. I worked late into the night and most of the day on weekends. Although I felt my students were successful, parents liked me, and the staff had accepted me, by year's end, I was exhausted. Depleted. The idea of doing this all over again was hard to bear, and I was only finishing my first year of teaching.

But a relationship moved me to a new town several hours away, and I was able to get a new teaching job there. From my first interview with my principal, I knew things would be different. My new principal was enormously helpful, answering questions before I had a chance to ask them. She gave me her personal phone number and told me to call anytime. She introduced me to several teachers she knew would be glad to informally mentor me. And she checked in often—both casually and by inviting me to talk about how I was feeling. She understood the emotion, stress, and pressure of being a new teacher, and she made it her business to help me manage. I'm not sure I would have stayed in education if it hadn't been for her taking such good care of me.

I've never forgotten how much the support of a principal means to a beginning teacher, and I try to do my best to emulate what was done for me. What can you do to help new teachers stay on top of their workload, manage their stress, and remain happy with their career choice? Here is my advice.

**After the hire, outline next steps.** When you offer a candidate a job, he or she will be full of joy and relief, and then will wonder, "OK, now what?" Be prepared to have a thorough answer to that question. You will need to explain the process and time line for being approved by the Board of Education, identify any orientation or training requirements for new teachers, and talk about payroll and insurance paperwork. Typically this happens through a human resources department or central office, but if you are in a very small district, some of this responsibility may be yours. Teachers will be most interested in how and when they can get into their classroom to get started, so you will want to set up a time to give them a tour of the school and get them keys to their room.

**Give them what is needed.** When you meet with new teachers to get them settled in their classroom, take a look at the room together and determine what they need to get started, from furniture to pencil sharpeners. Depending on the situation, the departing teacher may have left many resources and supplies—or left none at all. Create a list of things that may need to be moved from other classrooms or, perhaps, purchased. I always budget extra money for supplies for new teachers; although they are often willing to spend their own money, they are the least equipped to afford it. I find that when I am willing to purchase what they need, they are always extremely grateful, and it is a great first step in building a relationship of trust and loyalty.

**Hook them up with a great mentor—or three.** Your district and state may have a required mentor program, which will be an excellent resource for the new teacher. Make sure you have done what is required to get the two connected and working together. Beyond formal mentors, though, it's also a good idea to connect the new teacher with several informal mentors. I do this by selecting veteran teachers whom I think will have a compatible personality and will grow into friends as well as colleagues—veterans who can help the new teacher learn the culture of the school and all the little nuances about how things work. I'll call the veteran teachers and say, "I've just hired a new teacher, and I really think you will get along well. Would you be willing to reach out to her and take her under your wing?" They are always happy to help out the "new kid," because they are complimented that I trust them to do so; it also makes the new teacher feel like he or she has a few friends when school starts.

**Check in often.** I think back to how lonely I felt in my very first year of teaching. I was quite a bit younger than most of the other teachers in the building, and my principal definitely had a sink-or-swim approach. That's why I always assume new teachers are feeling a bit like that, and I work hard to make sure they don't feel alone. I stop by their room in the mornings or after school, I sit with them at lunch and ask how they are doing, and I invite them to my office to talk through any stressors or struggles they are having.

**Make a special effort to acknowledge their hard work.** I make sure I recognize the efforts of new teachers. I'll say, "I see how hard you're working in the evenings, and I've seen your car is in the parking lot often on Saturdays. I appreciate the extra time and effort you are putting in." I tell them that the first year is the hardest, but reassure them, "Trust me. It gets a little easier each year."

**Encourage often.** I try to be as positive and encouraging as possible to new teachers. When I see something good happening as a result of teachers' work, I write a quick note and slip it in their mailbox so they know that I noticed. I give them frequent feedback when I see them in the halls or in between classes. "I really enjoyed watching you interact with your kids this morning" or, "That was a really powerful discussion occurring in your Honors English class" takes just seconds for you to say, but it will make the teacher feel so good to receive your approval.

**Act quickly if there is a problem.** If I see a teacher struggling, I act quickly to provide support—someone to help plan, an observation with a master teacher, access to better resources—and check in often for signs of improvement or growth. I feel that if a teacher fails in the first year, it may well be my fault for not offering the necessary support.

**Remind them about balance.** Sometimes, new teachers will work themselves at a frenzied pace—teaching, coaching, advising clubs—and may need you to step in and give them permission to step away. I recently hired a teacher who, quite literally, stayed at school every night until after dark and worked most of the weekend, too. I encouraged her to take time to enjoy her family and friends, but she seemed unable to. I finally sat her down and told her I wanted her to take a personal day. "You are on a direct path to burnout," I told her gently. "If you don't fill your life with other things that are important to you, I guarantee you won't last as a teacher." She cried and confided that she had too much guilt to step away. I replied, "Well, I'm insisting on it. So guilt doesn't really have a role in this, OK?" I also told her I'd help her find ways to be more efficient, because it shouldn't be as hard as she was making it.

In time, with many reminders, she was able to find a good balance between her teaching and the other parts of her life.

**Know when to dial back the support.** As you see your newer teachers gain confidence, make strong collegial relationships, and excel in their work, it will be time to step back and relax your supportive net. You can continue to help them grow by looking for leadership responsibilities, or provide different kinds of professional development to stretch them as teachers, but they will need you less and less as time goes on. When this happens, you can applaud yourself for a job well done. Much like a parent watching a child leave the nest and enter the "real world" with confident readiness, you will feel proud to see your new teachers growing into veterans.

## Building a Solid Staff: Conversations to Help You Hire, Support, and Retain Quality Teachers

The tips in this chapter are all meant to help you in one of the central responsibilities you will have—the hiring and retention of quality teachers. It's important to dedicate the right amount of time and energy to the process so you make sure you get the right people in the right positions.

We will now revisit the scenarios listed in the beginning of the chapter. In each scenario, we will go through a conversation that may occur as you work through your hiring process.

### Scenario 1: The Hiring Process

In this scenario, you are talking with your district's director of human resources, Jim, about a teaching vacancy that is coming as a result of a retirement. You ask for his perspective on your plans for hiring the new teacher.

**Jim:** *Hi! I'm calling to tell you I got an official retirement resignation letter today from one of your teachers.*

**You:** *Yes, Gloria had told me she was sending it in. I hate to lose her; she's been a great teacher for us. She's excited about retirement, though.*

**Jim:** *Good for her. It's an opportunity for you to hire someone to fill her spot, though. I wanted you to know that now that I have her letter in hand, we can post her position on our district website and begin reviewing applications. Then, it's up to you to hire whoever would be a good fit for your building.*

**You:** *That's great. Since I'm new to this, though, would you mind talking me through the process I'd like to use? Since she told me she was retiring, I've thought a bit about how I'd like to approach it. But I'd love your perspective.*

**Jim:** *Of course! That's what I'm here for.*

**You:** *Well, first, I'd like to make a committee of several teachers and support staff—people who are going to work with the new teacher frequently. We'll get the committee together to talk through what qualifications and qualities we want our candidate to have. We will go through some of the résumés I feel are strong ones, and select about six candidates to interview. Then we'll work together to write interview questions that will give us great information on our candidates.*

Your approach is a solid one: develop a diverse committee that will determine what type of candidate you are seeking, help sort through résumés, and develop interview questions.

**Jim:** *That's a great start.*

**You:** *We'll block off a day to interview all of the candidates, and then debrief and decide who our favorites are.*

**Jim:** *And then? Will you interview the top two or three candidates individually?*

**You:** *Yes. Especially if the committee doesn't have a clear favorite.*

The committee has a vital role, but the ultimate responsibility and the final decision lies with you.

> **Jim:** *If you follow those steps, you'll be sure to get someone who is a good fit in your building.*
>
> **You:** *That's my hope. When I have determined whom I'd like to hire, I'll check references to make sure there's not something I missed.*
>
> **Jim:** *I think that's one of the most important steps in the process. It's what people say—or don't say—about your candidate that will solidify your choice.*
>
> **You:** *I agree. So you think this all sounds good?*
>
> **Jim:** *Yes. It sounds like you have thought out all the important steps. Give me a call if you have any questions, OK? Good job on creating a good, strong process.*

## Scenario 2: The Candidate

You have interviewed a candidate, Ajay, who impressed you a lot. Everything seems like it should be just right—but something feels a little off. As you are calling references, you realize the candidate did not list his previous principal as a reference. You do some quick research and find the principal's name—Senita—and phone number. You pick up the phone and give her a call.

> **You:** *Hello! Let me introduce myself. I am a principal at Riverview Middle School, and I'm calling about a reference check for a candidate at our school. His name is Ajay. Would you know him?*
>
> **Senita:** *Oh, yes. I know Ajay.*
>
> **You:** *He taught at your school this past year, correct?*
>
> **Senita:** *He did, that's correct.*
>
> **You:** *Do you know why he left?*
>
> **Senita:** *Well, he didn't. He's still under contract here.*
>
> **You:** *Oh! Did you know he was interviewing?*
>
> **Senita:** *Yes, I did.*

**You:** *Oh. Can you tell me a little bit about him?*
**Senita:** *Well, sure. What would you like to know?*

Note how the reference is being quite vague. This is a definite red flag.

**You:** *Well, first, do you know why Ajay is seeking to change jobs?*
**Senita:** *I sure do. It's something I encouraged him to do.*
**You:** *Do you mind telling me why?*
**Senita:** (Sigh) *Ajay is a complicated guy. He has worked here almost five years, and in that time, I haven't really been able to figure him out. His students like him, but that's mostly because his classes are seen as a bit of a joke. There is more casual conversation than there is teaching—a lot of "hanging out," I'd say.*
**You:** *That isn't good. Can you tell me more?*
**Senita:** *He doesn't seem interested in growing or making changes in his instruction. And when I meet with him and tell him I'd like to see improvement on what he is teaching—a more rigorous curriculum, for example—he nods and agrees and promises he'll change. But nothing changes.*
**You:** *Have you seen lesson plans? Are they well done?*
**Senita:** *I ask him to turn them in to me. He does it on an intermittent basis. When he does turn them in, I suspect they are plans from one of his colleagues and he has just changed the name at the top of the page. So they appear fine, but based on what I see in observation, it's not translating to the classroom instruction. And when he doesn't turn them in, he claims he has forgotten, but I don't buy that excuse because I send him frequent e-mails to remind him.*
**You:** *You say he's good with students?*
**Senita:** *Yes, they like him. And parents like him, because they hear their kids saying good things and all the kids get As. So they don't see a problem. The thing is, Ajay really is a great guy. Everyone likes him. Heck, I like him! He's funny and creative and completely laid back. He*

gets along with everyone. But in terms of being an effective teacher? I don't see it.

**You:** I'm so glad I called you. He didn't have you listed on his reference form.

**Senita:** I would be shocked if he did. I put him on an improvement plan this year, and it didn't go well. I did encourage him to seek other job opportunities, because if I don't see some improvement this next school year, we will probably not renew his contract.

You have discovered someone who was not on the candidate's reference list but should have been—and by making the call, you've gained valuable information as to why.

**You:** This has definitely been illuminating!

**Senita:** I wish I could be more positive—after all, it would behoove me if Ajay found another job—but I don't believe in doing that to another principal. We have to watch out for one another, you know?

**You:** I agree, and I'm grateful. If I can ever return the favor, please give me a call. Thanks so much, again, for your honesty.

## Scenario 3: The Brand-New Teacher

This scenario describes a teacher, Owen, who has just started his career as a social studies teacher. You help him get started in his classroom, give him curricular resources, and introduce him to the department head so he has a colleague with whom to work. Soon after school starts, you stop in to check on him; you are surprised to find him a bit of a mess. He's anxious and seems shaken up.

**You:** Hi, Owen! I stopped in to see how you're doing.

**Owen:** Oh, hi! Good . . . I'm good, I guess.

**You:** You sound unsure. Why don't you tell me more?

**Owen:** Well, I just didn't expect . . . well, I don't know. I guess I should have expected—it's just a lot, you know? I get here really early in the *morning, and I stay very late, but I can't seem to keep up. It's . . . well, I feel like I'm already behind, and I don't know why.*

**You:** *Well, first of all, this is a normal feeling, especially for a new teacher. And I'm here to support you; I'll make sure you get what you need. In order to do that, why don't you tell me where, exactly, you feel like you're behind?*

**Owen:** *I feel like my colleagues are much more efficient than I am; like, they can balance the grading, the planning, the classroom management, and the extracurricular activities they are charged with. I wish I had a better handle on all those things.*

**You:** *I remember that feeling myself. I remember looking around and feeling like everyone had it figured out except me.*

**Owen:** *Yes! That's how I feel.*

**You:** *Tell you what. I will secure a substitute for a few days, and you can shadow a veteran teacher, Mr. Phillips, for a day or two. You can ask all the questions you want about efficiency and management.*

## When you recognize there's a problem, take action right away.

**Owen:** *That would be good. It's really hard for me to admit I need help, but I am feeling a little lost.*

**You:** *Well, don't forget the positives. There are some great things going on in your room. I can tell your students enjoy your class, and I've heard them talking about it, so you are making nice connections with students. That's really important.*

## Noting the positive things you have seen in a new teacher's work is essential encouragement.

**Owen:** *Thank you. It's nice hearing that.*

**You:** *I know you're working really hard, too. I see you here late, getting your plans ready for the next day and keeping up with your grading. I know it's a lot to manage as a new teacher. Over time, it will get better because you'll learn some tricks on how to be really efficient in your* *work. Remember to make time for other things, too—family and friends and hobbies. I don't want you to burn out.*

You are acknowledging this teacher's hard work and reminding him that the first year is the most difficult. You are also reminding him about keeping balance between work and other things in his life.

> **You:** *Is there anything specific I can help you with? Maybe a particular task that you're struggling with right now?*
> **Owen:** *Well, soon I'll have to write my first assessment for our opening unit. I am a little nervous about doing it well.*
> **You:** *Why don't you have Mr. Phillips look it over? I've asked him to check in with you; I know the two of you will work well together. And if you need any other help with assessments, let me know. There are also some other experts on staff who would be glad to help.*

Note how you are bringing in mentors, both formal and informal, to support your new teacher.

> **You:** *I'll continue to check in with you, Owen. I think you're doing a great job, and I really think you will have a successful year. So I'll pop in often to see you, and you can always feel free to stop by my office, too.*

Notice your plans to check in often.

> **Owen:** *I appreciate it. It's nice to feel your support!*

Hiring quality teachers and effectively supporting new ones will have a direct correlation with the number of staffing, student, and parent problems you will need to solve. And it will have a tremendous impact on the overall success of your students. It's worth investing the time and effort to get it right.

# Maintaining Balance

## Scenario 1: A Scheduling Glitch

*You are a beginning administrator with three school-aged children and a spouse whose workday starts even earlier than yours. Your schedule is relatively predictable during the week. You are fortunate to have your mother-in-law living nearby. She gets the children fed and on the bus in the morning and ferries them to things like doctor's appointments. After school, you pick up the children from their after-care program, and together with your spouse, you oversee their homework, prepare dinner, and go through a bedtime routine. If you have a school event to attend in the evening, your spouse handles these duties solo. All is going well— until your mother-in-law calls and tells you she will not be able to help out this coming week. You and your spouse look at one another in alarm. What are you going to do?*

## Scenario 2: A Staff Member's Unexpected Absence

*You are the principal in a high school, and you have an excellent assistant principal who helps you lead the building successfully. Late one night, you get a call from your assistant principal. His wife has gone into labor a few weeks early, and they anticipate their baby will be born within a few hours. You can pick up in his voice—mingled in with his excitement and worry—a note of concern about everything that will be happening at school over the next few weeks. "Don't worry; we'll take care of everything," you assure him. "You just focus on your family." The next morning, you pull up the building calendar for the next three weeks. You make a plan and then draft an e-mail to your staff.*

### Scenario 3: A Predicament

*One evening after a long day at work, you arrive home to your wife, who meets you at the door with a happy smile on her face. She has wonderful news, she says: her sister is engaged to be married! This is wonderful news, but your heart sinks when you hear the date of the wedding. It will be the same Saturday as your high school's graduation—an event you are absolutely expected to attend. There are also the resulting graduation parties—all-day affairs held in homes throughout your community. It's a tradition for the principal to stop in at various parties to help celebrate the graduates' special day. How can you possibly do both—be there to support your wife and family, while also fulfilling your graduation obligations?*

When I speak to beginning administrators, time and time again I hear about how they are struggling to maintain balance between their work and home lives. Without setting some limits, the job of a principal can become all-consuming and exhausting. When that happens, people burn out, losing their love for educational leadership. Unhappiness on the job spills over into life in general, challenging relationships with family and friends. Of all the things to think about in this position, this might be the most important one of all.

But it's difficult to quiet the swirl of questions that pop up when we are advised to "seek balance." What will happen if you don't throw every ounce of your energy into your work? Will your school community think you aren't committed to them? Will your supervisors think the same? Will your teachers begin to question you? What if limits you set for yourself affect the students' educational experience? And if you don't set limits, what will happen to your relationships with family and friends? What will happen to your health?

When I talk about balance with colleagues who are entering the administrative field and they question how they are supposed to set limits while still giving the job the very best of themselves, I always respond the same way, and I'll respond that way to you now: *Relax. You're not that important.*

Don't misunderstand: you *are* important. You're the principal, and a lot of people are looking to you to be their leader. They need you to support them, solve problems, and make decisions. They expect you to endure and be strong and tough. But no one expects you to do this at the expense of your personal relationships and things you value outside of your work.

When I transitioned from the classroom to the principalship, I threw myself into the job with every bit of my time and energy. I arrived at school long before staff and students. I attended every after-school event, I worked late into the night, I came in on weekends to catch up on e-mail and make plans for the upcoming week. I spent all my time at school, only catching up with my friends in fleeting phone calls or dinner dates.

At the time, it wasn't actually a problem. I was in a place in life where I wasn't in a meaningful relationship, and my friends were largely doing what I was doing, so they understood limitations of time. I didn't have children. I lived in an apartment that required no maintenance. I was young and energetic, and I had ample time and enthusiasm to pour into my new job.

And for me, it ended in the best way possible because I was lucky enough to catch the attention of a crazy-handsome athletic director who was working the same outrageous hours. And he really understood the stress of my job, since he faced the same requirements and demands. Shared lunches turned into spending lots of time together, and eventually led to a wedding. But as our family expanded to four, my husband and I learned how important it is to step away from our work. We learned that to be our best selves on the job, we had to set boundaries between ourselves and the job.

## Strategies and Solutions for Maintaining Work/Life Balance

The solutions my husband and I figured out together are still in place in our home, and they've helped us both be better people— better spouses, better parents, and, yes, better administrators. Here is the advice we have to share.

**Put your family first.** As important as it may seem now, at the end of your career, you will find your job was just—yes, *just*—a job. Your family, in whatever form "family" takes for you, should be your highest priority, above everything else that consumes you during a day. Don't miss your son's tennis matches or your daughter's piano recitals. Go on a date with your spouse or partner. Stay with your mother or your best friend after her dental surgery. Attend your cousin's wedding. Make yourself a mental compass that has your loved ones firmly set due north, and check your direction regularly.

**Stay connected to your colleagues.** Being a principal can be a lonely job, especially if you do not have assistant principals working alongside you. You are alone in making decisions that may not be popular, you receive very few accolades for the things you do, and no one acknowledges the difficulty of your job. Nor should they, by the way—you are paid to do this work, and maybe even paid quite well. But there are times you will simply need to talk to someone who understands. Those are the times you pick up the phone and connect with a "principal friend." You may be seeking advice or perspective, or you may just need to spout off about how you're feeling to someone who will listen and, perhaps, offer insight. I have several "principal friends" I can call depending on what I need, and when I do, I come away from the conversation feeling supported and uplifted.

**Find activities outside of school that you enjoy.** Stay in touch with things you love to do that have nothing—nothing!—to do with your job. Reading, hiking, writing, gardening, cooking, vacations and road trips, sports, crafts, hobbies, watching movies— it doesn't matter what it is, only that you enjoy it and that it will stretch your mind in new ways. And when engaged in these activities, do all you can to be fully *there*, not distracted by things you are worried about at work.

**Don't eat like you work in a school.** It's a cliché, but clichés have immense wisdom in them: you must stay well to keep your mind focused and your body sharp. It's all too easy to get caught up in the whirlwind of your job and, at lunchtime, wolf down a cafeteria-issued corn dog or, worse, skip a midday meal altogether and then find yourself ravenous beyond logic as the day winds down. Don't live on a diet of coffee, cafeteria food, and whatever snack you can get your hands on when you have a few moments. Eat a healthy breakfast before work, pack a good lunch, and make time to unwind with a nice dinner. Allow your meals to be a time when you can slow down and take a few deep breaths.

Oh, and one more thing. If you are the principal of an elementary school, avoid those ubiquitous birthday treats. When a proud and lovely child comes to you with a cookie, donut, or brownie perched awkwardly on a paper napkin—*It's my birthday,* she will say with a sweet smile—give her the hug she deserves and wish her the best day ever, and then, when you're alone again, discard the treat or pass it along to someone in the office. In a large school, you'll get four or five of those treats a day, which could leave you wondering at year's end how you came to be carrying an extra 20 pounds.

**Exercise.** Being a principal is an active job; if you're doing it right, you won't spend much time sitting at your desk. You'll walk a *lot*. But to stay your best, healthy self, it is a good idea to regularly participate in an additional form of physical activity that will give you all the benefits of an exercise plan—stress relief, increased strength and flexibility, and the habits to keep you healthy for a very long time. Developing a regular, targeted exercise plan and carrying it out in whatever pocket of time that's available to you will be a great complement to your near-constant movement at work.

**Sleep.** Enough said.

**Turn off the technology.** It's very difficult to disconnect from the noise of life with technology so attached to us. We've got our laptops, tablets, and smartphones at our fingertips, and each device will pop up alerts every time someone contacts us. Social media can keep us in constant reach of the very people it would behoove us to take a break from. Do your best to leave your laptop in your office and refrain from checking e-mail or logging on to complete work-related tasks when you're at home. In my experience, doing so will allow you to return to work sharper, refreshed, and more effective.

**Make some regularly scheduled sacred time, and stick to it.** In our family, Sundays are days we Do Not Do Schoolwork. We laze around the house in the morning, and then we find something to do together that has nothing to do with work. Unless there is a true crisis (which is so rare I cannot even recall one), we do not work. Period. I recommend this plan for anyone starting an administrative job.

**Learn when it's time to walk away.** A wise mentor once told me, "You're never going to be everything to everyone, so don't kill yourself trying." There are times you should just get up, walk out the door, and go home—even though that means leaving tasks incomplete, leaving people dissatisfied, and postponing decisions and conversations. It will all be there when you get back. I've learned that, for me, the time to walk away is when I'm too tired to be productive, when my day has been a long one and I'm craving time away, and when I want to see my loved ones. Know your times when you should just *go*. Don't worry—you'll be back.

Similarly, after a long day (or week or month), when things have been especially challenging, I can get more exhausted than I realize—and, therefore, more emotional. It's best to avoid tricky or complicated conversations and decisions when you're not feeling mentally sharp. Try saying, "I recognize this is something important we need to address. Can we wait until I get some rest (or take a shower or have something to eat) so I'm in better shape to talk this through?" You'll avoid misunderstandings and arguments if you table conversations until you are prepared to handle them well. Moreover, taking time away from the conversation gives you an opportunity to pause, reflect, reprioritize, and come up with viable solutions to a problem.

**Get help when you need it.** One of my friends hired someone to clean her house twice a month because she was running herself ragged trying to manage the demands of her job with her need to have a sparkly clean home. She has often quipped, "The cleaning lady saved my marriage." She says it with humor, but it is a genuine truth for her. Hiring someone to clean her house helped her relax and enjoy her life—and be a better wife and mother. She also loosened her strict rules on having healthy home-cooked food for every meal; now, she and her family eat out twice a week and order takeout a couple times on weekends. Her kids don't always have packed lunches; now, they sometimes buy school cafeteria lunches. And things are much, much better. This applies at work, too; if you feel you won't be able to tend to all the things on your list of responsibilities, seek support from any of the capable people who surround you. You'll find colleagues and friends who will be happy to help when your load gets too heavy.

**Recognize—and accept—when you are not in total control of your time.** There's no way around it: there will be days as a principal when you're not in control of your time. Things will just *happen*. Your neatly planned schedule might be torpedoed by an unexpected parent phone call, a discipline issue involving students, or a teacher coming to you with a problem. Something as simple as a substitute teacher shortage can mean putting off a number of administrative tasks in order to be a social studies teacher for the day. It's best to accept this lack of control with a shrug and a laugh; there's nothing you can do about it except embrace it and adjust your plans.

That is why it is so important to seize control of your time outside of work. You can make your own decisions about how to spend your time—when to get up, when to eat and sleep and go out, when to see your favorite people. Enjoy being your own manager when you can.

**Use the free time you are given if you need it.** Your contract undoubtedly allows you to take a few personal days throughout the year, a certain number of vacation days, and some sick days. I strongly advise taking advantage of these days and not getting wrapped up in the anxiety of missing a day of school (even as I struggle to do it myself). You are entitled to these days; they are there to help you take care of yourself and avoid exhaustion and burnout. Use these days appropriately. As the leader, the way you manage your personal days will serve as the model for the people on your staff. Taking a full day off when you are feverish and contagious is necessary (and considerate). Taking a full day off for a simple dental cleaning is taking advantage of the sick day system.

## Doing It All, or Not: Conversations to Help You Maintain Balance Between Work and the Rest of Your Life

This chapter's opening scenarios all outline a situation you may find yourself in at some point in your career as a principal. In the following conversations, you'll see how you can put the suggestions above into place and make choices that will help keep your personal life balanced with your work.

### Scenario 1: A Scheduling Glitch

This scenario describes a situation in which your mother-in-law, who normally makes sure your children get on the bus to school in the morning, calls unexpectedly and tells you she will not be able to help out this coming week. You and your spouse sit down with your calendars and get ready for some problem solving.

> **You:** *I have early morning appointments every day this week, too. I guess we're both going to have to move some of those around.*
>
> **Tracey:** *Several of mine are conference calls that I can postpone; one of them can be done at home before the kids get on the bus, if I can keep them quiet! I'll let them have some extra time on the iPad.*
>
> **You:** *No harm in that. OK, so, let's sit down and go through everything we need to cover this week. Then, let's compare calendars and come up with a list of things we can both adjust at work.*

Here's how the reversed plan looks in your schedule:

| | Me | Tracey | Grandma |
|---|---|---|---|
| MON | 6:00: Workout<br>8:00: IEP meeting | 8:00-9:00: Kids' breakfast and bus<br>~~8:00: conference call~~ | ~~8:00-9:00: Kids breakfast and bus~~ |
| TUE | 6:00: Workout<br>8:00-9:00: Kids' breakfast and bus<br>~~8:00: Parent meeting~~<br>11:50: Take over at dentist. Take kids to lunch before going to school?<br>~~12:00: Lunch/Study Hall~~ (get coverage) | ~~7:00: Workout~~<br>8:00: Rescheduled conference call<br>~~11:00: Meeting~~<br>11:30: Dentist for kids<br>12:00: Rescheduled meeting | ~~8:00-9:00: Kids' breakfast and bus~~<br>~~11:30: Dentist for kids~~ |
| WED | ~~6:00: Workout~~<br>~~8:00: Meeting with union representative~~<br>8:00-9:00: Kids' breakfast and bus<br>3:30: Assembly<br>**Leave right at dismissal—kids to gymnastics<br>Dinner out? | Training out of town (leave 6:00 a.m.; return late!) | ~~8:00-9:00: Kids' breakfast and bus~~<br><br>~~4:30: Kids to gymnastics~~ |
| THU | 5:30: Workout<br>8:00: Rescheduled meeting with union representatives<br>*Leave work @8:30. Get kids on bus. Back to work for 9:00 bus evacuation drills | 6:30: Workout<br>7:30: Conference call at home (kids get screen time!)<br>8:00: Kids' breakfast<br>~~8:30: Review goals from call~~<br>9:30: Review goals from call | ~~8:00-9:00: Kids' breakfast and bus~~ |
| FRI | ½-day personal day<br>8:00: Kids' breakfast and bus, errands, groceries, etc.<br>10:30: OT appointment for son | 7:30-noon: Team meeting | ~~8:00-9:00: Kids' breakfast and bus~~ |

**You:** *This seems to work well.*

**Tracey:** *I agree. There are a couple phone calls and e-mails we'll need to send, though.*

**You:** *I'll work with my secretary to reschedule my meetings, and I'll e-mail my support staff and superintendent to let them know when I'll have to slip out for a bit and ask for help in coverage.*

**Tracey:** *And I'll do the same with my colleagues. It looks like we have a plan!*

Note how you have adjusted your schedule, recognizing that your presence isn't needed every moment of every day. In making your adjustments, you have stayed true to your priorities—putting your family first, teamwork with your partner, your exercise plan. You have also utilized a half personal day to help you complete some things you need to do for your family.

## Scenario 2: A Staff Member's Unexpected Absence

You are the principal of a high school. Your assistant, Rick, calls you one evening; his wife has gone into labor prematurely. You can sense the angst in his voice—he is worried about his wife and baby, and he is concerned about all the things happening at school. You reassure him that he should focus on his family and not think about work. After getting his assurance that he will step away for family time, you make a plan and draft an e-mail to the staff.

### E-mail to Staff

To: City High School Staff
From: Principal Evans
Re: Upcoming Weeks

Good evening, everyone,

I wanted to let you know that I spoke with Rick late this evening. As you know, Rick's family is expecting a baby. The baby has decided to come early—Rick and his wife are at the hospital now. Rick is optimistic that the baby will be healthy and all will be well.

I have encouraged Rick to take some time to focus on his family and the health of the new baby. I reassured him that we would come together to cover his responsibilities. By working together as a team, I know we will carry on as always!

To that end, below you will find a list of coverage we will need. As you know, Rick's responsibilities included discipline, facilities, freshman scheduling, the summer internship program, testing, and overseeing the English, science, and performing arts departments. I have divvied up his upcoming commitments. Please read below and let me know if you have any concerns with coverage. Note that in some cases, I have left responsibilities to departments. I ask that you work together to determine who, specifically, can step up and fulfill each task.

**Myself and Office Staff:**
Call Rick's contacts and reschedule meetings that aren't urgent
Complete scheduled walk-throughs
Cover discipline that is typically Rick's
Take over facility management
Dismissal

**Guidance:**
Lead freshman scheduling meeting
Continue Rick's work planning for summer job fair
Continue planning for PSAT administration

**English, science, and performing arts:**
Develop agenda for weekly meeting
Send minutes to administrative team

**Other departments:**
Provide coverage as needed

Thank you all for stepping up and allowing Rick this time with his family. I trust you will send any inquiries or concerns to me and avoid e-mailing or calling Rick until further notice. He deeply appreciates our willingness to come together to support him at this time, and he knows we are keeping him and his wife in our thoughts. He will pass on news as soon as possible. Hopefully it won't be long until we hear news of a healthy, happy baby!

Here you are modeling several of the suggestions listed above on behalf of your assistant. You are standing by your convictions that family comes first while reinforcing to your assistant principal the importance of balancing home life and work life, and you are mustering help and support from other members of your staff.

## Scenario 3: A Predicament

In this scenario, you have come home from work to find your wife eager to share good news—her sister is engaged to be married! Although you are thrilled for her and her family—this engagement has been eagerly anticipated—you are dismayed when you discover the wedding is scheduled for the same day as your high school's graduation. You are expected to be at graduation, and you know many students hope you will stop by their graduation parties to congratulate them after the ceremony. Your wife, Anne, notices your troubled expression, and you explain the dilemma.

> **Anne:** *No! Are you serious?*
> **You:** *Yep.*
> **Anne:** *Is there any way they can switch it?*
> **You:** *Graduation? No way. Graduation dates are set several years in advance by the Board of Education. Hundreds of students, faculty, and families have big plans for the weekend, not to mention reserving*

*the space for the graduation. And most of the students have parties planned afterwards.*

**Anne:** *Are you saying there's nothing to be done? You know how important this is for me. I do not want to go to this wedding without you. I hope you won't put your job ahead of this wedding. It is too important to my whole family.*

**You:** *I know you don't. (Deep breath) Listen, I feel like we can come up with a solution to this. I'm just not sure what it is. Could we wait until after we've had dinner and I've taken a shower? I'm wiped out after today, and I don't feel like I'm thinking straight. Can we talk about it in a little bit?*

Here, you recognize you aren't at your sharpest and decide to take a break before continuing this tricky conversation.

**You:** *OK, I've had a little time to think, and I may have a solution.*

**Anne:** *What is it?*

**You:** *Well, as you know, I need to be at your sister's wedding.*

**Anne:** *Yes.*

**You:** *And I need to be at graduation.*

**Anne:** *Yes, I know.*

**You:** *And I can't do both. That's a fact, too, right?*

You have recognized and accepted that this is a situation in which you do not have control of your time.

**Anne:** *Yes, I know. I'm sorry I was a little unreasonable earlier; I know you're in a difficult position.*

**You:** *Well, what about this: I'll stay here and go to graduation, which is at 11 a.m. I'll leave right after and drive to your parents' place, change into my tuxedo, and meet you at the reception hall.*

**Anne:** *But then you'll miss the actual wedding! And the photos!*

**You:** *Yes, I will. But I really don't see a way around it. It would be unacceptable for me to miss graduation. It truly is expected of me, not only by the superintendent and the Board of Education but also by the hundreds of people who will be there to see the ceremony. And I can make it in time for the wedding reception. I may even beat the wedding party there. And if you could convince your sister to wait to take some photographs until I get there, I can be with you for that part of it.*

**Anne:** *So you'd be skipping all the graduation parties?*

**You:** *Yeah, that's something I will have to let go of this year. I hate to miss them—I really feel it's important to go—but I also believe this wedding is important. I obviously can't do both things that day, but I can do half of both.*

**Anne:** *I guess that's the best solution. I don't like it, but it's probably what you have to do.*

**You:** *I think it is. I appreciate your understanding—I really do. I promise I will make it work in the best way possible.*

Note how you have reprioritized and come up with a solution that works for everyone.

As a new principal, there will be times you feel you can't get away from your job. It can feel all-consuming, as if things can't possibly carry on without your input in every decision. To balance these demands, it is important to keep focused on your core values and priorities. Your job will stretch you to your personal and professional limits, but by putting some limits in place, you will reduce the risk of burnout and will avoid alienating yourself from things that matter the very most to you.

# Concluding Thoughts

So. You're the principal! *Now* what?

You are embarking on a new and exciting adventure. It is a job that will challenge you, stretch your thinking, and open your mind. You will find fun, success, trials, angst, frustration, and triumph. Ultimately, being a principal will reinforce your commitment to young people, to the power of teaching, and to the work that is done every day by good, good, good people.

This book is meant to be the friend you can call upon along the way for an answer to a question you didn't know you'd be asked. It's a source for solutions anytime you encounter a problem and think, *"Now* what?" It's the beginning of an ongoing conversation about the wonderful work of being a principal.

I wish you the very best of luck throughout your journey!

You're going to be great.

# Index

# About the Author

 **Jen Schwanke** began her career as a language arts educator in 1998, developing a particular passion for literacy instruction and pedagogy along the way. She is currently a principal for the Dublin City School District in Dublin, Ohio. A graduate instructor in educational leadership, she has written frequently for literacy and educational leadership publications.

When not working or spending time with her husband and two children, Jen is a reader and fitness enthusiast. She blogs about her experiences in learning and leading at jenschwanke.com. Follow her on Twitter @Jenschwanke and Instagram @jenschwanke.

## Related ASCD Resources: The Principalship

At the time of publication, the following ASCD resources were available (ASCD stock numbers appear in parentheses). For up-to-date information about ASCD resources, go to www.ascd.org. You can search the complete archives of *Educational Leadership* at www.ascd.org/el.

### ASCD Edge Group

Exchange ideas and connect with other educators interested in school leadership on the social networking site ASCD EDge® at http://ascdedge.ascd.org

### Online Courses

Leadership: Effective Critical Skills (mobile friendly) (#PD09OC08M)

### Print Products

*100+ Ways to Recognize and Reward Your School Staff* by Emily E. Houck (#112051)

*Balanced Leadership for Powerful Learning* by Bryan Goodwin, Greg Cameron, and Heather Hein (#112025)

*The New Principal's Fieldbook: Strategies for Success* by Pam Robbins and Harvey Alvy (#103019)

*The Principal 50: Critical Leadership Questions for Inspiring Schoolwide Excellence* by Baruti Kafele (#115050)

*The Principal Influence: A Framework for Developing Leadership Capacity in Principals* by Pete Hall, Deborah Childs-Bowen, Ann Cunningham-Morris, Phyllis Pajardo, and Alisa Simeral (#116026)

*Short on Time: How Do I Make Time to Learn and Lead as a Principal?* (ASCD Arias) by William R. Sterrett (#SF114044)

For more information: send e-mail to member@ascd.org; call 1-800-933-2723 or 703-578-9600, press 2; send a fax to 703-575-5400; or write to Information Services, ASCD, 1703 N. Beauregard St., Alexandria, VA 22311-1714 USA.

# THE WHOLE CHILD

ASCD's Whole Child approach is an effort to transition from a focus on narrowly defined academic achievement to one that promotes the long-term development and success of all children. Through this approach, ASCD supports educators, families, community members, and policymakers as they move from a vision about educating the whole child to sustainable, collaborative actions.

*You're the Principal! Now What?* relates to the **Safe, Supported,** and **Engaged** tenets.

# WHOLE CHILD
# TENETS

**1** **HEALTHY**
Each student enters school healthy and learns about and practices a healthy lifestyle.

**2** **SAFE**
Each student learns in an environment that is physically and emotionally safe for students and adults.

**3** **ENGAGED**
Each student is actively engaged in learning and is connected to the school and broader community.

**4** **SUPPORTED**
Each student has access to personalized learning and is supported by qualified, caring adults.

**5** **CHALLENGED**
Each student is challenged academically and prepared for success in college or further study and for employment and participation in a global environment.

For more about the Whole Child approach, visit
**www.wholechildeducation.org.**

**ASCD**
LEARN. TEACH. LEAD.